Twisted Links

Anthony and Donna Pelham

Sweet Justice Press, Inc.
www.sweetjusticepress.com

First Printing, 2011

This is a work of fiction. All places, events and characters appearing in this work are fictitious. They are either a product of the authors' imaginations or are used fictitiously. Any resemblance to real places, real events, business establishments, or to real persons, living or dead, is purely coincidental. Nothing in this book should be construed as legal advice. While legal topics are discussed, the information should not be relied upon in any way, or applied to any specific situation. If you have a legal issue, consult a licensed attorney in your jurisdiction, not a novel.

ISBN 978-0-9836169-9-3

Library of Congress Control Number: 2011909725
Library of Congress Subject Headings.

Thomas, Desmond (Fictitious character) -- Fiction.
Golf - Fiction.
Virginia -- Fiction.
Counterfeiting – Fiction.
Detective and mystery stories.
Golf stories.
Legal stories.

Cover art by Alexandra Cerovac.

First Edition

10 9 8 7 6 5 4 3 2 1

Acknowledgements

Many people generously gave their time and talent to this project.

We would like to thank Methodist University, and the Reeves School of Business, including, but not limited to the following people: Wendy Vonnegut, JD, Theresa Clark, JD, Pamela Strickland, DBA, Jeffrey Zimmerman, PhD, Mary Kirchner, PhD, Warren McDonald, PhD, and Anne Way, MBA Coordinator.

Special thanks to the Methodist PGA Golf Management program and PGA Professionals - Jerry Hogge, Steve Conley, and Landon Bentham.

Wonderful experts offered informal advice, encouragement, and review. Any representations or inaccuracies in content are ours, not theirs. Thanks to: Roy Pedretti, Sgt. Jim Goodman, Eric Eshleman (PGA Professional), Thomas Colclough, Anthony Troeger (fraud investigator), Robert G. Ray, Esq. (Ray and Pennink, PLLC), Pamela Villegas, CPA (Comstock and Villegas, CPAs), Deborah Gerhardt, JD (UNC School of Law), Judith Welch Wegner, JD (UNC School of Law) and Cynthia K. Kirby, MD.

Thank you to the Wisconsin Tri-County Readers and Professor Pelham's student reviewers: Ashley Skipper, Ashley Baggett, Nicholas Sauls, Rachel Evans, Tyler Arnold, Lindsie Bentham, Larry Nance, Ashley Evanich, and the Summer 2011 MBA Business Law Class.

Our family members who reviewed the book put up with us as we incessantly debated characters, plot and word usage. All exhibited great patience over our sometimes single-minded focus. We love you all.

Brenda Pedretti, David Pedretti, Marilyn Pelham, Matthew Pelham, Benjamin Pelham, Morgan Kirk, Corey Kirk, and Taylor Kirk.

Chapter 1

Frankie Brooks had no way of knowing that he was minutes away from a horrific death. After all, he was simply enjoying a round of golf.

As he looked down over the famous green, the cool breeze on his face reminded him of his daily ritual.

Check the wind.

Kneeling down, he grabbed a few blades of dried grass, tossed them lightly in the air, and watched as they landed almost two feet to his left.

Nothing to worry about.

The 14th hole on the Chesapeake Bluffs' "No. 3" course, was, without a doubt, Frankie's favorite hole. In fact, it was everyone's favorite—to look at. What many called it after playing was an entirely different matter. Fourteen was the crown jewel on what was arguably the most famous and distinguished course on the Eastern seaboard. On this sunny spring morning, as he did on nearly every morning, Frankie had the entire course to himself. There were a few perks to being a course pro at the Bluffs. Mere mortals had to pay upwards of $400 a round for the privilege.

In this one, small, nearly perfect setting, the confluence of emerald grass, golden sand, blue water, and black, basaltic rock created a private heaven on earth, at least to the golfers of the world, of which there were more than a few who could afford the steep entrance fee. The fairway hugged tightly along the rocky Virginia shoreline. A scant five yards of rough on the right quickly gave way to a short guard rail, a few small rocks, and then sheer descent into the watery depths below.

Frankie had played this hole at least a hundred times, and many more than that in his head. Even though he was familiar with almost every square inch of the fairway, bunker, greens and rough, he'd still only managed to par the hole about sixty percent of the time. On only four occasions had he managed a birdie. Reaching the green on the first shot was well-nigh impossible, as it required hitting a nearly 320-yard drive over the water, landing and then sticking onto the postage stamp green. He had never seen it done, and doubted that even the best player alive could manage such a feat.

His ball was situated 120 yards from the pin, an ideal lie. He could have, in theory, hit his tee shot some 15 yards farther, but doing so would have put the ball past the hump at the end of the fairway, the point after which a drive tended to gain more momentum than it lost, which usually resulted in a long, unceremonious drop down to the rocks.

He waved to the two maintenance workers ahead. He hadn't seen their cart, so he was a little surprised to come across them. Starting his round at 6:00 a.m., Frankie was accustomed to encountering golf course workers as he played. He knew most of them by sight, but didn't recognize this pair.

Must be the new guys.

He lined up beside his ball, ever-so-lightly gripping the leather-wrapped handle of his club, and smiled to himself as he remembered the advice he gave his students: "When you grip the club, imagine that you're holding a bird and trying to keep it from flying away." Maybe he had a bird right now, maybe even an eagle. He calculated that the wind would move his ball right to left about 6 feet, although calculating was hardly the right word. Frankie just knew.

He drew back and lofted a nearly perfect pitch high into the morning sky. Looking up to admire his shot, he felt an odd pressure on the small of his back, a tingling. Instantly, his body tensed. He tried to speak. "What the...," but no sound emerged. He felt himself fall to the ground, powerless, muscles frozen by the high-voltage charge. Stunned, he was only dimly aware of the two uniformed men hovering above.

They wasted no time. Each grabbed an end as they lifted him, moving quickly to the guard rail. In unison, they swung the bewildered golfer toward the fairway, then, swinging harder, they propelled him rapidly toward the water. And then they just let go.

Frankie knew for certain he was about to die.

The events of the last few minutes replayed in Frankie's mind. He struggled to comprehend, to glean anything that would explain his unimpeded plummet toward the sharp rocks below.

But his last precious seconds yielded no clues as to the cause for the men's actions. As his rapidly accelerating body twisted during the fall, he briefly caught sight of his ball, now on the green, rolling the last few inches to the hole.

It would be the last eagle that Frankie Brooks would ever make.

"They had no right to read my emails, Mr. Thomas," the young woman whined. "They're private, and I didn't say anything bad about the company, just my manager. Everybody already knows she's a sorry-ass bitch."

"But your employment agreement," I reminded her, "states that the company has a right to view all emails that utilize your company's email address or anything that is sent to you or received by you on company computers or phones."

Clearly, she hadn't read her contract.

Although I was Susan's attorney, right now I was playing the devil's advocate, a position, I had been told on more than one occasion, for which I was eminently qualified. But, in actuality, my temperament tended more toward reconciliation. I considered myself a peacemaker.

During my initial consultation, I'd give every client the same advice—"You'll get much better results if you can put away any hostility and bitterness, and at the end of the day, you'll feel better, too."

Not to mention your attorney.

But right now, my client was on a rant. She hadn't yet come to the place where she could see things from a slightly more objective perspective. Susan didn't seem like a bad person, but my initial impression of her was that she was somewhat self-involved. Her current performance only reinforced that view.

Indignantly, she continued. "Yeah, but then they looked at my Facebook, and then they got my tweets. That's spying. I feel violated! I have rights, you know. That's gotta be illegal. I might sue. Maybe even a class action."

Clearly, she also had no idea what constituted a class action lawsuit.

As for myself, only a few short months ago, I wouldn't have known a tweet from a twit, but the burgeoning number of cases dealing with cyberstalking and internet privacy issues had forced me to get up to speed. I had my own Twitter account now. I even had one follower.

"Was your Facebook page limited to friends only?" I asked.

"It is now."

"How about your Twitter account? Was your profile locked?"

"I'm not sure."

"Can anyone follow your tweets, or do you have to approve who receives them?"

"You mean I can set it up so not everybody gets them?"

"Uh-huh." I was suddenly feeling very "with-it" at being more knowledgeable than a twenty-something about any aspect of social media. "I'll show you how to do it. It'd be a good idea for you to lock it down."

I was interested to find out how much information she would offer freely. "Did you say anything bad about the company on Facebook or Twitter?"

"Well, yeah, I kinda called our current product some names."

I knew exactly what she had said, having the printout directly in front of me. I read aloud.

"According to the records, you said your company's product was 'extremely lame,' 'a guaranteed rip-off' and that 'you'd never buy it.' You also called your boss 'Cheapy McCheaperson' when complaining about your lack of a raise. I can see why your company might be upset."

Her mouth dropped open.

A tad too dramatic.

"I thought you were on my side."

"Yes, but I have to evaluate it from the company's point of view, to gauge the strength of their case."

Susan had been terminated by her employer for poor performance. During her dismissal, her manager had alluded to the fact that she had violated her employment agreement by publishing harmful and negative opinions of the company via email and on public forums. A defamation suit from her employer wasn't out of the question.

"You say that you'd never received a poor performance evaluation during y—"

I stopped when I saw Jaclyn poke her head in the conference room door. Jaclyn never interrupted during a client meeting, unless it was urgent.

Despite my best efforts, I found it impossible to still my thoughts.

Had something happened to Bertha? My parents?

In the few short seconds it took for me to get up from the table, mumble an apology, and walk out of the room, I had already braced myself for the worst possible news.

"I'm so sorry to interrupt. Mr. Thomas, I have Lisa Brooks on the line. She said something about her husband. I tried to take a message, but she started crying. She begged me to get you on the phone."

Lisa Brooks. She and Frankie were my oldest friends. I grabbed the phone.

"Lisa?"

I heard only a quiet sob from the other end of the line, followed, after a time, by a weary voice. "Desmond. Oh Dez. It's Frankie. He's, he's..." She trailed off.

"What is it, Lisa?"

"He's gone. Some golfers found him on the rocks at the bottom of the cliff on fourteen."

Nothing could have prepared me. Frankie Brooks. Dead? I had just talked to him a few days ago.

"Are you s—," I stopped myself.

Stupid question.

"Tell me what happened."

"I don't know, I don't know. The police just came over here and told me that Frankie was dead. I heard one of them talking to someone on the phone. They said that it looked like a… a leaper. You know him, Dez, Frankie wouldn't do that."

"Of course not, Lisa. Where are you?"

"I'm home. What am I supposed to do? How can I tell the kids? They'll be home from school soon."

"I can be there in an hour." If I took the back roads and floored it, I could shave ten minutes off that time. "Hang in there. I'm leaving now."

She began to ramble. "Maybe it was my fault. I probably shouldn't have given Frankie those pills."

Instinctively, I shifted gears. "Lisa, listen to me. Do *not* talk to anyone, not the police, not the investigators, not anybody, till I get there. Do you understand? Not a word. Tell them your attorney is on his way."

Frankie Brooks had been a great friend. We'd first met as students at Virginia Lutheran. He was a wild, life-of-the-party guy. We were both on the team that won four straight national championships. He became a club pro; I was lucky enough to go on tour for a while, that was until "the incident."

Later, while I earned my law degree, Frankie moved up in the ranks and eventually got the plum job at Chesapeake Bluffs.

Lots of pros would kill to have a job like that.

I pulled into the Brooks' driveway. The detectives were waiting in their car, as I knew they would be. Lisa had called when they'd arrived, and said that they wanted to ask "a few questions."

Although I'd never met these detectives, I knew how they worked. They were experts at catching people off guard. "Not to take up any more of your time, Ma'am, but one more thing, did you and your husband have any fights recently?" or "We've got to get going, but where did you say you kept that revolver, again?" Before you know it, your client has already confessed to half a dozen unsolved homicides.

As I ambled over, the car window rolled down. "Detectives, I'm Desmond Thomas, Lisa Brooks' attorney. I'll need a few minutes alone with my client." They knew exactly what I was going to say, and would have been shocked if I had deviated by more than a few syllables from the standard greeting.

The detectives resumed their attempts at tackling today's crossword puzzle.

Lisa met me at the door, tissue in hand, eyes red and swollen. I stepped inside, out of the detectives' view, and closed the door. The first thing that Lisa needed right now, I knew, much more than an attorney, was a sympathetic soul.

"I'm so sorry, Lisa." I wrapped my arms around her. She said nothing, but the deep sobs spoke volumes.

She struggled to catch her breath. "I had to call Dick and Jeanine. They had to know that their son was... gone."

"You did the right thing. That must have been hard." The sobbing resumed. After a minute or so, she began to quiet.

"The detectives are here to do their job, which is to find out what happened to Frankie, so they may be blunt. At this point, everyone could be a suspect. I'm not a criminal attorney, but if you think that you need one, I can recommend some good ones."

And some to avoid.

"Does that make sense?"

She nodded.

"Do you think you need a criminal attorney?"

She shook her head.

Good sign.

"Is there anything you need to tell me about Frankie? What about the pills?"

She retrieved the medicine from the kitchen, handing the container to me. I glanced at the label. "Eletrex. Take one daily." Eletrex, as I'd learned from the hundred or so repetitions of an annoying TV spot, was one of the "new generation" of anti-depressants. "When you just can't lift yourself up, talk to your doctor about Eletrex."

"Frankie'd been feeling down. He wasn't himself. I finally talked him into seeing a shrink, who gave him the prescription. After Frankie started taking them, he seemed to get better. He said he didn't notice a difference, but I did. He just thought they hurt his sex drive. After a while I had to remind him to take them. I put a pill out with his breakfast every morning. I told him, 'You're not going to get any better if you don't do what the doctor says.'"

"Anything else?" I prodded. "The detectives are going to ask you about everything. It's better if I hear it first."

"We had a few money problems. Frankie made good money at the Club, you know. But he liked nice things. Take a look in the garage. That's his latest toy."

I opened the door from the laundry room and peeked into the expansive three-car garage. A shiny red Corvette looked like it was ready to leap out.

Nice.

When I returned to the table, Lisa resumed. "Some guy called up a few times, asking me when Frankie was going to be paying his debt." He wouldn't say where he was from. He just told me to tell Frankie that 'Mr. Tom Jones' called to ask about the money he owed."

"Did you ask Frankie about it?"

"Yeah. He said that he had made a few bets with this guy, that he was going to pay him back next payday. I didn't care for that, not at all. I told Frankie that he needed to stop with the betting."

"Is that it?"

"Well, for a while I thought Frankie might be having an affair. He would stay late at work. When I asked him, he said that he was giving private lessons. I checked at the Club, but you know how those guys stick together. They'd never tell me if he was up to something. Finally, I got sick of it and hired a private investigator."

This was news.

"You hired a private investigator? What did he find out?"

"He followed Frankie for a couple of weeks. One night, Frankie met a woman at a restaurant. They were talking, mostly arguing, actually. After they left, my guy followed Frankie, but Frankie came straight home. I'll get you the pictures.

"Another time, he followed Frankie to one of his 'private lessons.' It turned out to be at a bar. He was just drinking and talking to some guy there.

"After a couple of weeks, the investigator said it didn't look like a typical affair. He hadn't seen Frankie meet the woman again. Said he could keep going, but he didn't want to waste my money. I didn't have any more money to pay him, anyway, but I still think

Frankie was up to something."

Wow. Private investigators, gambling debts, and clinical depression. The detectives might be here for a while.

After helping Lisa make arrangements for her kids to stay with a neighbor, I waved the detectives in. They were an odd pair. Reed, short and stocky, looked like an ex-marine with his closely cropped hair. Johnson, younger and of the female persuasion, was tall and vanishingly thin. Popeye and Olive Oyl. All that was missing was a can of spinach.

They covered a lot of the same ground with Lisa that I had. They copied information from the Eletrex container. They also got the name of the physician Frankie had been seeing. When Lisa mentioned the PI, I could see by their raised eyebrows that we had hit an area of particular interest.

"Do you recall the name of the private investigator, Mrs. Brooks?" Reed asked.

"It was Durham, Bill Durham, but they call him Bull. I guess it's kind of a joke, but I didn't catch it."

The detectives nodded their heads in recognition, while Johnson wrote down the information in her book. "Did Bull, I mean, did Mr. Durham find out who was calling you about the gambling debts?"

"No, the calls happened after I hired him."

"Mrs. Brooks, did your husband have a life insurance policy?"

"Yes, we just got one about a year ago. I'd been after him to buy it. We have two boys, you know, and I told Frankie, what if something happens..." She stopped there, lost in thought.

"What was the benefit on the policy?" Johnson chimed in.

"I think it was for $500,000."

"Do you happen to know," continued Johnson, "if the policy had an accidental death benefit, what they sometimes call a 'double indemnity'?"

A shock of realization registered on Lisa's face. "You think I had something to do with this?" Her voice grew louder as she wound up. "I'm trying to help you find out what happened to my husband, and now you're going to accuse me of... bumping him off for the life insurance money?"

"Lisa, stop talking," I commanded in my best calm but authoritative attorney voice. "Detectives, a moment with my client, please."

The detectives had sat still and stony-faced during Lisa's monologue, soaking in her every word and inflection. Either Lisa was a fantastic actress, or she really had no idea that she was suspect number one, barring a suicide determination.

"We'll be outside." The detectives headed toward the door.

After giving her a moment to unwind, I explained to her that this was standard procedure. In unexplained deaths, the spouse is often the first suspect.

And for good reason.

The coroner's findings cast a large pall over Frankie's funeral.

Suicide. No one wanted to talk about it, much less believe it. The coroner had found no evidence of foul play, and, in fact, had indicated little likelihood of an accident given Frankie's intimate knowledge of the course. An accidental fall would have required him to first climb over the guard rail, which seemed unlikely. That left just one alternative.

The fact that Frankie had been taking anti-depressants probably sealed the deal. Eletrex was now under suspicion of causing increased suicidal thoughts and tendencies. The attorney in me couldn't help but think that there might be a lawsuit in there somewhere, but now was not the time.

I scanned the packed church and saw more than a few familiar faces. Lisa was there, of course, dressed in black, along with her two boys in the front row. Frankie's parents, whom I had met many times, sat alongside her.

A large banner was draped over the casket. It was a picture of Frankie on the tee box, leaning on his driver, sporting that trademark grin of his that could charm your socks off. The Frankie we knew and remembered. It was a nice touch.

Many of our old classmates from Virginia Lutheran had come out, and it helped when they got up and told stories from our school days, like the time Frankie had lost a bet at the wayback and had to swim across the pond at hole 10 in his boxers.

Frankie was a good guy. Far from perfect, but you'd have to go a long way to find a better friend.

Lisa had asked me to give the eulogy. I reminisced about how much Frankie's friendship had meant to me, starting off as college freshmen, and now, fourteen years later, still close.

I talked about how he took time off from his job to caddy for me when I went to qualifying school, and how we both celebrated when I finally got my tour card. And after I developed a case of the dreaded "yips," suffering the humiliation of losing a major by one stroke after three-putting from three feet, Frankie was there. He wouldn't let me dwell on the negative. He helped me to see there was a new career waiting for me.

Thanks Frankie, you were a great friend.

After the service, I saw Evan McDermott walking purposefully my way. Evan had been the Director of Golf at Chesapeake Bluffs when I interned there ten years ago. In fact, he was the one who had selected me for the internship. A stand-up guy.

"Desmond. Nice speech. It made this day a little better for quite a few people here. He'll be missed."

"I'll miss him, I know. Good to see you again, Evan. I understand you're the head honcho at the Bluffs now. Congratulations."

"That's what I wanted to talk to you about, Dez. I've got a proposal for you. It's right up your alley. In fact, it's right up two of your alleys."

I didn't know I had two alleys.

"Since you're in town, let's talk at my office. It'll just take a half-hour or so. Then we'll stop by Lisa's house."

I had to wonder what was so important that it had to be crammed between Frankie's funeral and the reception.

Chapter 2

Cody glanced up and saw Sherrie walking by, wearing her trademark smile and tight shorts. He paused his iPod.

"Hey, Sherrie. Where ya headed?"

"The Caf," she replied. "Text me when you're done. Maybe we can hang out."

He smiled and nodded.

A little Sherrie after dinner sounded pretty nice.

She didn't need to ask where Cody was headed. The golf bag strapped onto his back, along with his upbeat disposition, testified to only one possible destination. Wayback, they called it at Virginia Lutheran, as in "wayback" at the far end of the campus. It was the nickname for the University's private golf course.

Even though he played nearly every day, golf never got old for Cody. His dad had told him at least a hundred times, "You don't play the course, you play yourself. If you're not up to the challenge, you shouldn't be out there." He hated to admit it, but the old man was right, even though he had long ago surpassed his dad's golfing abilities.

Cody Corrigan didn't look like the number one player on the University's golf team, much less an All-American for two-years running. Tall and skinny, his wire-rimmed glasses and quiet demeanor led most people to assume that he was anything but an athlete. But the strong, wiry muscles wrapped around his thin frame often left his golf partners staring in amazement at his spectacularly long and accurate shots.

This consistent, almost robotic shot-making ability had earned him a nickname. The "Wayback Machine," they called him, although recently this had morphed into "Mr. Peabody," in honor of the glasses-wearing 60's cartoon dog who controlled the machine.

College life at Virginia Lutheran University, or "the Big Val-U" as it was affectionately referred to by students and alumni, was tailor-made for Cody. He'd done his research before he enrolled. Their Professional Golf Management program was the best in the country. One hundred percent of their graduates found jobs in the golf industry, and even with his natural modesty, Cody knew that, at the top of his class, he could pretty much write his own ticket.

This summer would be his third internship. He'd worked at two local country clubs his first two summer breaks. Now, after his junior year, he'd set his sights on the country's most prestigious courses. He'd gotten interviews at Pebble Beach, Winged Foot, Baltusrol, Pinehurst, and Augusta National, before deciding upon Virginia's own Chesapeake Bluffs. This was going to be a summer to remember.

Lost in contemplation, Cody stepped off the curb and crossed the street toward the clubhouse, already envisioning the thrill of teeing-off on one of the most celebrated courses in the world.

Hot and sweaty, Assistant Coach Jake Harden hopped into the Blainesville University van with a single goal—get back with the food, fast. His Cougars were the visitors at the round-robin baseball tournament being held at Virginia Lutheran. The players were going to be hungry after their practice, and needed to eat something substantial before their next game, scheduled to begin in forty-five minutes.

The team's head coach had sent him out to pick up subs. Jake wondered why the coach couldn't have ordered from some place that delivered, sparing him the twenty minute roundtrip. With no time to waste, he hit the gas, and the van shot forward as he fished his cell phone out of his pocket. He just needed to text one more time to make sure they'd gotten everyone's order.

"Damn it," he muttered as he glanced down at the phone. "I can never get a signal when we come to this place." He checked

again, this time taking his eyes off the road for a split-second too
long.

When he looked up, it was too late. Five feet in front of his
speeding van, a tall, lanky student in a white polo shirt, with golf
clubs strapped on his back, turned and looked at the approaching
vehicle with ever-widening eyes.

After talking with a few old friends at the funeral, I had to
hustle so as not to be late for my meeting with Evan. As I
approached the entrance to the Bluffs, I was reminded once again
that even the guardhouse was impressive. For it, like every other
permanent structure in Chesapeake Bluffs Golf and Country Club,
was constructed entirely of stone. No bricks, stucco, siding or any
other exterior building material was allowed. Stone houses, complete
with slate roofs.

With the exception of the newer houses that lined courses 5
and 6, no driveways marred the front lawns, for each house had a
detached garage that connected via an alley behind the house. Some
of the oldest houses had two-car garages, which, at the time they
were built, seemed like an unspeakable luxury. Of course, all the
newer houses had three car garages or even more, some sporting five
and six car mega-garages, larger than many of the older houses here.

There was also a small airfield within Chesapeake Bluffs. The
jet-setter could buy or build a house that included a hanger for his
plane, and then taxi directly from house to airstrip. A famous movie
star had lived here for a while, until he started landing his private
62,000 pound Gulfstream II jet at the airfield, prompting what his
lawyer called "an extreme case of jet-envy." The homeowners'
association passed a resolution restricting the use of the airfield to
planes weighing less than 12,500 pounds. The actor moved on.

The cumulative result of the houses, the landscaping, the
meticulously maintained golf courses, and the view overlooking the
Chesapeake Bay on the only rocky section of the entire Virginia
coastline, was breathtaking.

It was no wonder that the "Bluffs at Chesapeake," as the
residential part of the Club was officially known, was the home for so
many millionaires, multimillionaires, and even a few billionaires. A lot
of the Bluffs' residents were from old money, but a few of the newer

breed of wealthy pro-sports stars had recently bought houses, providing the membership with an unending source of gossip and gawking.

The guard checked my ID and waved me in.

"Have a good day, Mr. Thomas."

I drove the winding road to the clubhouse and office complex, as I had done so many times in the past during my internship, and as I had done those four fateful days during the US Open event that had begun my rapid descent from the pro tour.

I found Evan in his corner office on the third floor, his door reading "VP of Golf Operations." Two sides of his office were windows, overlooking the 18th green of course No. 1, with a view from the top of the hill overlooking the Chesapeake Bay in the distance. This panorama would be hard to top.

"How do you ever get any work done with a view like that?" I asked as I entered the expanse, more like a suite than an office.

"It's tempting just to sit back and enjoy it, but then I realize how much work I have to do, so I turn around and stare at my wall."

It was true, I realized. His desk and chair were positioned so that his back faced the windows.

"Sit down Dez, or should I call you 'Clearly Dez?'"

He was referring to my old nickname, bestowed on me as a result of my persistent, perhaps even annoying, habit of starting off way too many observations with "Clearly, you've never...."

"Dez will do fine."

"Ok, I'll cut right to the chase. Our in-house counsel, Alex Van Avery, is retiring next year. In truth, he's just about retired now, but he's hanging on until he hits fifty years of service this fall. They're going to make a big to-do about it then."

I was quite familiar with Van Avery, as were most people who had anything to do with the Bluffs. He was practically a legend.

"But right now, he's only working a couple days a week, and by working, I mean he shows up and takes a nap, and then maybe goes to a meeting. We've got a few legal items that we need to take care of, and honestly, Van Avery's not up to it. We need to hire some new blood. At this point, it wouldn't be full-time, but when he retires, there's an opening."

"And you thought of me for this?"

"Here's the thing. You could handle our legal needs, and you could also work part-time as a pro here, taking Frankie's place. It'd be an ideal way to see if you want to get back into golf." He turned his chair and swept his arm around the idyllic view. "You gotta admit, you can't beat the work environment."

I did have to admit. And I also had to admit that working in my current law office, although lucrative and not too taxing, wasn't always a perfect fit for an outdoor guy like me. It was too often... what's the legal word for that? Oh yeah, *boring*.

"Wow, I'm going to have to think about this."

"Don't think too long. We're going to have to replace Frankie pretty soon. I can't hold this open forever."

He handed me an envelope.

"Here's the package, I think you'll be pleasantly surprised. Plus, I can throw in a few perks. There's a house for rent right off the third green of course five. It's being handled by our property management company. We can let you stay in it rent-free for the next year. Of course you can play at any of our courses as much as you want for no charge."

"How much legal work do you think there'll be?"

"Oh, not too much. Just the simple things that we need an in-house counsel for. Review documents, make sure contracts are ok, that kind of thing. We have an outside firm for the heavy lifting, you know, litigation and all that."

It sounded pretty sweet. It wasn't until later that I would find out that Evan had been lying through his teeth.

Consciousness returned slowly to Cody Corrigan. He couldn't place his surroundings. He tried to turn his head to look around and felt only agonizing spasms of pain, which, now unleashed, coursed freely from neck to torso. His head hadn't budged. His arms met with similar resistance.

Where am I?

He struggled to clear the haze that enveloped his mind. Slowly, memories trickled back. He recalled his last accounting class, and then grabbing the golf clubs from the dorm. He'd seen Sherrie on the walk down to the course. The sudden recollection of the white van closing in on him caused his body to jump reflexively. Or at least attempt to. The only tangible result was another round of searing pain racing through his body.

"God," he moaned. "Oh God." And then he realized. God was not going to help him here. Grandma had been right. She had told him where he was heading. He should have paid more attention while he had still had the chance.

So this is what it's like to be in Hell.

The familiar voice awakened Sarah Upton from her fitful slumber.

Was that Cody?

She willed herself to alertness, nearly jumping out of the soft recliner that had provided her with little comfort during her anguished wait.

"Cody? Cody, are you awake?"

"Mom? Is that you? Are you here too?"

"It's me, baby. I'm right here."

The sound seemed to be coming from behind him. He couldn't see her, though.

"Are you dead too? What's going on?" His confusion gave way to despair.

"Oh, honey, you're not dead. You're in the hospital."

"I can't see you," he said, "What's happening to me?"

As Cody waited for a response, a head moved into his line of vision. First the hair, then a forehead, then the familiar face—it was his mother, sideways, suspended in some bizarre fashion. He struggled to make sense of the scene.

"Cody, I'm here. Oh, my baby." She was crying, now, the tears running oddly down the sides of her face.

"I don't understand, Mom. I can't move my head. I'm stuck."

"I know. You're in a bed. It turns around. They've got you upside down now and you're strapped in so you can't move. I'm on the floor so I can see you."

"I thought I was dead. I thought I was in Hell," Cody said.

Despite her resolve to remain strong and in control for her son, these words tipped his mother from her delicate balance. Curling into a fetal position, she began sobbing.

Cody couldn't watch his mom like this. He exercised the only control he seemed to have at the moment. Closing his eyes, he gave her a moment of privacy.

"Cody," a man's voice intoned. "Cody, it's your Dad."

The voice came from beside him.

"Dad, I hear you. I'm scared."

"I know you are, son. It's alright. You're going to be alright. We're going to tell the nurses that you're awake. They'll get somebody to turn your bed so you can see us. So *we* can see *you*."

His Mom and Dad had long ago divorced, and rarely even spoke to, or even about, one another. It must have taken a lot to get them back together in the same room.

This. Whatever this is.

With eyes opened again, Cody now saw an empty floor in front of him. "Dad, am I gonna be para..." He couldn't bring himself to say the word.

"They don't know for sure," his father answered honestly. "They said after more testing we'll know where we stand."

But you're the only one standing now, Cody thought.

"But your fingers are working." His father tried hard to sound encouraging, doing his best to erase the pessimism that threatened to envelop them. "I can see them moving. Can you feel my hand?"

His Dad's grip felt strong, and Cody was surprised by its warmth. This time, he resisted the urge to nod.

"Yes," he replied, "I can feel it."

But it wasn't hard for him to read between the lines.

"What about my legs? Can I move them too? This can't be permanent, can it?"

"You're strong Cody. We're strong. We'll get through this. I love you, son."

"I know Dad. I love you too."

The room became silent. Mother, father and son each lost in private thoughts, the only sound, the soft, steady splashing of teardrops against the tile floor.

Chapter 3

The Chapman County Sheriff's office looked all too familiar, as if it were plucked *in toto* from some generic crime drama. The sterile metal desks, differentiated only by the heights and locations of their stacks of papers, formed the requisite rows and columns that created the appearance of organization in the expansive room. Stark fluorescent lighting provided the final institutional touch, painting occupants on both sides of the law with the same dull gray pallor. It was not a place where you'd want to spend a lot of free time.

This was the detectives' house, their home turf, so I knew my only chance at gaining the upper hand was to start on the offensive. A full frontal attack. So immediately after occupying my seat in front of Detective Reed's desk, I launched in.

"Detective, from what I've learned from Mrs. Brooks, and from my long association with Frankie Brooks, I think that the finding of suicide might be premature."

"You base this on what in particular, Mr. Thomas? You have some information?"

Gruff and confrontational, and most definitely not a people person, Reed had old-school written all over him. His tone conveyed his message clearly.

You're wasting my time.

"Frankie owed money to some person who was harassing Lisa Brooks for payment. Maybe that guy had something to do with his death. Frankie didn't leave a suicide note. He left behind a wife and two kids. He was still making plans for the future. He'd called me to play golf with him next weekend. These aren't the actions of a man getting ready to dive off a cliff."

"So let me get this straight," Reed said. "The guy owes money, and one of his creditors calls his wife. Plus the guy had a golf date for the weekend. Why didn't I see it? Of course, it's a murder plot."

"Hey Bill," he yelled over to one of his colleagues, "Matlock over here's solved the Brooks case. Can you believe it?" Their laughter grated on me.

"Counselor," he went on, "why don't you do your job, and let us do ours? We ran an investigation into the death, we went to the site and we found no evidence of any foul play. The coroner did an autopsy and found that the cause of death was extreme trauma. In other words, his head hit the rocks. He owed money, and he was taking anti-depressants known to cause an increase in suicidal tendencies. Maybe he was just having a really bad day and something pushed him over the edge."

He paused, perhaps thinking about his choice of words.

"I mean," he continued, "he snapped, and the opportunity to end it was right there in front of him. And he took it."

"I don't see it that way," I replied. "Did you investigate this Tom Jones guy?"

"We know who he is. He's a bookie. He doesn't kill people."

"How do you know?"

"*Because we've been around.* We know things. Look, I know you don't want to believe it. You were his friend. You know how many people come in here trying to convince us that a murder was a suicide?"

I'm sure you're going to tell me.

"That's right, none. You know how many people come in here trying to convince us that their friend's death wasn't a suicide? Lots. That's just the way it is."

I was getting a little ticked at this prick's dismissive attitude.

"Well, I'm going to keep working on it, since you guys appear to have given up on the case."

"Look Thomas, you go sticking your nose where it doesn't

belong, you're gonna get yourself in trouble, or you're gonna get hurt. You're not a cop, you don't know what you're doing, so why don't you stick to your legal work, and we'll stick to the police work."

Cleary, I wasn't getting anywhere.

"Fine," I said, meaning nothing of the sort. I got up and headed out.

"Asshole," I muttered quietly.

I could have sworn I heard Reed do the same.

It had taken me less than a day to accept Evan's offer. I think he knew that bringing me out to the Bluffs again would plant a seed, and damned if he wasn't right. In truth, I hadn't realized how much I missed being in the game. Plus, he would be paying me more than I was getting at my firm, for a lot less stress. I mean, really, how difficult could the legal problems at a golf resort be?

I loved being an attorney, but for me, nothing could beat getting out in the fresh air and swinging the clubs. If I hit it right, I could make the ball do magic.

Of course, if I didn't, the results were anything but magical. In the course of my golf career, I'd seen countless persons mishit the ball in every conceivable way, using every club in the bag.

The first time I ever picked up a club and took a swing was when my dad took me to the local driving range. Like so many others before and since, my first attempt missed the ball entirely. I whiffed. My father, in an attempt to lighten the mood, put his hand to his forehead in an exaggerated fashion as if watching the flight of my imaginary ball soaring through the air.

But I kept at it, and after a few weeks, I got to the point where I could make contact with the ball almost every time. The ball wouldn't go very far or very straight, but at least it was moving forward.

And then, one day—everything changed. I brought back my club, swung, and felt… magic. At that very instant I knew my golf game had changed forever. It wasn't just the sound, which was telling—an exhilarating, soul-satisfying crack. It was the feel. The power of hitting that ball was transmitted directly through the club straight to my hands. I looked up and saw my drive arc through the sky and land hundreds of yards down the center of the fairway. I was hooked.

After that one swing, I knew that I possessed the physical ability, the strength and coordination to hit the ball like that every time. I knew that it was theoretically possible that I could par every hole of every course in the world if I could only string together a series of shots like I had just made. Golf is a game of wonderful possibilities.

Possibilities, I reminded myself, which still applied to me. Even after my rapid fall from the pro tour, I had never truly given up hope of going back. I certainly wasn't getting any younger. I needed to push myself to see what I was still capable of, and taking this job just might be the kind of push I needed.

Hopefully, not over the edge of a cliff.

Carolyn Andrews loved her home. Some might even have termed it a mansion, as it was, by far, the largest house in Chesapeake Bluffs. Built in her typical ostentatious style, the house shouted to the world "I have money." The rear grounds included an astonishingly ornate swimming pool and deck, which never failed to draw gasps from first time visitors. That particular combination of marble and granite luxury had set her back a cool million. But most of all, she loved the enormous windows that gave her an unsurpassed view of one of the most beautiful golf courses in the world, No. 6 at Chesapeake Bluffs.

Today she was determined to finish reading the novel she had started a week back. She brewed a hot cup of oolong tea, and made her way out onto her pool deck to enjoy the fresh air and distract herself from her current trials and tribulations. As she settled into her overstuffed patio chair, she began to lose herself again in her book, one in a long series of alphabetically-themed mysteries.

She heard the sounds of a golf cart nearby, a little closer than usual, and then men's voices. As she looked up, she saw a sight that she had, at first glance, a great deal of trouble believing. One of the golfers stepped over her decorative wall, stumbled up to one of her azaleas, and began to unzip his shorts. He intended to relieve himself in her yard.

Her jaw fell open in astonishment, closing only when the smoldering rage building inside her forced it into a tight clench.

Carolyn quickly retrieved her purse from the bedroom, then reached inside for the .22 caliber pistol she'd kept there ever since her husband's death, five years ago.

She stormed out the patio door, aimed the pistol straight in the air, and fired one shot. The golfer froze. Next, she aimed the pistol directly at him.

"Get the hell out of my yard," she growled. "Now."

When he saw the gun leveled at him, the golfer put his hands up in the air. This was unfortunate, as he had not yet had a chance to zip himself back up.

"And put that thing away," Carolyn continued, "you drunken bum."

He attempted to do as instructed, but in his hurry and state of anxiety he initially succeeded only in painfully jamming the zipper. He finally managed to put everything back in and immediately began a hasty retreat, keeping one eye on the crazed woman as he scurried out of the yard.

The six beers that he had already consumed that day most certainly did not help his efforts, for he failed to recall the presence of the short, decorative wall that he had initially navigated. In his panicked and distracted state, he rammed his shin into the hard concrete barrier, flipping over and landing, at long last, outside the yard. Not stopping for the pain or even to fully stand up, he half-crawled and half-ran the remaining distance to his golf cart.

His astonished friends waited impatiently in their carts, the drivers' feet hovering over their accelerators. As soon as he hurled himself into his seat, they shot off. After a few moments, believing himself at a safe distance, he finally bellowed.

"Woman, you're in big trouble. We're going to report you."

"You have no idea who you're messing with," she yelled back.

Carolyn Andrews was not frightened by the man's threats. As a member of the Club's Board of Directors, and the granddaughter of the founder of Chesapeake Bluffs, she easily carried enough clout to make this little problem disappear. In a short while, the brainless imbecile would be begging to apologize. Before this was all over, he'd be wishing that she *had* shot him.

He won't win this pissing contest.

Still, a change in plans might be good, she thought. Instead of reading, she would go to her afternoon yoga class. Some intense relaxation was in order.

My employment decision having been made, there was still the small matter of seeing if Bertha and I wanted to live in the rental home offered us. It had a lot going for it. It would be tremendously convenient for my work, and would allow me to investigate Frankie's death in my spare time, as well as help Lisa if she needed a hand. Plus, it was free. It was almost a no-brainer, but I wanted to at least see it once before pulling up with the moving van.

After getting the keys and gate passes from the management company, we trekked over early the next morning to see how the house looked at sunrise.

Bertha Thomas was the one true love of my life. We met just over two years ago, and it was, as the trite expression goes, love at first sight. Apart from the physical attraction, I'd found that we're alike in many ways. We both enjoy the outdoors, long walks on the beach and good food. She's got a figure that turns heads, a face that melts hearts, a great disposition, a strong athletic build, and of course, that gigantically enormous head and wrinkled face. Bertha was the loveliest English Bulldog I'd ever laid my eyes on. The first time I saw her as a pup, I knew I had to have her. Though fully grown now, she'll always be daddy's little girl.

We pulled up and found the house on Player Drive. Immaculately landscaped, as were all the houses in the Bluffs, this house had a stone driveway leading to a side garage, which allowed an unobstructed view of the golf course at the rear.

Bertha knew something was up, and heaved herself out my door as soon as I gave her the signal. I had trained her to wait for the leash before going anywhere, so she stood there rock-still until I secured her. A vigorous wagging of her butt where her tail used to be was the only sign of her excitement. That, plus the ever present drool, of course. We had a lot of things in common.

I fished out the key, and we entered through the tall, massive wooden doorway. I was struck immediately by the glorious view of the third green. Bertha lumbered around the house, sniffing in all corners, while I stood transfixed, staring out through the enormous expanse of picture windows, soaking in the view that was course No. 5 at Chesapeake Bluffs.

Bertha had finished her rounds, and I could tell by looking at her that preliminary indications were good. She came over and stood by me, her butt still moving at a furious pace, and she looked up at me as if to say, "Are we going out there, or what?"

At that moment, something outside caught our attention. A jogger was taking an early morning run along the cart path. Female, attractive—no, make that damned attractive—thirtyish, and very fit. Both Bertha and I followed her progress, heads turning simultaneously as we checked out the rear view until the runner disappeared.

We looked at each other. I raised my eyebrows. I believe Bertha would have raised hers too, if she'd had any. I checked my watch. 7:30 a.m.

I love jogging in the morning, I reminded myself, forgetting for the moment that it had been six years since I had last pulled on a pair of running shoes.

I was beginning to like this place. It definitely had possibilities.

The drive to Bluffs' attorney C. Alexander Van Avery's estate from the resort took about twenty minutes, primarily on two-lane country roads. En route, I saw a mix of horse farms, with charming white fences curving with the hills, and trendy new high-end housing developments with country names like Shenandoah Valley Farms, and The Stables at Roanoke.

I was pleased that Evan had arranged for me to meet with Van Avery at his home. Since I had just finished working my two week notice at the law firm, this weekend seemed like a good time to meet before starting work on Monday. It took the edge off of things. Evan had said that everyone should have a chance to visit Van Avery's estate at least once, just to get an idea how the "privileged few" lived.

When my GPS finally announced a turn right into what appeared to be a massive row of hedges, I thought it might have made a mistake. But coming around the bend, a tiny opening appeared in the greenery. Turning into the small, nondescript drive, a whole new world unfolded.

The driveway led to a gatehouse, beyond which, about a quarter mile away at the top of a steep hill, sat a massive antebellum mansion. Surrounding the house were acres of lush green grass, landscaped gardens with flowering shrubs, gazebos and blue sparkling ponds. And this was just the front lawn. A ten foot high wrought-iron fence surrounded the property as far as the eye could see.

I pulled up to the guard house. The crisp-uniformed security officer checked my credentials and sent me up to the house. "You can park in the circle. They'll be waiting for you."

Sure enough, as I pulled into the circle, the front door swung open and a very proper-looking woman stepped out. "Good morning, Mr. Thomas. Mr. Van Avery is expecting you. He's out back. I'll be happy to take you there. My name is Hillary." Hillary had an oh-so-slight British accent.

As Hillary led me through the massive interior, I tried to take in the enormity of this place—formal sitting rooms, dining areas, what appeared to be smoking rooms, more sitting rooms, offices, libraries and studies.

Eventually, we hit upon the door that opened onto the back porch, although porch was probably not the right word for the enclosed area that stretched at least 150 feet along the entire back side of the mansion. I wondered if mint juleps were in the forecast.

In the vast expanse of the back "yard," an infinity-edge swimming pool blended seamlessly into the remainder of the estate, which, from what I could see from my current vantage point, housed a croquet court, two clay tennis courts, and what appeared to be the starting and ending holes of a regulation golf course, complete with putting green, chipping green and driving range. Nice digs.

On the putting green, a tall silver-haired man was poised over his putter, face tight with concentration over his current challenge, a six-footer. So this was C. Alexander Van Avery.

My chaperone waited patiently until Van Avery finished the putt before announcing my presence.

"Mr. Van Avery, Mr. Thomas has arrived."

Indeed I had.

Van Avery's putt had rimmed the hole, but his brief scowl

disappeared when he looked up and saw us on the porch. "Over here." He waved me over with the putter to join him on the green.

"Desmond Thomas. That's a name I haven't heard in a while. Nice to finally meet you. I hear you're going to be helping me out this year." His voice reminded me of an elderly statesman, serious, dignified, authoritative.

"That's what Evan tells me. Quite the little place you've got here, Mr. Van Avery."

Maybe I should have upped my salary demands.

"Please, call me Alex. Yes, it's been in the family for quite a few generations, I can't take any credit for that. But I have made some improvements. Added the tennis courts, a new pool, and the golf course. Of course, it's only nine holes."

Only nine holes. What a dump.

"How far back does this property go?" I asked, scanning the horizon.

"It goes back almost a mile. I had 700 acres up until about five years ago. But the greedy politicians need their money. You wouldn't believe how much they sock me for in property taxes each year on this place. Had to sell fifty acres off to create a tax-fund, just to pay those fools in Richmond. That's going to be gone in a few years, too. Probably have to sell some more off."

Gosh, it must suck to be you.

"So, Desmond, I recall that you always were pretty good with the putter, that was until...."

He left that hanging out there.

After a moment of awkward silence, he extracted three balls from a waist pouch and dropped them at our feet. "Alright, young man, teach me how to putt. Let's see what you can do for an old man's golf game. We're going for that hole." He pointed to a flagstick about forty feet away.

Van Avery had thrown down the challenge. Apparently, he needed to verify my golfing credentials before turning to the legal ones.

For teaching long putts, I'd always found that simplifying it down to only three rules allowed for the fastest improvements in most people's game.

"Ok. Hit one for me, and let me get a look at it," I

instructed.

Van Avery lined himself up and stroked the ball. It came up about eight feet short, and was off to the left by four feet. That left him with a very tough second shot. The goal from this distance was to get it close enough to two-putt. The line to this hole had a slight right-to-left break during the last ten feet or so.

The first thing that I had noticed was that his putter wasn't squared with his stroke path. On a putt, even if you swing the putter on the correct line to the hole, the ball will tend to go off in the direction of the putter face, not the swing, so squaring the putter face is essential. Even a tiny error on a forty foot putt can send the ball off by a foot or more. Rule number one, *square up the face with the line of the putt.*

For his next shot, I made sure Van Avery squared up his putter. This one ended up only about one foot left, but still about the same distance short. "Much nicer."

"I've found it helpful to visualize the path the ball will take as it travels to the cup. Formulate this path in your mind. The ball's direction at the start of the path will tell you the direction to hit. Make sure again you square the club up to that direction." Rule number two, *visualize the path and hit the ball in the starting direction.*

Van Avery putted for a third time, and hit it on a nice line, ending up about three feet short. "Excellent putt. Easy par," I said.

I wanted him to try one more. *"Your goal is to aim about a foot and a half beyond the pin."* Rule number three.

Van Avery produced another ball and dropped it down. He stroked this one along almost the same line, but with just a little more pace. The ball rolled to within one foot of the hole.

He seemed satisfied. "Let me see you sink one," he said, handing me his putter.

"You know," I said, dredging up a golf fact I had learned during my university years, "the odds of sinking a putt this long are less than ten percent. And that's for a pro golfer."

"I don't want to hear any mathematical mumbo-jumbo, just let me see what you've got. And you are a pro golfer, aren't you?" Another challenge. He dropped three more balls in front of me.

None of his balls appeared to be directly in the way of a line to the pin, so we left them there and I hit my first ball. It ended up about two feet past. The second shot ended up even with the cup, just a bit on the high side. My third shot had the line all the way. It was one of those shots that you know as soon as you hit it that it's going to drop. I didn't even have to look. But I watched anyway, enjoying every moment as I saw the ball curve perfectly toward the pin, then drop out of sight with a satisfying rattle.

Van Avery nodded, with just a hint of a smile. Initiation successfully accomplished, we retired from the green.

After giving me a brief tour of the extensive grounds, we settled into his office. I hadn't caught the archery range, indoor bowling alley, sauna, and racquetball courts on my first go round. I could see why Van Avery didn't want to go in to the office every day.

As I sat down, I glanced at the sole picture occupying his large mahogany desk, that of a young woman in a cap and gown, smiling brightly, sun illuminating her long blond hair.

"She's my only child," he said, now looking at the picture. "Seems like that was taken such a long time ago. She's all I have now. Mrs. Van Avery, her mother, died eight years ago. Cancer." Van Avery appeared lost in thought.

"I'm sorry to hear that," I said. The words snapped him back to the moment.

"Well, anything else you need to know, Desmond?"

"I thought we could go over any outstanding legal issues at the Club."

"They're all pretty trivial. Small stuff. Evan can fill you in. I'm sure you can handle whatever comes up. All the current cases are in the file in my office. Sharon, the secretary, she's the one who filed them. She can give you the whole bunch. Look them over. You can always call me if you have a specific question on any of them."

And with that, I could see that Van Avery was finished.

In more ways than one.

I wanted to give the news to Lisa myself, rather than over the phone, so I arranged to meet her at her house.

This wasn't going to be much fun.

When I arrived, Lisa had sandwiches and tea waiting. I decided to start right in with the bad news.

"I've looked over the First Virginia Casualty life insurance policy, and talked with their representative," I explained, "and I'm afraid, the way it stands, they're not going to pay out for a suicide. This policy's not even a year old. They won't pay out for a suicide death until after two years."

Lisa's face turned white. "You mean just because the coroner made a bad decision, I get nothing? I've got no income. How am I supposed to pay the mortgage?"

"The insurance company has their own investigators. We can take them to court and try to convince a jury to force them to pay. They would have to prove that Frankie committed suicide. That's going to take time. It may cost a lot of money to fight. But it may make them amenable to a settlement.

"Chesapeake Bluffs carries a life insurance policy on their employees. For Frankie, it was sixty thousand dollars. That policy doesn't have a suicide clause. You'll be getting a check from them any day."

A bit of color returned to Lisa's face. "That will help for a little while, but Frankie owed a lot of money. And we've got the kids in private school and everything."

Any solution I could propose would probably involve a pretty radical change in Lisa's lifestyle. "How much did he owe?"

"About forty thousand by what I've seen so far in the credit card statements."

Yikes.

"Were the statements in both of your names, or just Frankie's?"

"We've got quite a few. I'm not sure which is which, let me check."

When she returned, she handed the pile to me.

"It appears that the majority of these are under both of your names," I said after a quick review. "It looks like there is about thirty thousand dollars that you'll have to pay off. The rest are in Frankie's name. You didn't know about these joint accounts?"

"Frankie took care of all of the bills. I had no idea. I don't even remember signing up for these cards. Why should I have to pay when I didn't even apply?"

"We can check and see if your signature was on the application. Maybe Frankie signed your name."

"There's another thing," Lisa said. "I went to the bank this morning to take his name off of our joint checking account. They told me that Frankie had another savings account there, in his name only. It was payable on death to me."

"How much was in it?"

"Only about three thousand."

"Did they give you any statements from the account?"

"They said they could only give them to me if I was named in the will. As the...."

"Personal representative."

"That's it."

I'd already looked over the copy of the will that Lisa had given me. It was a pretty basic one, and it named her as the personal representative, what used to be called the executor or executrix.

"You are the personal representative. Why don't you let me take care of getting the records. Who knows what we might find there. "

"There's also this," Lisa said, holding up a key. "It was in our safe deposit box. I don't know what it goes to."

The key itself was nondescript, but attached to it was a tag with the number 412 printed on it. It wasn't another safe deposit key, maybe a locker or hotel key. Not much to go on at the moment.

"Let me see what I can find out," I said.

"I've got Frankie's laptop," Lisa said. "But I don't know his password. Do you think you could get into it?"

"What do you hope to find?" I asked her.

"Emails, Facebook, any other things he might have been hiding."

"Are you sure you want to know what I find out? Sometimes, it's better "

"I need to know. I just need to."

I nodded. "Ok. You'll need to decide pretty soon whether or not you want to fight the insurance company. First, let me see what I can get off of the laptop. It may help provide some more information."

I knew the exact person to call to access the laptop. And it didn't hurt that he happened to be my brother.

Chapter 4

Monday morning at nine marked the start of my first day at Chesapeake Bluffs. I was enthusiastically anticipating the change in venue. No more long hours, demanding clients, rainmaking, and partners breathing down my neck to charge more billable hours. There were going to be benefits to moving out of the law firm and into the position of in-house counsel at a golf and country club, and the benefits couldn't be expressed in dollars. It was a matter of lifestyle.

As was necessitated by circumstance, Van Avery kept his luxurious corner office. Dripping with power and authority, its dark wood, leather furniture and backdrop of legal books perfectly complemented his pre-eminent status as the most senior member of the Bluffs' staff. Too bad he was barely here to use it.

I was shunted off into the spare office, whose white walls and more modern furnishings were perfectly suitable for my work, but not enough to make women's knees quake when they entered. I'd have to do that part myself.

My initiation began in the conference room. When the large, expanding portable file suddenly appeared next to me on the table, the tiniest bit of trepidation began to infuse itself into my newfound hopes and dreams.

That sucker was full.

"These are our active cases, ordered by priority," she said, sitting down in the chair next to me. "She" was Sharon Connolly, whom I had just met a few moments earlier, the administrative assistant for the main offices at the Club, which included the director's office as well as finance, and legal. An attractive woman, in her mid-forties, Sharon definitely seemed to know what she was doing. She spoke in the authoritative manner of someone who had the utmost confidence in her abilities.

The expression on my face must have clued her in.

"Yes, Mr. Thomas, these are all active cases," she said. "We've got a bit of a backlog."

You don't say?

Both Evan and Van Avery had led me to believe that there were just a few simple things that needed to be looked at.

Thanks a bunch, guys.

"The good news is that some of our older issues may have exceeded the statute of limitations for filing a lawsuit, which is two years for many civil cases. We'll go over those next week and see if we can't move them into the inactive file. For our current cases, I wrote a summary for your review.

She extracted a thick folder from the file and dropped it the front of me.

These were the summaries?

"Each case is summarized on a single page," she said. "You'll find an overall description of the case, followed by the names of the relevant people involved. At the bottom is the current status of the case, along with what actions we've already taken."

Despite my dismay at the unanticipated workload, I was already greatly impressed by Sharon's acumen and attention to detail.

"This will be tremendously helpful. Thank you," I said to her, remembering to smile.

My guess is that she didn't get a lot of positive feedback from Van Avery.

"Why don't we get started while we're waiting for Evan," I said.

"Mr. McDermott's going to want to go over the Bristol case today," she said. "We had a drowning in one of our ponds, three months ago. The dead man's name was Peter Bristol. He was diving in the pond to retrieve golf balls, when he apparently became entangled on a sunken piece of machinery in the pond."

"Did we know that there was machinery in the pond?"

"Yes. It's an old lawn tractor. I'm told it's been down there for at least sixty years. It even has a name. They call it the 'Pond Deere.'"

"Was Bristol authorized to dive for balls here?"

"That's the problem. His business partner claims that we gave him authorization. He said that he talked to one of our maintenance workers, Juan Ortiz. Mr. Ortiz had been employed by our lawn care contractor, Fairview Greenery Services."

"You say he *had* been employed?"

"It appears that Mr. Ortiz has disappeared. There is some question of his residency status."

An illegal immigrant.

"And Mr. Bristol's business partner, was he with the diver at the time?"

"Yes, Donald Atkins. Apparently, he helped Bristol set up the equipment, and carry away the balls. After Bristol didn't surface at the appropriate time, he called 911 for help. By that time, it was dark. It took the emergency crew an hour to get here and find them in the dark. Susan Bristol has filed suit against us."

"What's the amount?" I asked.

"She wants twenty million."

I suppose she wants it in small, unmarked bills.

"Yikes. How old was the guy?"

"Thirty-one."

"Any kids?"

"Three kids, all under six."

I winced. "How did these guys even get on the property? Clearly they didn't come in through the front gate."

"Apparently, they came in through the back woods off of Old Fort Road," Sharon answered.

"Do we actually permit anybody to collect water balls from our courses?"

"We have a contractor that comes in once a month, who gives us half the balls back, cleaned and prepped, in return for the privilege. Bristol must have known the schedule. The accident occurred the day before the contractor was due to come in. The contractor knows about the 'Pond Deere,' and his men know enough to keep away from it."

Damn, she knows her stuff.

Although not a paralegal, Sharon might just as well have been. Diligent, organized, and serious, I could see she was going to make my new job a lot easier.

"So tell me," I asked, "what's your overall assessment of the Bristol situation?"

She took a moment before answering, and I noticed the look of intense concentration on her face. At last she spoke.

"We're fucked."

I think I'm going to like working with Sharon.

Evan had scheduled my welcome reception to run two hours or so, starting at five. Chesapeake Bluffs was, all-in-all, a fairly large place, and to facilitate the meet-and-greet, he had billed it as an informal affair. Free food and booze were an added enticement. It promised to be an impressive ending to my first day at work.

The reception room at the Clubhouse was definitely up to the elegant standards set by the Club as a whole. Ornate fixtures decorated every single wall, while immense chandeliers loomed overhead. For an informal gathering, the assortment of food was staggering. An entire buffet lined one wall of the large room, complete with meat-carvers, seafood, soups and hot and cold salad bars.

Three bartenders were kept occupied by the attendees, even as waitresses circulated to supply simpler needs such as champagne and wine.

Of course, for the first hour, Evan chaperoned to make sure I met the "appropriate people" as he put it, in the "appropriate order." First up were the bigwigs. I noticed Van Avery was part of this group.

The patriarch of Chesapeake Bluffs was one Charles McClelland, now over ninety years old, and son of the original founder of the Club. Confined to a wheelchair, Mr. McClelland was the first person to whom I was formally introduced.

"It's an honor to meet you, Mr. McClelland," I said, after introductions. He was a legend around the Bluffs, having been the chief architect of the rapid expansion of the club into preeminence in golfing circles. I had been told he only made rare public appearances nowadays. I felt honored to be in his presence.

He extended his hand toward me, but instead of shaking, he beckoned me toward him. I moved closer, placing my ear near his mouth in accordance with his commands.

In a voice that was so faint it was almost a whisper, he finally spoke.

"Your fly's open."

"Thank you sir," I nodded as I deftly and discreetly zipped. "It's a pleasure to finally meet you."

I'd learned that Charles McClelland had sold the Bluffs in the seventies to FirstResorts, a large, publicly-held corporation that built and managed several other ultra-high-end golf resorts. Part of the sale stipulated that the McClellands retained seats on the Board of Directors. His two children, Robert and Carolyn, now in their late fifties, were the current board members. They seemed more interested in my capacity as legal counsel than in my golf prowess.

"Have you had a chance to review the expansion plans yet?" Carolyn asked.

By "expansion plans," I assumed she was referring to the 500 or so acres termed the "North Property." Fortunately, I had been briefed on it this morning.

Thank you Sharon.

From what I'd learned so far, the Board of Directors of FirstResorts had wanted to expand Chesapeake Bluffs to build a seventh and an eighth golf course, along with an extremely ambitious housing development on the coast.

There was only one problem. The land which encompassed the north property also happened to be the habitat of the northern flying squirrel, which was currently listed as an endangered species. For the sake of protecting this furry flying rodent, the $300,000,000 expansion plan had been stopped in its tracks.

FirstResorts didn't yet own the property in question. The planned purchase had been immediately halted after the environmental impact study uncovered the squirrel habitat.

"I've seen the plans," I said. "They're quite impressive. I plan to review the issue this week."

In truth, I had no idea what I would be doing on this

problem, but at least I hoped I sounded like I had a clue.

"That's good news, Thomas," Robert said. "We've been sitting on this thing for far too long."

"We should have bought that property and bulldozed it years ago," Carolyn said, "back before the liberals got into office."

After exchanging further pleasantries with some of the other Board members, I was shuttled over to meet my golf colleagues. First in line was Rodney Collingsworth, Director of Golf, and also the Head Pro for No. 3, the Club's most prestigious course. I'd already met Rodney prior to coming to the Bluffs, and the best I could say about him was that he was a first class jerk. On this evening, at least, he appeared to be on his best behavior, and he introduced me to the rest of the golf pros, who just so happened to be clustered together in his little clique.

I'd met a few of them before, mostly when I'd played golf here with Frankie. I'd also heard some of them speak at Frankie's funeral. There were six pros, including myself, one for each of the courses.

I was the new pro for No. 5. It was one of the two courses that had homes surrounding it. The older courses had been built before the developers realized how much money could be made in selling real estate with golf course views.

We exchanged condolences about Frankie, and then talked shop. One of the pros, Dave Arnold, wanted to consult with me about a "legal matter." We set up an appointment. I had tentatively arranged my schedule to work mornings in the office in my capacity as attorney, and afternoons teaching lessons, and other golf-pro work. Of course, Evan had assured me that my schedule was very flexible.

I'll believe that when I see it.

After a few more escorted introductions, Evan left me to my own devices. I tried to make the rounds and meet as many different people as I could while I had the opportunity. It was toward the end of this process that I noticed a familiar face, now alone at the buffet serving table. It was the lovely jogger that Bertha and I had seen from the house. I'd recognize those well-toned glutes anywhere.

Quickly seizing the moment, I made a beeline for the buffet table, grabbed a plate and moved expediently down the line, finally catching up to her at the soups.

"Good evening," I said, getting her attention. "I don't believe we've met."

She turned toward me, and after a moment, realized that she was talking to the guest of honor.

"Darby St. Claire," she said. "I apologize for not finding you sooner, but I just got off work, and I'm famished. I was going to say hello after I had a quick bite."

"No apology needed. Why don't we sit down somewhere? I haven't eaten either, and I think I've met just about everyone else here."

We grabbed an open table.

"I'm the women's tennis pro," Darby volunteered. "I came right over from lessons. I probably smell like a pig."

"Not as bad as some of our golf pros, and they've already showered," I said, eliciting a chuckle.

Good sign.

"Tennis is a great sport," I continued. "Not quite as big as golf here, but the players generally look a lot better."

Especially the ones in skirts.

"I must confess," I went on, "I'm a bit of an amateur psychic. I believe I can tell just by looking that you're a jogger." I touched the sides of my head, as if I were Johnny Carson channeling the great Carnac. "And I'm thinking you probably like to run in the mornings, on the golf course, yes, I'm getting a time, yes, probably around sevenish or so. Am I right?"

By the look she gave me, I realized I'd just cast myself in the role of "creepy stalker." Quickly backtracking, I explained the circumstances behind my eerily accurate assessment.

Clearly, I need to work on my technique.

"I'd like to get back into my running routine," I said. "It's been a little while. Would you mind if I joined you on your next morning run?"

"That might be possible," she said. "I run No. 5 just about every morning. Tomorrow..." she thought for a moment, "I'll be somewhere near your place around quarter after seven or so. If you like, we could meet-up there."

"It's a deal," I said.

My plan for tonight was to use my psychic abilities to figure out which of my many unpacked boxes contained my ancient running gear.

I wasn't in horrible shape, but I hadn't been exercising regularly in quite some time. Even when on the tour, golfers aren't particularly known for being the greatest specimens of athleticism. Golf doesn't really require aerobic stamina; it's more of a coordination sport, using some finely tuned muscles. The new generation of younger golfers on tour includes a much higher percentage of well-toned jocks. But a lot of golf fans can still relate to some of the heavier touring pros from generations past. Plus-sized, with ample beer guts, they were still able to play at the highest levels of the sport, becoming the perfect role models for millions of out-of-shape guys who still believed they had what it takes.

Nonetheless, I was prepared for my early morning run, having decked out in air-dry running shirt, sunglasses, ball cap, and shorts that were a just little too short by today's standards, exposing my glaringly pale upper thighs. Bertha was particularly fascinated with my running shoes. She sniffed them incessantly, then rolled on her back and rubbed herself all over them, the way dogs do when they encounter some decaying animal corpse out in the woods.

"C'mon, they don't smell that bad," I said, exiting through the patio door into the back yard to begin a few stretches. Looking back at the house I saw Bertha's huge flat face plastered against the bottom of the picture window.

That's going to need to be cleaned.

I glanced down the cart path and sure enough, right on schedule, I saw a tiny figure off in the distance, heading this way. I stepped out and waved. After a moment, the runner returned the favor.

I ran in place to get loosened up. A few moments later, Darby reached the house. She wasn't even breathing hard.

"Good morning," I said.

"Good morning to you."

"You look warmed up. How long have you gone so far?"

"About four miles. Today I'm only doing eight."

What have I gotten myself into?

"Great," I said, trying to force a smile. It was too late to back out now.

"This place is fantastic," she said as she surveyed the property. She stopped when she reached the picture window. "Awww."

Bertha has a way of doing that to people. She was watching us intently, even more so when she saw Darby looking straight at her. I could tell by the rapid fire bobbing of her head in the window that, hidden from our view, Bertha was excitedly wagging her butt.

"That's Bertha," I said, "my baby."

"She's beautiful," Darby said, already smitten.

"Would you like to meet her?"

"Of course."

Bertha was thrilled when I opened the patio door, and bounded out to see the wonderful new creature in our midst. She flopped down at Darby's feet, allowing Darby the privilege of showing her some love.

"She's two years old. My only child."

Darby looked up at me, then back down to Bertha. "Why yes, I do see the family resemblance."

Smart-ass.

Even for dogs as wonderful as Bertha, all good things must eventually come to an end, and after a minute or so more of loving attention, I led her back inside. She did not go willingly. But after all, I had some serious running to do.

We started down the cart path. Darby ran with a fluid, effortless stride. Me, not quite so effortless. I could tell at this pace I was going to get winded pretty fast. After a few minutes of running in silence, I finally broke the ice.

"So, how long have you worked at the Bluffs?" I asked.

"Almost two years. Before I came here I was coaching tennis at McKean University," she said.

"Did you play there too?"

"No, at Virginia, four years."

The University of Virginia was a top-tier division-one school. She'd have to have been a pretty highly-rated player to play on that team.

"What'd you play?"

"Number one singles and doubles."

"I'm impressed," I said. "I played on my high-school team…. In college, I concentrated…on golf mostly." It was getting a little harder to talk now.

"I was thinking," I continued, pausing every few words to catch my breath, "you know, since we're already running partners… and everything, maybe we could play some tennis… get to know each other a little better."

"I already know I'm a little better," she retorted. As if to prove her point, she sped up the pace.

I was beginning to like this gal. She played hardball.

"Just to let you know," I huffed, "I wouldn't pass this up… if I were you…. I've got women… breaking down my door."

"Are they trying to get in or out?"

I had to laugh at that. And that made it impossible for me to keep running, not that I had much left in the tank anyway. I was done. Darby kept right on going, not breaking a stride.

"What about our match?" I called out to the rapidly receding figure.

"How about Thursday. Seven?" she said, turning back to yell, "Bring your 'A' game."

"You're on," I yelled back.

Now if I could only remember where I'd left it.

Kevin laughed when I asked him if he could break into Frankie's laptop. "Bro, if it takes more than ten minutes, I'll buy you a beer." Of course, since we were sitting in my house, and he was already drinking one of my beers, it wasn't too much of a risk on his part.

Kevin was my only sibling, not quite three years older. While I had received my share of smarts and athletic talent from my parents, Kevin had inherited the big brain. And by big brain, I mean the kind that goes to MIT and just about aces every course. He was in Mensa; I was a little "densa." While at school, Kevin was fraternity brothers with some of the guys who were part of the blackjack team that cleaned up in Las Vegas for a while.

He could tell me all the intricate probabilities involved in their card-counting scheme, and I had asked him once why he hadn't joined the team. He was honest, and told me that he tried, but that he failed the "boobs test."

"After weeks of training, they run you through the final test, the gauntlet. You've got to keep an accurate count in the face of every distraction they throw at you. I was doing great, keeping the count, playing the hands perfectly, all the while they were yelling in my face, spilling drinks on me and playing loud bells and sounds. Finally, they pulled out the big guns. They had some of the girls take their tops off, right in front of my face. Just for a moment, I lost track, and I forgot the count. You might say I was having a little trouble keeping 'abreast' of the situation."

"Stop," I groaned. Kevin was the master of the truly horrible pun. The sad part was that he sincerely believed that they were funny. He felt that if you didn't laugh at his humor, it was because you were in some way deficient, not quite mentally capable of appreciating his pure, true wit. He felt sorry for you. What he didn't know was that the feeling was most often mutual. Plus, he'd never come to grips with the fact that I held the bulk of the family's humor genes.

But all in all, my brother was a pretty good guy, genuinely kind-hearted and down-to-earth. He worked over at some think-tank near DC, not too far away. He tried to explain to me one time what he did. After a fifteen minute dissertation, I nodded like I understood.

"Rocket scientist," I had decided to explain to anyone who inquired. That was impressive, and probably sufficiently close that it wasn't a complete fabrication.

Rubbing his hands together in anticipation, Kevin opened the laptop, ejected up the CD-tray and plopped in a CD.

"What's that do?"

"That's a password cracker. It contains a small Linux kernel. We'll boot the PC from the CD, and then we can start the cracker program from there."

"How does it work?"

"Well in theory, it just guesses the password."

"And then it tries to log in with the guess," I said, trying to impress Kevin with my astute powers of logical deduction.

"No, not really."

Here it comes. I asked for it.

"The passwords are stored in encrypted form, so they just look like gibberish. When you type in your password to login, the computer transforms your password into the encrypted form, and compares it to the stored encrypted value. If they match, you get in. That transform is called a hash."

"I've seen lots of people who've been transformed into gibberish by hash."

Ignoring my attempt at levity, Kevin continued. "Look, do you really want to know how this works, or not?"

I was already very sorry that I had ever asked.

"Not?"

Kevin wasn't one to take "not" for an answer. This I knew from frequent, painful experience.

"This program uses hash values that are precomputed, so it doesn't have to take the time to compute hashes for all the guesses. Because even at billions of operations per second, that could take days, or weeks, even. The precomputed hashes are stored in what is called a rainbow table."

Rainbows are cool.

The computer had finished booting up, and Kevin selected the option to crack passwords and hit enter. "Ok, let's get crackin'," he said, looking at me to acknowledge yet another of his groaners.

Help me, please.

In no time flat, the program was printing stuff out to the screen. In about two minutes, it was completely done. The results looked like this:

User	Password
Administrator	MyLaptop
Frank	HoleInOne

"There you go," said Kevin triumphantly. "Write those down."

He had to admit that, yes, even one so technologically limited as I, was capable of writing these two things down on paper.

He removed the disk and restarted the machine. When we got to the login, Frank was already selected as the user. Kevin typed in "HoleInOne" and we were in.

Even though Lisa had given us permission to break in, this

somehow felt a little wrong, like snooping in someone's private matters. It was also, I had to admit, quite exhilarating, in a voyeuristic kind of way.

"Where do we go first?" I asked eagerly.

"Email, always email." Kevin clicked on the small icon, and in a few seconds, Frankie's electronic record sat staring us in the face. Among the thirty or so messages on the first page were a few that I recognized.

"Hey, that's from me," I said, pointing to the last email I'd sent confirming our planned golf date.

"Well, now that we've got that cleared up," Kevin said, as he pantomimed the motions of closing down the laptop and getting up to leave.

"Really," he continued, "it may take a while to go through the emails, especially since we don't know exactly what we are looking for. There're likely to be a lot of passwords stored on the computer, plus the web browsing history. It's probable he also had some webmail accounts. If he had anything to hide, it could be in one of those.

"I'm going to make a ghost clone of the laptop's drive, that way I'll be able to bring the copy back to my place and do some forensic computer analysis from there, where I have all my tools. I'll leave the laptop here with you, so we can work in parallel. May save some time that way, since you knew Frankie and all."

And you have the tools.

But I still had a few tools of my own.

Bertha had been alerted when Kevin had pretended to get up. She came over and looked up at him for attention. I went to the kitchen to get more beer. When I came back, the two of them were wrestling on the floor, like kids, a fierce battle between two gigantic heads.

As beverage-cart attendant Caitlyn Ross squeezed herself into her polo shirt, she performed her daily self-ritual, evaluating her "look" using the full-length mirror in her small bedroom. The open collar dipped down precipitously, providing an exceptional view into the abundance of cleavage that defined her upper body.

The bigger the dip, the bigger the tip.

It was a sight, she knew from long experience, that most males were utterly powerless to ignore.

As usual, the tight stretchy fabric showed off every curve of her well-toned body. But today, for the first time, among those curves was one that Caitlyn didn't necessarily want to reveal to the world. As she looked down at the reflection of her torso, she noted that the growing presence inside her was starting to make itself known.

Caitlyn was acutely aware that she was a fantasy figure. That was an unspoken, but well understood, part of her job description. Tall, blonde, with ample breasts and long trim legs showing just a hint of muscle, all packaged up in a tight shirt and those short, short pants, she provided for golfers a different kind of refreshment than the food and beverages she sold from her cart.

On a good weekend, Caitlyn easily made $200-$300 a day in tips. Even on weekdays, she averaged well over a hundred. On her best day ever, during last year's members' tournament, she had made over $500. And almost all of her income was tax-free, that is, as long as she didn't bother to tell the IRS. Her job was simple, sell the product—beer, soft drinks, crackers, snacks—and keep the golfers happy. The latter part was the most important, for the happier they were, the better the tips.

Flirting with the male golfers came easy for her. She smiled, joked, and stroked their egos, making sure to bend over just a little bit more than necessary to provide a good view to all those who were interested, which generally meant just about anyone who toted a penis along with their other woods.

The members at Chesapeake Bluffs were, in general, pretty sweet people. Having worked there for more than three years, she knew almost all of them by name, including what they liked to eat and drink. It got to the point where she even knew what they were going to say most of the time. Naturally outgoing, Caitlyn found it easy to socialize with her clientele. They loved her for it.

Some men lingered at the cart, wanting her to stay and chat. While golf was recreation for them, it was her livelihood, and dawdling any more than necessary on any hole meant cutting into her income. So Caitlyn devised ways to extract herself without seeming rude or rushed. Often she told them that if she got going now, she would see them again in five holes. The promise of another visit by such a vision of loveliness was enough to get most of them on their way.

When the men golfed with their wives, Caitlyn wisely modified her approach. She greeted the women first, respectfully, by their last names. "Good morning, Mrs. Halston. How are you today? Can I get you anything?" Then she would move on to the husbands, "And for you, Mr. Halston?"

These women knew that their husbands liked to ogle the beverage cart girls, but at least while their spouses were around, Caitlyn reined it in, and the wives appreciated that. They tipped her well.

Most of the golfers realized that the beautiful beverage cart girl was just a fantasy, but there were always a few who got carried away. Members at the Bluffs were wealthy and powerful men, accustomed to getting what they wanted, and every once in a while, what some of them wanted, was her. Looking at her made them feel young and virile. Having her, they thought to themselves, would prove it.

They would try to corner her and suggest in not too-subtle ways how they could "help her out." The price of this "help" was not mentioned, but was well-understood. She would usually attempt to deflect their advances by smiling and telling them she would think about it, and usually after a time they came to their senses and forgot, or maybe they began to focus their attention on one of the other cart girls.

But the greatest pressure, by far, had come from management. They had real power over her, given their ability to set her schedule and to determine the course on which she worked on any given day. She regretted giving in to the pressure those few months ago. Although not her direct supervisor, the man had tremendous influence at the Club. He could get her moved to Course No. 3, *weekends*, if she'd "go out" with him. Reluctantly she'd agreed, desperately needing her car fixed to get to and from work. And he'd come through on his promise. Her tip income had grown by almost fifty percent with the move to her new route.

But that wasn't the only thing that was growing, she reminded herself, glancing again at the reflection of her belly.

She pulled off her top. Patting her bare abdomen, she smiled as she thought about the new life present within. Moving to her closet, she found a similar shirt, one size larger. This top, though still attractive on her, wasn't quite as form-fitting as her usual one, but the looser fabric around her waist proved effective in hiding her secret, at least for now.

I bet my tips will be way down today, she thought to herself, *just because of this big-ass shirt.*

On Wednesday morning, just as I had promised the Board members, I delved deeper into the issues surrounding the Bluffs' northward expansion. Having only seen a summary on Monday, I had barely learned enough to avoid seeming like a complete idiot at the reception.

Unfolding the set of oversized documents in the file, I looked over the artists' renditions of the proposed golf courses and the "Riviera on the Chesapeake" development. The poster sized pictures were apparently computer generated, but so realistic that it looked like this thing had already been built.

Utilizing the rocky coastline, the development called for the natural hilly terrain close to the shoreline to be artificially enhanced, boosting the elevation up to 200 feet above the water. Artificial cliffs and rocks were seamlessly integrated into the landscape, providing the basis for the construction of 300 seaside homes winding down from hillside to the bay.

The plans called for the Bluffs to build and sell all of the homes through its construction and realty subsidiaries, ensuring that the villas would conform precisely to the desired Riviera look. And judging from these renderings, the development bore a striking resemblance to the rocky coastal villages in Northern Italy that I'd seen in countless travel posters. And that was certainly no accident. Complete with waterfront shops and marina, this development was unlike anything seen on this continent.

But unlike their European counterparts, these houses had all the modern luxury appointments expected by today's ultra-wealthy buyers. The price of such luxury ranged from two to five million and up.

The two new golf courses, numbers No. 7 and No. 8 at

Chesapeake Bluffs, were closely integrated with the village topology. Both designed from scratch, the two courses couldn't possibly have been more different. No. 7 was to be a true "links" course, built in the style of the original, ancient, Scottish courses. Close to the beach, a links course was built on sandy soil, on the strips of land that "linked" the beach to the inland areas, hence the name.

In Scotland of old, these strips were not suitable for farming, so they lay dormant until some bright chap thought about hitting a ball into a hole with a stick. The rest, they say, is history.

No. 8 was radically different, as it took full advantage of the rolling terrain to create what looked to be a scenic masterpiece, fairways winding up and down the natural and man-made hills, many holes ending at the bay with island and peninsula greens. Almost all of the holes had an unobstructed view of the water, the marina and the natural cove that housed the village.

I could almost imagine the view from inside my private Italian villa on the Bay....

The wall of windows was filled by the brilliant orange and purple sky reflecting on the water, signifying the day's end. Sailboats made their way back to the marina, spinnakers in full blossom. The day's final golfers finished their putts on 18, defeating the darkness.

I took another sip of wine as I devoured the view. This bottle was near perfection, rich, fruity, full-bodied with great legs, words that also happened to perfectly describe my dinner companion, who had just slipped out of her—

"Mr. Thomas?"

Sharon's voice over the intercom jolted me out of my transcendent daydream.

One of my better ones.

"Yes."

"You asked me to remind you of your one-o'clock meeting with Mr. Collingsworth. I'm going to lunch now."

"Thanks, Sharon."

I had really wanted to finish my thought. Perhaps one day I would get to live there, that Italian Riviera next door on the Bay.

That is, if it ever got built. And right now, I seemed to be the only person doing anything at all to make it happen.

Director of Golf Rodney Collingsworth could have been the poster boy for narcissistic personality disorder, if such a diagnosis still existed. If vanity, conceit, egotism, and obsession with oneself were symptoms, Rodney was all that and more.

A little self love is probably not a bad thing; but in Rodney's case, it completely defined him. He was a total, absolute, without any doubt about it, jerk.

Ordinarily, I try to stay as far away from these people as possible, as I've found that distance is the only real cure for this particular affliction. Unfortunately, there was one underlying circumstance that made this solution somewhat difficult.

Rodney was my boss, at least on the golf side of things. As the Director of Golf at the Bluffs, he dictated much of my day-to-day activities in the golf arena.

On more than one occasion, Frankie had told me stories about Rodney, and in an odd way, I felt that I had come to know him through these tales, developing a fearsome dislike for the man without ever actually having seen him in person.

I finally did meet him last year, when Frankie invited me to play at a tournament at the Bluffs. After a last-minute scheduling change, Rodney's name appeared in our foursome. I think he wanted his chance to show up the "big name" pro on his home course.

Rodney was everything I expected him to be, and more. He could be smooth as silk when he wanted to, pleasant and charming. He'd have a nice chat with someone, just shooting the breeze. As soon as they were out of earshot, he would take me aside and tell me what a douche bag, dumb shit, or moron that guy was. Of course, I knew that as soon as we were done talking, he'd be saying those same things about me to somebody else.

He talked incessantly about his romantic conquests. He seemed be acquainted with nearly every woman we encountered during our match, describing to me, in very specific terms, intimate details about each one. Of course, they all had some fatal flaw that had required him to dump them. Most of the beverage cart girls didn't seem to care for him too much, I noted.

We sat down around the big conference table, and after introductions, Rodney outlined his philosophy of the pro life.

"You gotta sell the product, whatever that product is, whether it be lessons, golf equipment, your course, whatever. You're always selling. That's how you're going to keep your job, that's how you're going to make your living, and that's how you're going to define yourself."

After his spirited motivational talk, I felt like throwing up. I'm sure Rodney did define himself by how well he could sell, but that was his problem; his whole life was just one big con job.

Next, Rodney went over the big upcoming events, including tournaments, and this month's group packages. At Chesapeake Bluffs, a corporate group could buy a package which included lessons by one of the pros. These were pretty lucrative for the Club, and usually resulted in some fairly substantial tips for the pro. I noticed Rodney assigned himself the choicest opportunities.

"Thomas, I'm starting you off with the youth clinic next week. It's a good opportunity to break in at the ground level." He said this with a straight face.

Teaching youth golf classes was generally considered the worst assignment for a pro. Twelve year olds don't usually tip too well. But I really didn't mind. I kind of liked working with the kids.

And this brought Rodney to his last topic. Summer interns.

"So, Big D, I understand your intern ran into a little problem, or should I say, a problem ran into him." He chuckled.

Big D? I really disliked this guy.

This was news to me. I hadn't heard anything at all about my intern.

"I'm not sure I follow," I said.

"Oh that's right, you probably haven't heard. Your Virginia Lutheran home boy got hit by a truck. Word on the street is that he's paralyzed, in a wheelchair for life. That's too bad. I heard he was a pretty good player."

"Has anybody from here talked with him since the accident?"

"What for?" he said. "We can't use a kid like that around here. He's got to be able to hit the ball, stock the merchandise, drive the carts, and collect balls at the range. You think there's a chance in hell we're going to hire him when he graduates?"

"Maybe we should see if he still wants to work this summer,"

I said.

"We're not running a charity ward around here, Thomas. Didn't you just hear my speech? It's all about moving the merchandise. He's dead weight. The kid needs to move on and find something that's… within his reach now, which is a quite a bit lower than it used to be."

Clearly, Rodney had never heard of the Americans with Disabilities Act.

I was trying hard to remain calm. "That's pretty harsh, don't you think? I need to talk with him. It sounds like the kid's been through one of the worst things that anyone could ever imagine. I think he deserves that much. Plus, if we made him an offer for employment before the accident and he's still capable of doing the work, he may have a case for an ADA complaint if we retract the offer because of his disability."

"Now don't get all lawyerly on me, Thomas. Ok, you go talk to him, if that makes you feel better. Just don't come complaining to me when you get stuck this summer with an even bigger handicap than you've got right now."

You don't have to worry about that. I wouldn't come to you if I were choking to death and your last name was Heimlich.

If it worked for Disney, why not for us?

Before there was any such thing called Disneyworld in Florida, Walt's crew had quietly formed real estate companies that combed the area outside of Orlando. Their goal was to purchase the 27,000 acres needed for the new theme park at the best possible prices without having the original property owners discover who exactly it was who wanted to buy their parcels.

Nothing wrong with that.

Walt knew that once the owners "got wise," they would use their newly discovered leverage to jack up the prices. With company names such as "M.T. Lott," their plan had been a huge success. Almost all the land came cheap. The first acre of land had cost him $80. After their plans had finally been unveiled to the public, the going rate rose to $80,000.

As I continued my research through the paper trail of the northern property expansion, I realized that FirstResorts had attempted to do something similar to Disney's strategy, establishing three Limited Liability Companies in an effort to procure the land discretely. They only needed 500 acres, one-fiftieth the size of Disney's purchase. There was only one problem; it looked like something had gone horribly wrong.

Searching through the stack of proposed sale documents, I discovered that the parcels in question, those 500 acres bordering Chesapeake Bluffs on the north, were already owned by four *other* LLCs.

Now there was nothing all that unusual about property being owned by an LLC. The flexible tax treatment, which combined certain aspects of partnerships and corporations, was fairly popular with individuals who owned multiple properties and wanted to manage them together as one entity.

But there was something odd about these particular companies. According to the online property records, each LLC had purchased its parcels in either late 2001 or early 2002. Prior to that timeframe, most of the parcels hadn't changed hands in well over ten years, some for more than twenty.

If it looks like a duck, and swims like a duck....

The markup on the properties had been ridiculous. Having access to all the records for the proposed sale, I was astounded to see that in the two years or so between the LLCs' purchase of its parcels and the proposed sale to FirstResorts, the prices for the acreage had risen by 500 to 1,000 percent. We were talking tens of millions of dollars in increased property valuation.

That was crazy.

Even during a boom time in real-estate, that appreciation was exorbitant.

I was surprised that all these irregularities hadn't been red-flagged by the FirstResorts' purchaser prior to the sale.

Maybe his name was M.T. Head.

I needed to ask Van Avery about this. My other concern was the status of the land's endangered species classification. Looking through the file, I found a series of letters and responses to the EPA, the state DNR, and our state and federal representatives. We'd put all our muscle and resources into trying to get the land reclassified, or at least to get some sort of relief.

Almost all of the responses started off with *"I'm sorry"* or *"It is with some regret."* I'd been around long enough to know this was generally not a good sign.

The trail of letters seemed to have tapered off after about two years. It appeared as if, after that, we just threw in the towel. There had been nothing new for the last three years. But now, *Desmond Thomas* was on it.

I needed to do some more research on that land acquisition. Something about it just seemed a little "squirrely."

Chapter 5

On Thursday morning, Dave Arnold arrived for his appointment. The pro on No. 2, Dave was a fine golfer, at least that's what I recalled from having played in a foursome with him and Frankie some time back. Only five-foot-eight or so, he had terrific swing mechanics and hit the snot out of the ball. He out-drove me on most of the holes that day.

He'd seemed somewhat tense when I'd talked to him at the reception. Clearly, he'd had something he wanted to tell me.

Dave sat down, and fidgeted.

"So, there's a legal issue you want to discuss?"

"Yeah, sort of," he said, pausing. "I don't want to say anything bad about Frankie or anything, but I think we've got a little bit of a problem."

"How so?"

"Well, Frankie was our contact guy. When we wanted to, you know, make a bet on a game or something, Frankie knew a bookie. Frankie set us all up with accounts, so we could bet through him. He'd take care of collecting the money and paying out and everything."

"So far I'm with you."

"Frankie liked to gamble a lot, a whole lot. He played for the big stakes. When he told me how much he put down sometimes, I just couldn't believe it. Me, I just do it for fun. I never bet more than fifty bucks on any game. I usually just bet on the Redskins to win.

Makes the game more interesting."

"I'm aware that Frankie had some gambling issues. You can be assured that I'll keep your information confidential, Dave. How much would you say he bet?"

"Sometimes he'd bet five hundred, maybe a thousand on each game, a couple games at a time. Way over my head."

How had I missed this?

"So how does this involve you, Dave?"

"Well, I got a call last week, after Frankie died. It was from the bookie. Said I needed to pay up my debts. Now that Frankie's gone, he said he had to contact me directly. He wanted five thousand bucks."

"Five thousand?"

"I told him he's crazy, I never bet five thousand in my whole life. He said he's got the records. If I don't pay up, he said he'd call my wife, and then work."

"How did you know it was Frankie's bookie?"

"He told me his name. Tom Jones. That's the same as Frankie's bookie."

"Did he threaten you in any other way?"

"He said he'd give me a week to pay, and then he'd start calling people. He said if I still didn't pay after that, some of his guys might be by."

"Did you have his number?"

"No. His number was blocked."

I didn't like the sound of this. Had Frankie placed his own bets using Dave's name? Maybe Frankie had tried to recoup his losses by placing bets in the names of his co-workers. Whatever it was, this latest development had Dave Arnold scared witless.

"You mentioned that some other people were involved in this. If anyone else has gotten these calls from Tom Jones, tell them to get in touch with me, soon."

"Jeez, I never expected this," Dave said glumly. "It was bad enough Frankie dying and all, and now this shit. You don't think...."

"Right now I'm not sure what to think."

Dave thanked me and left quickly. I had a feeling I would be hearing from a few of his co-workers very soon. Of course, it was also entirely possible that Dave was lying to cover his own debts.

Maybe he really did owe Tom Jones the money, and Frankie's death provided the perfect opportunity to shift the burden onto a dead man. That seemed pretty callous, but money, or rather the lack of it, sometimes made people do strange and awful things. That much I was sure of.

There was one guy who might help me get to the bottom of this.

Where'd I leave that number?

Lucas had never set out to become a bookie. It just sort of happened. Actually, it was his Uncle Danny's fault. Danny had run the books as long as he could remember. His father had always told him that his uncle was the black sheep of the family, but to Lucas, his father's brother seemed way cooler than his dad.

Uncle Danny even drove a cool car, a convertible Triumph Roadster. When Lucas was only fourteen, his uncle taught him to drive. After only a few short weekends, Lucas had mastered the transmission, steering, gas and brakes and was tooling around the countryside with the wind blowing through his hair, Danny smiling next to him, giving the occasional bit of advice, always on the lookout for the cops, who wouldn't look too kindly on the under-aged pilot.

His father never found out about these weekend excursions. But when Lucas turned fifteen and got his learner's permit, his dad took him out for the first time to "teach him how to drive." After a few minutes of watching Lucas' flawless operation of the family station wagon, he'd pretty much figured it out.

"Uncle Danny taught you to drive his car, didn't he?" his father had asked with more than a hint of disgust. A shrug of Lucas' shoulders told him all that he needed to know.

"Damn it!" He slammed his fist on the car's dash, a flash of red briefly coloring his face, now mindful that his brother had robbed him of this time-honored father-son ritual.

It had been one of the few times that Lucas had heard his father curse.

Always good with math, Lucas was thrilled when his uncle began to let him in on the secrets of his trade. Lucas peppered him with questions.

"What if your team loses?" Lucas had asked him. "Won't you

owe a lot of money?"

"That's the beauty of it. You do it right, you make money no matter who wins or loses." You try to get the same amount bet on each team. You take a percentage off the top when you pay out the winnings. If you take ten percent, and each person bets a thousand, you make a hundred bucks."

"How do you know that people will bet the same amount on both teams?" the boy persisted.

"Good question. The official line comes out of Vegas. They just set the odds and watch how much money gets bet on each team. If more money gets bet on one team, they change the odds until the bets even out. Like I said, they don't care who wins, they make money either way."

"What if people don't pay up when they lose? What do you do then?"

"I knew you were a smart kid. You've figured out what the toughest part of the job is. Most of the time, I tell the guy that I'll call his wife, or his work if he doesn't pay up. They don't like that. These guys don't want their wives to know they've been betting the mortgage money. If that doesn't work, I might go to his next-door neighbors and ask if they can help somehow to convince him to pay his bills. They don't like that at all."

"What if none of that works?"

"Jeez, I can see you're really thinkin' ahead. Well, I happen to know a few guys I can call. Big guys, you know?" Lucas nodded. "After they go pay a visit, our guy usually pays up pretty fast." The young man absorbed the information.

He liked to hang around Danny's office, hear him talk with his clients on the phone, see him write the wagers in his book and watch him lock away the records in his safe after each transaction. After a while, Lucas had memorized the combination.

It was a few years later, after Lucas had gone away to college, that his father called him one day with the news. Uncle Danny had been in a car accident. His Triumph hadn't stood a chance against the big SUV that t-boned him. He'd been killed instantly.

Lucas volunteered to help his father clean out his uncle's place. After they got there, he waited until just the right moment, while his dad was busy in the basement, to slip into his uncle's old office. Once there, he moved to the safe and quickly worked the lock.

The satisfying click told Lucas that the combination hadn't changed. Inside, Lucas found the book, along with his uncle's client records and other priceless information. He stuffed them quickly inside his jacket.

A few months later, Lucas told his dad that he was taking a break from college. Truth be told, by that time, with his growing clientele, he was already making more money than both of his parents. He bought himself a shiny new convertible, a Japanese model though, a little more reliable than the British ones. When he came home with his new set of wheels, his father took one look. "Oh Lucas," was all he could manage to say. He knew.

Lucas' uncle had told him that he never let his clients know his real name—a safety factor, he'd said. Driving home one evening, Lucas had pondered what he should call himself. As he listened to the popular singer's hit song on the car radio, it dawned on him that a simple, easy to remember name would work well for him.

From now on, he thought to himself, I'll just be Jones, Mr. Tom Jones.

⸻

"Are you here as her lawyer, friend, or what?" Bull Durham didn't pretend to engage in small talk.

"A little of both," I replied.

William "Bull" Durham was the stereotypical private investigator. Bald, stocky, muscular, without even a hint of the beer gut that plagued most fiftyish males, he looked like the kind of guy you didn't really want to mess with. I'd heard he was a former police officer. They usually make for some of the best PIs, I'd found.

His office was small, but sufficient to hold his desk, computer, files, and a couple of well-worn guest chairs. It was located in one of those nondescript strip malls that plague every city nowadays. In fact, everything about this place was nondescript. That seemed to suit him quite well.

As an attorney, I'd already had a bit of experience working with private investigators. As far as lawyers are concerned, PIs exist in the gray area between legal practice and professional pragmatism. Lawyers need information, PIs supply it. The methods and mechanisms that they use to get this information may not always be one-hundred percent kosher. They may call up agencies, hospitals, friends, misrepresenting who they are, and as a result, get access to privileged information.

One of the most common uses of privately licensed investigators was for spousal infidelity, which was why Bull had initially been retained by Lisa.

Bull began paging through the documents and photographs sitting in front of him. "As Mrs. Brooks probably already told you, I didn't uncover a whole lot on her husband. For a little while, I thought I hit pay dirt when I caught him at the restaurant with the broad."

He flipped an 8x10 photo my way. It was taken through the window, of Frankie and a woman sitting in a restaurant. By the intensity of their stares, neither appeared to be there for pleasure.

The woman looked familiar, but I couldn't place her. Dark brown hair, mid-forties maybe, I tried to think if I'd met her before with Frankie. Stylish, affluent, but not garish, definitely not trailer-trash. If this was Frankie's paramour, she had to be one high-maintenance honey.

"Apparently, the dame left through the back, 'cause I didn't see her go. When Brooks took off, I followed him. He headed straight home, so I never got any more dirt on the female. After that night, I tailed him for another week, but she never resurfaced."

Bull appeared to be disappointed.

"His only other extra-curricular activity was knocking back a few at the Stone Street Tavern. I got a shot of him talking to this guy." He flipped me another photo.

"Who is he?"

"If I was a bettin' man, I'd say that he was Frankie's bookie, judging by how much he liked scribbling in his little black book."

Perfect. That's what I wanted to talk about.

"Lisa Brooks said a guy named Tom Jones had called her about Frankie owing some money. According to the detectives, Tom Jones was Frankie's bookie. He's trying to shake down some of Frankie's friends at work now. I bet this is the same guy."

"Bookies have been known to do that when they don't get paid on time. That's step one on their collection checklist. Tom Jones? Sounds like a fake name if I ever heard one," he said.

"Wouldn't it be funny if his real name was Engelbert Humperdinck?"

Bull didn't smile. "Want me to track this guy down for you?"

"Yeah," I said, "see what you can find out."

"Will do," he said, "I'll get right on it."

"How's business?" I asked, assuming it must be slow if he could start so quickly.

"Lately I've been sniffing out employees taking fake sick leave. You know, they call in sick, then head out to the dog track, go on vacation, that kind of thing. It's easy work, and it's getting to be a big business."

I had no idea that companies were now hiring investigators to check up on their employees' personal lives. That was somewhat disturbing.

"Anyhow, if you need an investigative partner for any of your work, keep me in mind. Or for any other attorneys you know. I like referrals."

"I'll do that," I said. But first I needed to find how this job would pan out.

After a brief discussion about finances, as in "Who's going to be paying for this?" my "Bull session" was done.

George Robinson didn't speak a word of Korean, but then he really didn't have to. The shiny new electric vehicles that surrounded him told him all that he needed to know.

George loved golf carts. He even kept a scrapbook in his office that he populated with pictures and articles of these strange beasts, all the way from the earliest models up to the present day.

His favorite—and the one generally acknowledged as being the first commercially available golf cart—was the Autoette. This odd looking creature, sporting three wheels and a tiller control, had an appearance that could best be described as a self-powered Tilt-a-Whirl. George had spent many hours trying to track down a working Autoette, or at least one he could fix up and restore, so far with little success.

He did have one of the earliest production carts in his collection, dating back to 1954, the year Mr. Beverly Dolan formed the E-Z-GO company in Augusta, Georgia. Beverly had begun operations by using surplus B-17 wing-flap electric motors hooked up to the drive wheels of his small carts. In 1960, E-Z-Go was producing 60-70 carts a month; by 2010, they were up to 600 a day. George's first-edition cart was both rare and valuable.

George also owned a 1976 Club Car, produced during the company's first year of operation after Beverly's brother Billy defected from E-Z-GO and bought the struggling company, subsequently turning it into the largest golf cart manufacturer in the world, as well as E-Z-GO's chief rival. Yamaha, the third member in the golf cart triumvirate, entered the business in 1979, also basing its operations in Georgia. George had recently added a first-model-year Yamaha cart to his collection, completing the triple crown of cart collectibles.

As head of facilities at Chesapeake Bluffs Golf and Country Club, George was responsible for procuring and maintaining their fleet of nearly 400 golf carts, a huge number by golf club standards. These carts were one of the largest sources of revenue for the Club, bringing in nearly $4,000,000 each year.

The Bluffs completely replaced their fleet of golf carts every two years, and during each biannual bidding period, the three Georgia manufacturers waged a heated battle for what was undeniably one of the most prestigious product wins in the golf world. George used his leverage to squeeze every financial and service concession he could from the eventual winner.

This year, however, George had been in contact with a new company, Korean-based KG Limited. KG was a growing concern in South Korea, but had, as yet, no real US presence. The company was eager to break into the American market, which accounted for over fifty percent of the world-wide sales of golf carts.

When KG offered him the opportunity to tour its manufacturing facility near Seoul, George jumped at the chance. After an extensive product presentation and financial briefing, he found himself staring down over the assembly line, and liking what he saw.

George reviewed KG's offer. The two-year lease featured the top-of-the-line Elite cars, complete with state-of-the art 48-volt electric drive, regenerative braking, built-in GPS, Wi-Fi connectivity and all-weather flat-panel displays. Their electronic cart management system allowed each cart to be individually tracked and accounted for on the course.

The system knew when golfers had finished their 18 holes, and automatically charged their accounts if they "happened" to decide to play another nine holes, cutting down on a significant source of lost revenue for the Club.

While seated in their cart, Club members could access the internet, order food from the Club's restaurants, make dinner reservations after the match, use video chat to talk to their playing partners, make personal calls, and even access an electronic caddy that would suggest proper club usage for their particular lie, giving them warnings about water and sand hazards. Each club member's account could be stored in the system, which would automatically recall individualized information and preferences.

The interiors of these cars were unlike any other golf cart George had ever seen, rivaling the look of the finest exotic sports cars, with the additional benefit of being totally weather-proof.

The icing on the cake was that their two-year lease would save Chesapeake Bluffs nearly $750,000 per year. George knew that if he recommended going with KG, he would encounter some resistance from the old-schoolers on the board who wanted to go with a familiar name, but this level of cost savings would be nearly impossible to pass up.

After the final briefing, KG's president took George into his office and thanked him for his visit. Through his translator, he spoke about the company, and how much they valued their employees, even to the extent of paying for the educational expenses of each employee's family.

"In this spirit," he told George, "we have created an education fund for your family, as we desire to extend our company's educational arm to all our partners and associates. Of course, in order for you to share in this fund, your company and ours will need to become partners in business."

He handed George an ornate red silken envelope. Opening it, George saw a Korean bank account statement.

His eyes settled on the first entry, and George initially thought that he had misread the number. But it was no mistake. KG Limited had set up an account in the name of George Robinson containing two-hundred thousand US dollars.

I arrived at the tennis courts around 6:30, a little early, to warm up, and maybe get in a few practice serves. Unlike jogging, I had actually played tennis fairly recently, having participated last season on my law firm's team.

I played at a solid 4.0 level in singles, maybe a little better in doubles. Unlike golf, where a player's proficiency is specified in handicap strokes above par, there is no practical way to evenly handicap players in tennis. As a result, players are placed in levels, and a player competes in league play or tournaments against others at his or her own level. At least that's the way it's supposed to work.

A beginning player would be rated at a 1.0. A 6.0 player, like Darby, could qualify for a scholarship at a top Division I school.

Players rated 6.5 and above can play at the professional level and perhaps compete successfully on tour.

Despite our significant differences in rank, I wasn't too worried about our match, since I knew that I held two distinct advantages over Darby. Number one, I was a man, and number two, she was a woman.

The difference between men's and women's tennis is much more than just power, strength, and speed. Women's tennis is played with a completely different style—much less aggressive, much more patient. Women players typically work the ball, hitting softly from baseline to baseline until one player finally makes a mistake.

Men, in contrast, usually resort to strength and speed, working the angles to hit winners, and slamming the ball at every opportunity.

Darby was just finishing up a group lesson with a band of energetic youngsters, none of whom seemed old enough to be out of elementary school. After all lessons were finished and all kids were safely accounted for, she transferred her gear to my court.

"How are you feeling after that run the other day?" she asked. "It's tough getting back into running, but you'll get there if you keep at it."

"Easy for you to say. I haven't played tennis in a few months, so it may take a little practice for me to get back into the groove."

"Take all the time you want," she smirked. "I wouldn't want you to hurt yourself."

We took our sides and began to warm up. She returned every ball with a soft, perfectly struck topspin shot. After a few minutes, my old stroke began to return, and I returned each ball with a little more pace. I tried some tighter angles and hit a few down the line that she couldn't reach.

When you're warming up, it's generally considered bad form to try and hit winners, since the goal is to hit the ball, not chase after them. But every now and then, you want to show your opponent just a hint of what you're capable of. It puts a little fear in them. Tennis is a thinking person's game.

We practiced some serves, and then we were finally ready to start. She spun the racquet, and I won. I elected to let her serve first. *Clearly, that would be the gentlemanly thing to do.*

I prepared myself just inside of the baseline, ready for a soft and accurate first serve. As she tossed the ball in the air, I did a little crow hop to get myself on my toes, ready to react. I was hoping to pound her first ball back down the line, just to get the match off to a good start.

I heard the noise first, the sharp crack of ball against tightly strung racket, followed immediately by a blinding yellow flash that was quickly speeding away from my forehand. Lunging to my right, I barely managed to get my racket on the ball, the result being a weak floater over the center of the net.

In a heartbeat, Darby was at the net. I saw her eyes widen in anticipation as the ball came into range. She took a full overhead swing, and blasted it down at a steep angle back into my side. The ball bounced high up into the air, completely carrying over the fence into the neighboring courts.

She had "fenced" the ball. On the very first point of the game, I had been totally emasculated. She might as well have just hung my balls in her trophy case.

Looking at her face, I saw no indication of any expression whatsoever, although I believe I detected faint signs of a smirk emerging as she turned around to walk back from the net. I was a little more prepared for her next serve, a high kick serve that I managed to get back at a decent pace, only to see her put it away for an easy backhand crosscourt winner.

She toyed with me for the remainder of our match, much as a cat plays with a small rodent that it has captured, running me ragged back and forth from one side of the court to the other with her ruthlessly consistent topspin strokes, until I reached a point where I could barely catch my breath. She mixed in slices, drop shots, overheads, and spin serves with such ease and grace that I would have applauded if her opponent had been anyone else. Since it was me, I simply said, "nice shot." And after a while, even that was understood.

Darby won 6-0, 6-1, with my only victory being in a game in which I managed to land four of the hardest serves I could muster just inside of the service line, although one of those was a generous call on her part.

She was gracious in victory, and even complemented me on "making some pretty good shots." Of course, after such a shellacking, she might have just as well have asked me what color panties I like to wear, such was the general state of my ego.

I did have to admit, she was a great tennis player, much better than I had ever been, or could ever hope to be. And my criticism of women's tennis as a whole may have been a tad overstated. Despite the drubbing, the whole experience had been immensely enjoyable. I felt it was time to take the next big step in our relationship.

It was time to play some golf.

After the tennis match, a check of my messages showed that I had a voice mail from Bull Durham. Earlier today I'd heard from two more frantic gamblers with stories similar to Dave Arnold's. Both had been contacted by Tom Jones and had been told to pay up on thousands of dollars in bets. Both claimed that they owed nothing. Thus, it seemed likely that Dave was telling me the truth.

There was another angle I considered, however. Jones might just have parceled up Frankie's debt and assigned it to his betting buddies, hoping through intimidation to get them to cough up part of the debt themselves.

In addition to the voice message, I also had a new email message. I knew exactly what it was. My brother had rigged up my

phone so that I got an email transcript of every voice message that
had been left. Kevin loved gadgets, widgets and all things
technological. His newest thing was writing smartphone apps. I was
his guinea pig, or beta tester, as he liked to call it.

"You've got nothing 'beta' to do," he'd always quip, this line
repeated so frequently that now I'd only notice if he didn't say it.

Whenever he would come over, he would install one of his
new brain farts, and then have me spend hours calling, punching, and
testing over and over. It would take at least three beers to numb my
mind after one of these sessions.

Nevertheless, some of his apps were pretty cool, and if I ever
suggested something to Kevin that sounded remotely plausible, in a
week or less he would send me a link where I could download the
new app and try it out.

I checked the email transcript. It read:

> US. I found Janet's arrange to meet tomorrow. You want
> me kinda little bar. You never know. Emily's guys are not
> always the most flexible. Characters, you can come up and
> to Customer, I do, this is where I didn't know you, which
> you know also found it. If you get this call me back there.

Now that was useless. These voice transcripts were cool, but
obviously still had a way to go, especially with guys like Bull who
talked in rapid, clipped sentences. I wasn't sure who Emily was, or
why I should care if her guys are flexible or not. I tapped the key to
listen to the actual voice message, which was somewhat more
understandable:

> Thomas. I found Jones. I arranged a meet tomorrow, you
> and me, at a local bar. You never know with these guys,
> they're not always the most reputable characters. He thinks
> I'm a potential customer. I had to do it this way or I don't
> think he would show. Also found where the key goes. Call
> me back. Durham.

That made a little more sense. I checked the time. Ten-thirty.
Not so late for a private-eye, so I returned his call.

"Durham," the voice snapped.

"Desmond Thomas," I said. "I got your message."

"Yeah, I checked out the bar where Brooks and the guy met. I asked the bartender if he knew a place a guy could make a few wagers. After a while, he told me about a guy named "Jones" who comes in here. After a few more beers, he gave me a number. I met with him tonight."

"Without me?"

"Right. I placed a bet. Just a small one, a hundred dollars out of your retainer. That way, he thinks I'm legit. After I left, I tailed him back to his house. Bingo, I got his address and his real name. From that, I got his social security number, credit reports, the works. Nice car, and nice place. His bookie business must be doing alright. His real name is Lucas Bennett."

He made a bet from the retainer? I guess that made sense.

"So what happens next?"

"You'll be happy to know that we won our bet. I'm meeting him Sunday night to collect and make a few more bets. He doesn't know you're coming, so I'll meet him like last time, and then we'll ambush him."

"Won't he be kind of pissed when he finds out you're not a customer, and I'm a lawyer?"

"He's gonna be pissed no matter what we do. If we told him what we really wanted, he'd never show up. This way, I already got the dirt on him, so he can't run."

That was actually pretty smart, I thought, the way Durham had planned this two part shakedown. Plus, I didn't mind that he was going to be there to cover my back when I met Bennett, aka Tom Jones.

"By the way," Durham said, "I found out where the key goes. I visited all the private storage facilities in the area, and on the fifth try, the tag matched the one used by the facility. I figured you could get in there with power of attorney and all, but to save time, I smooth-talked my way into the back and managed to open up Brooks' unit. You're not going to believe what I found there."

He was right. I didn't believe it.

Chapter 6

My active file was starting to get very active. After only one week on the job, I was already looking into the Bristol drowning, the Brooks' bookie ring, and the north property expansion plans. This morning, I had barely been in my office for ten minutes when Sharon hustled in, shutting the door behind her.

"We might have a problem," she said. "Milton Langford's waiting to see you. He's steaming. I told him to sit out there and cool off. Take a look at this."

She handed me a manila envelope. I extracted the glossy, spiral bound contents. After glancing at the cover, I cleared my throat and sat up.

"Wow," was all I could manage.

It was a calendar, with the provocative title "Cart Girls Gone Crazy." On the cover was a very attractive, and very nude, young woman, perched seductively in a spanking new golf cart.

I went through the pages. Each of the months was graced with a different beverage girl. All of them were stunning, and all had no, or almost no, clothing on, with the exception of visors and golf gloves. Strategically placed golf bags, beer trays, golf clubs and flagsticks kept the calendar from moving into x-rated territory.

"Are you about finished?" Sharon asked, with a hint of irritation.

"Hold on, I've only got three more months of research to go," I said, as I pondered how in the world Miss Cart Girl of September learned to do *that* with a ball retriever.

I quickened my pace over the last three pages, although a bonus, thirteenth picture was included, a group shot of the girls lined up, simultaneously placing their balls on their tees.

Nice touch.

I closed the calendar and looked up at Sharon.

"And you would like my choice for the top month?" I asked. "I've always been fond of spring." I started to open the calendar again, when Sharon grabbed it out of my hand.

"Not funny," she said. "Milton tells me that four of these young women are currently employed as Chesapeake Bluffs' beverage cart attendants. He wants to fire them immediately."

"I didn't recognize any of them," I said, "but then again—."

"You weren't looking at their faces." Sharon cut me off in mid-sentence.

"I was going to say that I've only been here for three days, and I haven't had a chance to meet everyone." I gave Sharon my best "hurt feelings" look.

"When did this calendar come out?" I asked.

"It just came out. Apparently, they're being sold in bars all over town. One of the caddies gave it to Milton."

Milton Langford was in charge of day-to-day operations of the food and beverage side of the resort. The beverage cart ladies fell under his purview, which was a pretty nice purview, now that I think about it. Milton was a good ole boy, with a big Southern drawl, who spoke slowly and deliberately in the finest tradition of the South. He was a true Southern gentleman. I was trying to imagine Milton being so upset. It didn't seem likely that he would talk any faster, that just didn't fit with that drawl. My bet was that he talked at exactly the same speed, only louder.

"I guess it's time," I said. "Send him in."

As soon as I saw him, I wondered what he'd looked like before Sharon had given him a chance to cool down. He had his suit coat off, his face was flushed, and beads of perspiration dotted his forehead. He had his handkerchief in his hand, mopping up the drips that threatened to roll down his chubby cheeks.

"Have you taken a look at it, Desmond?" Milton asked, wasting no time.

"I glanced at it."

"We cannot tolerate this at this Club. We have a reputation."

"What would you propose we do, Milton?" I asked.

"I believe those girls need to be terminated."

"The ones who work here. There're four of them is that correct?"

"Well they all ought to be terminated, but I can only fire the ones who work here."

"And what would you say would be the reason for termination?"

"They are an embarrassment to their employer. We have standards here. There are a lot of members who could be upset at this."

"Could I take a look at these standards?" I asked. "Since I've just started here, I'm not familiar with the contracts we give to our beverage assistants."

"It's not written anywhere. It's just understood that they need to watch what they do. They represent our Club. They represent us. And one of them there, she has on our Club visor."

He turned to Miss Cart Girl of July. Her visor did appear to have the blue and gold colors of Chesapeake Bluffs, but the logo was absent, probably removed via Photoshop.

"That'd be a hard sell, Milton. There's no logo visible. Just having the colors is probably not enough."

Clearly, it would take some fine-tuned finessing to get Milton to reconsider his current stance as "upholder of corporate moral standards."

"Let me ask you this," I continued. "You hired these four girls, is that correct?" He nodded. "And about how long have they worked here?"

"Some of 'em worked here for two, three years, maybe."

"Are any of them poor performers, miss a lot of days, unreliable? Anything like that?"

"No, I can't say so. When they work, they do a pretty durn good job. But still, look at this, Desmond," he said, pointing to the calendar. "I can't look at these girls the same way after seeing them in that calendar."

"You mean to tell me that you've never imagined any of these girls without their clothes on, at any time?"

"Well," he said, fidgeting, his discomfort evident.

"Do you want me to leave, Mr. Thomas?" Sharon asked.

"No, not at all. We're all adults here."

"Let me ask you Milton," I said, "when you hired these girls, did their looks play any part in the hiring process?"

"Well, they *are* beverage cart girls. There's an expectation."

"Would you have hired them if they were unattractive or overweight? Is it a coincidence that every one of our beverage cart girls is a big busted double-D bombshell?"

"Like I said, there's an expectation for a beverage cart girl. She can sell more product if she's attractive. It's a matter of sales. That's just good business."

"It's not my decision," I said. "I'll back you up on whatever you decide, since that's my job, to represent the Club in legal matters. I'd hate, though, to end up with a wrongful termination lawsuit against the Club from these four girls, especially after what you've affirmed to me about our hiring criteria. You'd end up having to go to court and testify to what you've just told me. And their lawyer won't be so nice."

The look on Milton's face as he pondered that eventuality spoke volumes. From here on out, we were just playing out the string. He *was* going to give in. Sometimes peacemaking involved giving the potential warriors a small taste of the impending battle. The wise ones chose alternate ways of resolution.

"Why don't you take a week before you decide, let things cool off. See how their sales do in the meantime. If you decide to keep them on, I'll tell you what I'll do. I'll bring those girls up here and have a chat with them. I'll warn them about the legal implications of their actions and that we decided to give them a break this time, but that it would probably be wiser not to do that again. Think of it as a legal spanking. I'm sure that'll put an end to this in the future."

The image of the girls being chastised in this way seemed to soothe Milton considerably. The red was gone from his face, and he was once again breathing through his nostrils.

"Alright, I can do that," Milton said. "I can hold off for a week." He headed out of the office, noticeably pacified.

"Legal spanking?" Sharon frowned. "Now I've heard everything. Did they teach you that in law school?"

"Yep, it's the legal principle of *poena ut patesco solum*. That literally means 'pain to the bare bottom.' There's quite a bit of legal precedent. "

"I'm sure there is," Sharon huffed.

Before Milton was completely out the door, I picked up the calendar off my desk and waved it.

"Milton, I'm going to hold onto this," I said. "For evidence."

Sharon headed back to the reception area, but she couldn't resist leaving a parting comment.

"Evidence, my *patesco solum*."

This kid was going to do alright.

In her fourteen years as Neurologist at West Hope Memorial Hospital, Dr. Cynthia Gallo had worked with hundreds of spinal cord injury patients. She could tell within minutes how quickly a patient would adapt to the challenges of their new condition.

Her job, although rewarding, was also, of necessity, extraordinarily intense, especially during those moments when she had to tell new patients they would never again have full use of their whole bodies. Almost all of them cried. Most went straight into denial. Many hoped for a miracle, and occasionally, a few seemed to get one. But for the vast majority, a severed spinal cord would permanently change the way they lived their lives.

She looked again at Cody Corrigan's X-rays. The injury had occurred at T5, in the middle of the thoracic vertebrae. That meant his legs would be fully paralyzed, but that he would have full use of body, arms, and hands. The higher up the spinal cord the injury, the greater the paralysis. Anything above C4, in the cervical vertebrae, usually meant complete paralysis. Dr. Gallo hated those the most.

Cody was one of her younger patients, but she had already noticed that he was an exceptionally bright young man. By the time she'd first met him, Cody had already pretty much figured out everything she was going to tell him. That was a very good sign. It meant that he had accepted his injury, and had already started his recovery. The doctor was reasonably certain that Cody would be very interested in what she had to show him today. Entering his room, she saw that Cody's mother and stepfather were visiting. Cody had received a steady stream of visitors from day one.

"How we feeling, today, Cody?" Dr. Gallo asked.

"About halfway," Cody replied, with a smirk.

"I'm glad you've still got your sense of humor." Dr. Gallo chuckled.

"I just wanted to check and see how things were progressing. Have the rehab people made a plan for you yet?"

"A plan? You've got to be kidding. They've already had me lifting dumbbells in bed. I think those guys get off on making us lame-o's suffer."

"Cody," his mom reprimanded.

"You'll appreciate them when you find out how strong they're going to help make your arm and torso muscles," Dr. Gallo said. "You're going to be extremely buff before they're done. Your situation is quite unique. Apart from the obvious spinal cord injury, other parts of your body suffered very little serious trauma, no broken bones or internal injuries. This means you'll be out of here in a week or so and able to get back to school very soon."

"Does anyone have any questions?" the doctor asked.

There was silence for a few seconds, and then Cody spoke up.

"Umm, I did have a few things I wanted to ask...."

That slight pause was a dead giveaway. Dr. Gallo was pretty sure she knew what Cody wanted to talk about.

"I just remembered, I need to run one more test," the doctor said. "Mr. and Mrs. Upton, could I ask you to wait outside for a few minutes? I'll let you know when we're done."

"Of course," his Mom said as they quickly made their way out of the room.

Dr. Gallo waited until they were out of earshot.

"You want to know if you can still get an erection."

"How did you...?"

"You're not the first twenty-one year old male I've treated. That's a pretty big thing."

"That's what she said," Cody quipped reflexively.

Dr. Gallo shook her head in amusement.

"Male sexual arousal is a pretty amazing beast. Even without the direct connection to the brain, the spinal cord itself can control many aspects of arousal, and of course the blood flow to the area hasn't been affected. But there's one way to test it." Out of the stack of papers and charts in the manila folder the doctor was carrying, she extracted a glossy package and handed it to Cody.

Cody took one look at it and smiled. "'Cart Girls Gone Crazy.' Now that's what I'm talkin' about."

"I appropriated it from the doctor's lounge, and I thought you might like a copy for reference, you being such a student of golf and all."

Cody nodded, accepting the sentiment.

"Here's what I want you to do," Dr. Gallo said, pulling the curtains around the bed. "Take your time, look it over well. Then I want you to do the Johnson maneuver."

"What's the Johnson maneuver?"

"You look at your Johnson, and see if it maneuvers."

Cody's face turned crimson red, unaccustomed as he was to discussing such matters with members of the opposite sex.

"I'll be at the nurses' station. Ring the call bell when you're done. One ring means no luck today; two rings means things are looking up. I'll leave you to your devices, then," she said, exiting.

A few minutes later, Dr. Gallo heard the nurses' call bell ring. There was a brief pause, then a second ring. She smiled, only to hear the bell ring a third time. This made the doctor laugh, along with a few of the nurses who were familiar with this particular procedure.

After an appropriate time, Dr. Gallo strolled into Cody's room. "Are you decent?" she yelled at the curtain.

"Better than that." Cody replied.

The doctor opened up the curtains.

"Now the calendar's yours to keep. You may want it for future research."

"Thanks doc."

"There's one more thing I wanted to show you," the doctor said, extracting yet another packet from her folder.

Cody scanned the pictures on the pamphlet.

"This is amazing," he said. "I never knew you could get such a thing."

"Now don't go getting yourself all excited again," Dr. Gallo said. "But take a good look at it. It might be just what the doctor ordered."

His smile told the doctor all she needed to know.
All in all, not a bad day.

My legal workload seemed to be getting no lighter, despite my best efforts. After another long day at the office, I arrived at the Stone Street Tavern around seven, as Durham had suggested.

I ordered a draft, an offering from one of the local microbreweries in the area, while waiting to be summoned to the big reveal. The light wheat beer wasn't half bad, but then again, I hadn't met too many beers that I couldn't say that about.

I scanned my surroundings, trying hard to be incognito, just like a normal bar patron, instead of someone waiting for an intervention with a dead friend's bookie. Unfortunately, the harder I tried to act normal, the more self-aware I became, like a bad actor who doesn't know what to do with his hands. Now, I was having a hard time remembering what normal looked like.

The place was fairly large, dimly lit, appropriately oaky, and appeared to have a pretty regular clientele, judging by the way the bartender and waitress greeted everyone. There were three guys cheering at the other end of the bar, watching the ballgame on TV, a group at a table, and a couple in a booth who couldn't keep their hands off each other.

Got to be some kind of secret affair going on there.

And there were four women in a booth. That had "girls' night out" written all over it. As soon as I spotted them, all four ladies turned and looked away simultaneously.

They were checking me out.

The women giggled. From the looks of their table, they had already knocked back quite a few, and it didn't look like they were ready to quit. That could mean trouble.

Bull Durham wandered in a few minutes later. He nodded at the bartender, then took a seat at a table in the far corner.

The next guy who comes in should be Jones.

I wondered if he looked like the singer. I was getting a little apprehensive.

It didn't take long to find out. Short and heavy, he looked as if he would burst out of his skin, like a jumbo-sized kielbasa. I couldn't imagine this guy belting out anything but a belch. He sat down at the bar, two stools away.

Not him.

I felt a tap on my shoulder. Turning around, I saw one of the women from the table.

"Excuse me," she said, with just a hint of a slur. "My friends and I wanted to know if we could buy you a drink."

She was pretty nice looking, as were two of the other girls at the table. I tried to think what a normal, inconspicuous guy would do in this situation.

Attractive—*check*. Inebriated—*check*. Free drinks—*check*.

"I never turn down an offer like that," I said. I turned to the bartender, who appeared to be monitoring this development with professional detachment, and raised my nearly empty mug. He nodded and went off to fetch a full one.

"Come sit with us," she said, "I'm Eileen."

"Desmond," I said. "It looks pretty crowded over there."

"Don't worry, we'll make room. We're very friendly."

I have no doubts.

I was sandwiched between Eileen and a curvaceous companion. It was a tight squeeze, but the ladies didn't seem to mind in the slightest. I had to admit, I'd been in worse situations in my life.

"So what do you do, Desmond?" Eileen asked. "We tried to figure it out already. It's a game we play. We think you work in DC. Some kind of political job."

I thought about what I should tell them, and then decided that there was no harm in the truth.

"Well, I have two jobs right now. I'm an attorney and golf pro."

The ladies sat in stunned silence for a few seconds as their alcohol-addled brain cells struggled to process this news.

Then, nearly simultaneously, they erupted, as if the slot machine they were playing showed up with three bars. They laughed and giggled and pumped their fists. One hugged me and gave me a kiss on the cheek.

"You're positively delicious. You aren't married, are you?" she said, quickly followed by "Ow, who's kicking me?"

Amidst all the merriment, Bull walked by the table and gave me a head signal.

"Ladies, I hate to run, but I've got to meet somebody," I said, attempting to edge Eileen out of the booth. She pushed back with equal force. Finally, I managed to slide out, but not without being the recipient of a few assorted gropes disguised as assistance.

"Thanks for the drink," I said.

"Awwww. No fair-sies." They giggled again. "Come on back. We'll be here."

Of that I could be certain.

Sitting down at Bull's table, I was introduced to Tom Jones, a relatively normal looking guy, who could have been a banker or insurance salesman. He was wearing a gold Rolex watch.

"Desmond Thomas, the golfer?" he said. His face lit up, with the kind of smile people get when they recognize a celebrity. "I made a lot of money off you when you played in the Open here. Lot of local interest in that one." Then his face changed to a more somber appearance.

"Tough break on that last hole," he said. "Gotta be a heart-breaker."

"I got over it."

It was time to come clean.

"Listen Jones, I was good friends with Frankie Brooks. I understand he was one of your clients."

His face fell.

"What is this, some kinda setup?" he said, looking over at Durham, then back to me. "Aw, shit. I ain't tellin' you guys nothing."

He started to leave, when Durham spoke.

"Hold on there, Bennett."

At the mention of his real name, Lucas Bennett froze. Slowly he sat back down, realizing that we held a few cards he didn't want revealed.

"Are you guys cops?"

"No, he's a PI, I'm an attorney."

"Shit, shit, and shit," he said.

"I understand Frankie owed you some money. His wife says you called her, told her that Frankie needed to pay."

"Owed me is right. He was in the hole for thirty grand."

"And the next thing you know, Frankie ends up dead," Bull interjected.

"And you guys think… Jeez, who do you think I am, Tony Soprano? I never touched Frankie. I had nothing to do with that."

"Maybe you sent out your boys to rough him up, scare him a little. Maybe they got carried away."

"You guys have been watching way too much TV. I got a business to run, and a customer who won't pay. If I… get rid of him, how am I supposed to collect money from a dead guy?"

"Maybe you call up his co-workers and try to harass them into paying Frankie's debts."

"You know something?" he asked.

"I know three workers at the Bluffs who've been getting phone calls."

"Frankie set up accounts for those guys. They each owed me for bets they made. I got records. I ain't trying to cheat people. Look, what I do's not strictly legal, but I keep an honest book. Ask anybody."

"Sure, would you mind if we took a look at your records?"

"In your dreams," he scoffed. "That's my bread and butter."

"Those guys claim they never bet anywhere near that much. They're all small peanuts," I said.

"So if they didn't make those bets," Jones said, "then Frankie would've had to make the bets in their names." He thought for a moment. "I'd cut off his credit since he owed so much. Shit. That guy, when he lost, he lost big."

"How much did he end up losing, all told?"

"I don't know exactly, maybe one-forty, one-fifty grand over the past two years. Plus what he owes now."

Durham and I looked at each other. No wonder Lisa was in such dire straits. Where had Frankie gotten the kind of money to fund losses like that? He didn't earn anywhere near that much. It was time to take another look at his finances. Something wasn't adding up.

"Right now, I want you to stop harassing these men, and Lisa Brooks. Their slates are clean, as far as I can tell."

"And I'm out nearly forty grand now?"

"Not much I can do to help you with that," I said. "But if I hear about any more phone calls or threats, I'm going to the authorities."

As I got up from the table, Durham looked at Jones and rubbed his fingers together.

"Shit," Jones said, as he pulled out his wallet and handed him two one-hundred dollar bills.

"Drinks are on me, gentlemen," Bull said smiling.

On our way out the door, I heard a woman's voice call out. "Oh Desmond."

Shit.

My legal world was populated with wars and battles.

One of the most frequent skirmishes involved the infamous Battle of the Forms.

The key to victory in this campaign came not in the fighting, but in its prevention. Always, always, use protection.

The conditions that created the encounter were simple. A purchase was made. The seller's sales form contained their terms and conditions, the buyer's purchase order contained different ones. The act of making the purchase created a legal contract, but one with two conflicting rules.

Resolving a dispute over such a purchase involved the so-called "Battle," where neither side acknowledged the terms of the other. I did my best to protect the Club from this occurrence by reviewing *all* sales contracts before any purchases were made.

Our largest pending contract was the two-year lease for new golf carts. This year, George Robinson had recommended a brand-new vendor, KG Limited, out of Korea. But a new vendor always required starting the paperwork over from square one. And this was a huge contract—in the millions.

I had made some last minute changes to some of the terms that KG had proposed, specifically, I wanted to be able to break the lease in case of defects found in these carts. George Robinson vehemently opposed such language. He was deeply concerned that it would be a deal-breaker. I was concerned with covering our corporate ass.

KG wanted the signed contracts back by 5:00 p.m. They hadn't bothered to specify whether this was 5:00 p.m. Korean time, in which case the deadline had expired, or our time, in which case we were well within the limit.

I called George and told him the contracts were ready to be sent to KG.

"But you need to contact them and clarify the expiration time issue, before you fax it."

"Ok," he said, in a voice that didn't instill confidence in me that he would follow through. "I'll come by and pick them up now."

At that moment, Sharon burst into the office.

"Desmond, you're going to want to take a look at this."

I followed her outside, where, in the parking lot, a battle of a different sort of forms appeared to be brewing. A group of angry Bluffs' caddies had congregated around a pink van. Pinned against the van were five women, four of whom were young and seriously hot, dressed in identical white polo shirts and short, no, make that very short, plaid skirts. The fifth carried a briefcase, complementing her business suit.

Painted on the side of the van was a blow-up of one of these girls, along with the name of her sponsor.

Virgin-ia "Fore" Play
Fantasy Caddy Assistants

"Holy shit."

"That's exactly what I said," Sharon intoned.

I found Paul Owens, the most senior of the caddies, and told him to back his guys away from the van. Reluctantly, he complied. I turned to the well-dressed woman.

"I'm Desmond Thomas, attorney for Chesapeake Bluffs."

"Thank you," she said, holding out her hand. "I'm Anna Martin, the founder of Fore Play."

And all this time I'd thought it'd been in the public domain.

She continued, "We have a contract, signed by your representative, authorizing us to caddy at your course."

"I don't think that's possible," I said. "All contracts go through my office. I'm pretty sure that I would have remembered this one. Can I have a look at it for a moment?"

She handed me the papers. At first glance, it didn't look like any contract that came out of our office. Looking at the signature line, I instantly realized the problem.

The contract had been signed by Randy Lewis, Business Director at Chesapeake Bluffs. The problem was that Randy was now the ex-Business Director, terminated three weeks ago, just before I came on board. I'd heard it hadn't been pleasant.

Apparently, Randy had been helping himself from the till, in a manner of speaking. The investigation into his alleged embezzlement scheme was currently being conducted by the Virginia Bureau of Criminal Investigation.

The contract appeared to have been signed on Randy's last day at the Bluffs.

A final act of revenge.

I glanced down at the contract's termination clause.

> In the event that the Chesapeake Bluffs Golf and Country Club shall refuse to permit Virginia "Fore" Play to utilize its caddies on their courses at any time during the agreement period, Chesapeake Bluffs shall immediately pay to vendor as liquidated damages and not as a penalty, that sum of money (the "…earnings") vendor would have been entitled to receive under the provisions of this agreement for the balance of the term hereof, that sum being no less than $500,000.00.

"How many caddies do you have booked for today?" I asked Ms. Martin.

"There are eight, pre-paid."

"And do you use this van to provide transportation for them?"

"No, I drove that today since it's the first day and I wanted to make sure there wouldn't be any problems. The ladies provide their own transportation."

By now, Evan had also arrived on the scene. Before he had a conniption fit in the parking lot, I pulled him aside and gave him the heads up.

"I'm going to recommend that we let those girls caddy today. This may, in fact, be a legal contract. Randy signed it before he left, and there appears to be a large payout if we break it."

"But Randy wasn't authorized to sign the contract," Evan said. "Isn't that illegal? Can't we sue him for malicious contracting or something? And what about *our* caddies? Paul told me they might walk off if we let these girls play."

"Malicious contracting?" I said, "I'll have to look into that one."

People always come up with new and novel reasons for lawsuits, but I had to admit, this was one of the better ones. I tried not to laugh.

"I'll talk with Paul," I said. "He won't be happy, but at least he'll know what's going on." I'd known Paul from years ago when I'd first interned here.

There was no doubt that our caddies were going to be upset at this intrusion onto their turf, but in reality, they had no legal justification to prevent it from happening. Caddies were independent contractors, not employees of the Club. I doubted that their contracts gave them all-exclusive rights.

After tying things up in the parking lot, I retreated to my office to study the contract.

The contract period was for twelve months, and allowed Virginia "Fore" Play caddies to work our courses. We received $25 for each caddy used. On their website, I found that they charged $225 per caddy for one round, not including the minimum gratuity of $100. According to the site, they already had privileges at four courses in the surrounding area. Chesapeake Bluffs was listed, next to a flashing red "NEW" icon.

As it read, if we broke the contract, we were on the hook for liquidated damages at a minimum of half a million dollars. At first glance, this seemed outrageous. But according to my calculator, if they averaged ten girls a day for a year, their annual gross would be $820,000, not including the gratuities of $365,000, which went straight to the girls.

With that kind of income, I began to think about whether I should be getting into this line of business myself. I'd been known to get into a short plaid skirt or two in my day.

The main problem was that even though Randy was not expressly authorized to sign contracts on behalf of the Club, it could be argued that because of his position as Business Director, he had implied authority to sign such a contract, and as such, it could be deemed valid by the courts, even if signed on his last day. Contract law and the law of agency can get quite complicated. Breaching a contract can have costly repercussions.

Premature termination of "Fore" Play might prove most unfortunate.

Finding myself with a free evening not occupied by a dinner reception, tennis match or clandestine private eye rendezvous, I reviewed the statements from Frankie's mysterious bank account, which had just arrived, after I'd faxed the bank the power-of-attorney. I was eager to see what this secrecy was all about.

Putting the sixteen monthly statements in chronological order, I began my first foray into forensic accounting. The account had been opened a year and a half ago, with an initial deposit of $500.

Nothing out of the ordinary there.

A few days later, a deposit of $50,000 had been electronically transferred in.

Definitely out of the ordinary.

Who could be giving Frankie this kind of cash? Maybe he was some wealthy widow's private boy toy.

Was Frankie a kept man?

Withdrawals from the account were made in cash, $5,000 at a time, with a single one of $9,000. At the end of March, the account balance was down to $2,000.

In April, another $50,000 deposit appeared.

Exactly six months later.

The same general pattern of withdrawals continued, except now there were more $9,000 dollar withdrawals, and the money was depleted by June, only three months after the April deposit.

Then in October again, a new deposit came in, this time for $75,000. A few days later, three large consecutive withdrawals were made for $9,500 each. This continued over the next few months until the balance was down to $3,000, where it remained until the account was closed after Frankie's death.

All told, there had been $175,000 in deposits made to Frankie's secret account, and all of it had been withdrawn in a little over a year.

It looked like he had deliberately kept all cash withdrawals under $10,000, most likely to avoid triggering a currency transaction report to the Feds, who looked at large transactions as possible indicators of drug-related or other illicit activity. Clearly, he had overlooked the fact that the large deposits into the account could have triggered this very same thing.

Maybe the Feds were onto Frankie. Could he have been dealing drugs and realized they were closing in on him? That might explain the sudden suicide.

What had he gotten himself into?

The amount of the withdrawals and the general pattern seemed in line with what Frankie's bookie had estimated. But I needed some corroboration. One thing I knew for sure was that bookies kept meticulous information on their clients. I called Jones.

"Yeah," the voice answered.

"Jones, this is Desmond Thomas." Absolute silence.

"Are you there?" I asked.

"Yeah, I thought I was done with you guys."

"Look, I need to know exactly when Frankie made payments to you, and for how much."

After a minute or two of spirited debate, Jones decided it might be in his best interests to provide the information, which he did.

"Thanks," I said. "If I need anything else, I'll be in touch."

"I'm sure you will," he said, a split-second before I heard the click ending the call.

The payments to Jones correlated precisely with cash withdrawals made from Frankie's secret account.

I realized that the cash deposits were at regular six-month intervals. The next deposit would have been due this month.

Maybe we shouldn't have closed out that account.

I was overdue to spend some quality time with Frankie's laptop. There were bound to be clues in there.

D. Thomas, super-sleuth.

I started with Frankie's email, as Kevin had suggested. Not having a better plan, I decided just to read all of them.

Some three hours and multiple beers later, I was having quite a bit of trouble staying awake, and all I'd found out was that Frankie received lots of spam and chain emails, and that he bought tons of stuff from Amazon and eBay. No lonely widows, mistresses, drugs, bookies, or mysterious bank accounts were mentioned.

So much for a smoking gun.

It was time to admit defeat and call in the egghead.

It turned out that Kevin hadn't yet applied his computer skills to his copy of the laptop. I clued him in on what I'd found out from the bank account statements, and what I'd found out from Bennett. I could almost hear the gears grinding away in his oversized noggin.

"Let's try the basics first," he suggested. "Let me take control of the laptop remotely. You can watch and help. Is the laptop on your network?"

"Umm, network," I said, looking at the screen for a big flashing icon, screaming "Network!"

"Can you get to the web?" Kevin sounded slightly exasperated.

"Sure, why didn't you say so in the first place?"

A few seconds later, the cursor on the screen started moving by itself. It clicked on the bar at the bottom, and windows began popping up. This was pretty cool, but slightly creepy.

"I'm in," he said. "Let's do some email searches to find the obvious."

I was about to tell him I'd already done that, but held back to see if his obvious was the same as my obvious.

To look for the money trail, he searched successively for emails with the words "bookie," "money," "transfer," and "bank." The only responses were a lot of spam on the order of "make money fast."

"It's unlikely a bookie would use email," Kevin said. "Too easy to trace. But of course, we already knew that."

"Of course," I said.

He entered the next search term—password.

"If you forget your password," he explained, "a lot of times they'll simply email a new one when you request it. Most people just leave the password sitting out there in their old messages."

We got quite a few hits on this search, and found out that Frankie had accounts at Amazon and eBay, among other places, but of course I had figured that out already.

I was quite proud of myself.

It was getting late, and I was ready to call it a night, but Kevin was still going strong.

"Ok bro," he said. "Chances are he used a web-based email for anything he wanted to keep on the down-low. I'm going to deploy some utilities to see if I can't find anything else related to the money."

"That's exactly what I was thinking of doing," I agreed.

"Right. I'll just stay on the laptop for a while, so leave it running. I'll email you if I find out anything interesting."

With that, I said goodbye to a very long day.

I woke to that timeless gravelly voice of Louis Armstrong. The only problem was that my alarm didn't play Louis Armstrong. Louis was my phone's ringtone.

What time was it?

The caller's name was McDermott, Evan. It was 7:04 in the morning. Reluctantly, I answered.

"Desmond. We've had a security breach. Apparently Janet, in accounting, took her company laptop home last night. She got up this morning, and couldn't find it anywhere. Then she remembered she'd left it in the car when she went shopping last night. She doesn't recall seeing it after that."

"Did she call the police?" I mumbled, still wondering why this event warranted waking me up from a very pleasant dream.

"Not yet. She called her boss in accounting. Then he called me. Apparently the laptop had the credit card information for all of our members and customers."

I was suddenly fully awake.

"She needs to call the police and report the theft," I said, "but that's not going to help with the loss of data. How many accounts were on the laptop?"

"I'm not sure of the exact number," Evan said, "but almost everyone in the Bluffs is on there, and that's well over a thousand."

It was way too early for this.

"I'll be in the office as soon as I can," I said, reaching down to rub Bertha's belly. She was not used to so much early morning excitement.

After walking Bertha and then taking a brief shower, I arrived in my office, clean and fresh, ready for an exciting day.

Sharon was already there.

"They're in the conference room," she said, almost in a whisper. "Some of them seem to be a little testy."

"Thanks for the warning," I almost whispered back.

In truth, Sharon hadn't needed to tell me where the meeting was located. The sound of loud angry voices echoing down the hallway would have led a sight-impaired person directly to the spot.

I opened the door and the din momentarily abated, as all heads turned my way. Around the table were Evan, Alan Roberts, head of accounting, our IT guy, whose name escaped me, Fred Burns, in charge of security, and of course Janet, whose swollen red eyes led me to believe that she had been on the receiving end of most of the hostility.

"Desmond. Glad you're here," Evan said. "We're not making much headway."

Now there's a real shocker.

"Justin believes there's no real chance of a data breach," Evan continued. "He says the data's encrypted."

Justin. That's his name.

Evan's lead-in gave Justin the cue to speak.

"The thief would have to know where the data resides on the disk," he said, in an authoritative tone. "Then he'd have to figure out the password to unencrypt it. I'd say it's virtually impossible."

"With all due respect," I began, "this is no longer a technology issue. It's a legal issue in terms of our Club's liability and the perception that we were negligent in dealing with our customers' sensitive financial data. The data loss opens the possibility of identity theft. Our only choice now is to perform some serious triage and make the best of the situation going forward. We have to assume that the credit card and personal information on the laptop have been compromised. With that assumption, what should we do?"

"We're going to need to contact every customer, so they can decide if they want to cancel their credit cards," Evan said. "That's what I was saying before you came in."

He settled back in his chair, apparently vindicated.

"How many accounts were on the laptop?" I asked Alan.

"And can we get a printout of all the customers, with contact numbers?"

"We have about 1,400 accounts. I can run that report in a few minutes," he said.

So why didn't we have that already?

"And how many people can we bring in to make these calls? Evan?"

"Well, there are four in accounting, plus the administration staff, and everyone here. That's about ten."

"We'll divide up the list into ten parts. Alan, you can manage the call list. Every caller we contact, we'll cross off. Then we'll have to decide what to do about the ones we can't get a hold of this morning."

"Not everyone's going to believe you," Fred chipped in. "We warn our people all the time about scammers who call up and try to get their information. We tell them they have to look up the number themselves and call it back to verify."

"Good point, Fred. We'll have to leave one accounting line open for people to call back, and have somebody to work that line."

Alan nodded.

"There are quite a few more things we're going to need to do," I said, "to remedy this situation and make sure it doesn't happen again. The fact that credit card information was even on a laptop computer points to a major failure of our internal accounting controls. There's no way that should have been allowed. And then to further allow the laptop to be taken off the property was just asking for something like this to happen. We're going to have to address these issues right away. Undoubtedly there are others. We'll also have to do a mailing to everyone who's been affected by this theft. But right now, we've got some calls to make, and the earlier the better to catch these people while they're still home."

I grabbed some donuts from the tray Sharon had brought in.

Better chow down now, because I was about to spend the rest of the morning eating crow with angry club members.

Chapter 7

The first thing I noticed when pulling into Lisa's driveway was the large "For Sale" sign on the front lawn. I had a sneaking suspicion that Frankie's new Corvette was no longer taking up residence either.

I'd been dreading this conversation. There was no easy way to tell Lisa about the extent of Frankie's gambling, or the bank account.

We met again around the kitchen table, now the default consultation room.

"I've looked over Frankie's bank records," I said. "It appears that Frankie had been receiving large amounts of money over the past year and a half.

"How large?"

"$175,000."

Bewilderment did not begin to describe her changing expression. It was more like a cross between astonishment and intense anger, quickly escalating toward fury.

"And where did it all go?" she snapped.

"His gambling problem was much worse than we thought. It all went to his bookie. We tracked down Tom Jones, the bookie, the guy who called you. Bull Durham helped me put a little pressure on him, and we were able to correlate the bank withdrawals with payments to Jones."

"I knew Frankie gambled, but this..., this is just too much.

$175,000? That sure would've come in handy right about now. Especially after seeing how he left us here with nothing."

She put her head down on the table. I gave her a few minutes. There was nothing I could really say to help. Finally, she resurfaced.

"I'm sinking fast, Dez, really. And now I find out this. I'd kill him myself if he weren't already dead."

"We talked to Jones. He shouldn't be bothering you anymore. Whatever debts Frankie owed were his, not yours."

"Do you think he had anything to do with Frankie's death?"

"There's a lot we don't know yet, Lisa. We're pretty sure it wasn't the bookie. We're still checking on things, though. Durham's pretty sharp."

Lisa was deep in thought. This was an awful lot to take in.

"Do you have any idea where Frankie might have been getting the money that went into that account?" I asked. "It came in every six months. The first two deposits were for fifty thousand, the last one was for seventy-five thousand."

"His paycheck went straight into our checking account," she said. "So that can't be it. Frankie never mentioned any other money. Of course, I can see why. He just pissed it all away. How could he do this to us?"

"We also found out where that key went. It fit a storage unit. The only thing that was there was a set of golf clubs. The set looked brand new."

Her puzzled look told me she knew nothing about them. "He keeps his clubs in the garage," she said. "There's a whole golf section near the cart. Why would he keep them anywhere else?"

She got up and headed to the garage. As soon as the garage door opened, I noticed the large space previously occupied by the Corvette.

I surveyed the golf equipment area. Golf pros in general tend to have lots of stuff, and Frankie was no different. He had three sets of clubs hanging on the wall.

"Here's the set Frankie used all the time," she said, pointing to the largest. "Those were the one's that he was using when he… when they found him. The other two are his older sets. He didn't like to get rid of anything."

I recognized one as the set Frankie had used when we played together in college. I know why he kept them. They brought back good memories. I still had my college clubs, even though I hadn't touched them in years.

"Is there anything missing?" I asked.

She thought for a moment.

"There was a set of clubs that Frankie got from work. They were a gift. He said that the Club gave them to all the pros on their one-year anniversary. Frankie said the Club thought they'd sell more new sets if the pros used them."

"And those clubs aren't here anywhere?" I asked.

"I don't think I've seen them in a while. I can't remember the last time."

Why had Frankie rented a storage unit just to hold clubs that he'd apparently never used?

Heading back to the kitchen, I still had one more thing to discuss.

"Have you given any more thought about the lawsuit with the insurance company?"

"I don't think I have any choice," she said. "I took the kids out of private school, and I'm selling the house. I've got a new job starting next week, working as an aide at the pre-school down the street. Even with all that, that sixty thousand won't last very long, especially with all these bills."

"Then you have a couple of choices," I said. "You could go with a firm that will work on a contingency basis. This won't cost you anything, but they'll probably take one-third of your award, plus legal costs. Or, you could hire an attorney on an hourly basis. You'll need to pay a retainer fee up front. It could be several thousand dollars right away, and quite a bit more after that."

By her expression, I could tell that neither of those seemed particularly appealing.

"Or," I continued, "it's possible I could initiate the lawsuit myself."

"How much would I be paying you?" she asked.

"Frankie was my best friend. He helped me out when I needed it. I'm just returning the favor. It may take me a little bit of time, since I've got a pretty full plate right now, but I'm willing to give it a try."

That evening, I finally got around to checking my personal email, and discovered a message from Kevin. He was short and to the point, as always.

> Bro:
>
> I found 3 web email accounts that Frankie had accessed in the past. Unfortunately, he only stored the password in the browser for one of them. That account was pretty old and not too interesting.
>
> The other two require knowing the password, or answering questions for a lost password. None of the other passwords worked.
>
> Call me.
>
> K

Kevin had sent the email over three days ago. I'd been so busy I hadn't even thought about the laptop since that night.

I rang him up.

"Where you been, Dez?" were the first words out of his mouth.

"Sorry, we had a crisis at work, and I just got to your email. My part-time lawyering has been anything but."

I brought Kevin up-to-speed on Frankie's bank account.

"I'm surprised," he said, "that those big deposits didn't trigger a currency transaction report. The Feds should have been all over that."

"They tend to be pretty busy trying to catch the big fish," I said, pulling a fact out of my posterior.

Who said sibling rivalry was dead?

"I'd like to find out where that money was coming from," I said.

"Banking's not my specialty," he said. "But I kind of believe that if the people who transferred the money wanted to remain secret, we're not going to have much luck finding out who they are. My guess is that if Frankie was carrying on some secret deals, he would have used a pre-paid cell-phone or webmail account."

Lisa hadn't mentioned anything about finding a second cell-phone of Frankie's. As far as Frankie's email accounts, I could try to contact the webmail providers using Lisa's power-of-attorney to request access as surviving spouse, but my experience in the past taught me that this was almost always a lost cause.

"How can we get into the webmail accounts?" I asked.

"There're two ways. We can try to guess the passwords, or we can go through the lost password process."

"How's that work?"

"There are questions and answers you supply when you create the account, questions that other people ordinarily wouldn't know. If you tell the system that you lost your password, it brings you up to a screen where it asks your questions back. If you type in the correct answers, you can reset your password and get back in."

"Ok, I've seen that before. What kinds of questions are we looking at?"

"There's one for each account. The first one is, 'Who is your all-time favorite movie actor?'"

I had really been expecting a factual question that I could look up, like his mother's maiden name. A favorite movie actor could be anyone.

"That's a tough one," I said. "It might take a while to figure out. How about the other one?"

"When did I make my first hole-in-one?"

Now that was more like it. I was there when Frankie got his first ace. It was during a college match. I could still, to this day, picture that hole. A downhill green with a big lake in front, it was a great vantage point from which to watch his shot hit and bounce on one hop into the cup. It hadn't even rolled. We had done quite a bit of celebrating after that match.

Figuring out the exact date might be a little trickier. I was having trouble recalling our opponent that day, and now even the exact year seemed a bit fuzzy. A voice interrupted.

"Dez, you still there?"

"Oh, sorry, but I think I might know that one," I said. "I was trying to remember the exact date."

"I'll email you the usernames to the three accounts and the one password I have, along with some instructions. When you figure out the answers to those questions, give me a holler."

The investigation into Frankie's mystery was progressing, but with baby steps. I was just hoping I wouldn't fall down on the job.

The promotion to third-shift factory floor manager was the greatest moment in Zhou Jindong's life. His new salary would allow him to buy a real house for his growing family, and finally get out of the crowded state-owned apartments where he'd lived nearly all his life.

The Kan-shoo factory in Tianjin, China, where Zhou worked, was state-of-the-art, producing nearly 400 sets of golf clubs every shift. The MacKenna clubs produced here were the most popular in the world. That fact was a great source of pride among all the workers. Zhou had been told that just one set of these clubs sold for over fourteen thousand yuan. That was hard for him to comprehend, the amount being more than his total wages for three months.

But Zhou was not complaining, nor were any of the other 200 workers who populated the plant almost twenty-four hours a day, churning out over 1,000 sets of clubs daily, six days a week.

Zhou had started out as an assembly line worker in the factory. But his productivity and intelligence, along with a rock-solid work ethic, had been noticed by the Kan-shoo management. He had been quickly promoted to line foreman. After only a few months, Zhou's line consistently out-produced all the others.

Management at Kan-shoo had been greatly impressed by Zhou Jindong's innovative methods, and even more impressed by his results. When the third-shift position opened up in the new plant, Zhou became the youngest floor manager in company history.

The third shift had only a few differences from the first two shifts. Most notably, the third-shift clubs used a cheaper grade of titanium for the metal castings. Also, the shafts came from a different source. Almost all other aspects of the production were identical.

The quality of third-shift employees was somewhat lower than that of the first shift. It was getting harder to find people who wanted to work in the middle of the night, such was the demand for workers in the many factories sprouting up all over Tianjin. As a consequence, there were more mistakes and line stoppages.

Occasionally, the third-shift would be shut down for days or even weeks. The management called these "vacation periods." Inevitably, they would correspond to the times when American corporate representatives were in the country. Although they cost Zhou wages, these breaks were a welcome respite from his busy routine.

Before he moved to third shift, he had often heard people talk about the jiahuò products that were made there, but Zhou didn't really understand the subtleties of trademark and piracy laws, never having learned these concepts in school. To him, these products were the result of hard work and honest labor, and whether or not anyone called them jiahuò, or counterfeit, did not change that fact in the slightest.

The caller id showed up as "blocked" on the bright blue phone display.

This had better not be another salesperson.

Reluctantly, I picked up.

"Chesapeake Bluffs, this is Desmond Thomas."

"Thomas. I believe I may have run across something of yours. I thought I'd do you a favor and let you know that it's in safe hands."

"Who is this?"

"It's Jones."

Tom Jones.

"What is it exactly that you've got?"

"It's a laptop. It seems to contain some information related to your club."

"You stole our laptop? You got some balls, calling me up and telling me that. I could go right to the police."

"Slow down. I didn't steal nothin'. An associate of mine came across it, said I might be interested. I just happened to browse through the files, and found some valuable records that looked a little interesting. By the way, you can tell your computer guys that their passwords need a little updating. There's a lot of information on here.

If this got into the wrong hands, people might get upset."

"What is it you want?"

"I'm offering you a chance to get all this back, at a cost of only, say, $25 a member. Call it a finder's fee."

Finder's fee my ass. This was extortion.

As I remembered, there was credit card information on something like 1,400 accounts. A quick crunching of the numbers told me he wanted in the vicinity of $35,000.

"You trying to recoup your losses from Frankie?"

"I'm just talking about a simple transaction. I found something that you want. I'm willing to get it back to you. You offer a reward, no questions asked."

"How do we know that you haven't already copied the information?"

"Look, I'm the only one so far that's cracked your file. You'll know I'm on the up-and-up because you won't be getting hundreds of calls from your members about funny charges on their credit cards. I'm a man of my word."

Who's currently trying to put the squeeze on us for $35K.

"I'll tell you what," I said. "I'll offer you a deal. You give me back the laptop, I won't call the police and tell them that you stole our laptop and tried to extort money from us. That sounds fair to me."

"Look, I don't use stolen credit card information. That's not my racket. But I can't control what other people might do. There're a lot of bad people out there, some who might just be willing to pay good money for this stuff. I'm offering you some peace of mind, so you won't have to worry about your data zipping around the internet."

Jones, or rather Lucas Bennett, had made a rather foolish mistake, calling an attorney to try to work his shady, underground deal. Did he really believe I was going to risk my job and my career by making extortion payments under the table? What would happen if he'd already copied the files, and then wanted another payment next month? I was obligated to tell our management about this, and go to the police.

"You're right. There are a lot of bad people out there. I know one in particular. What makes you think your scheme is any better than credit card fraud? You can expect a visit from the police pretty soon."

"You can play this however you want," he said. "But you know, I've got friends over in the police department, so I'm not too worried about that. You really think they're going to find the laptop here? But if I were you, I might watch my back. You wouldn't want to end up like Frankie."

The click on the phone once again signified the end of his call.

In my book, that constituted a pretty serious threat. Perhaps I had this guy pegged all wrong.

Chapter 8

ive years earlier - The thumping beat of the FM radio filled every available space in the luxury sedan's cavernous interior, interrupted only by the steady flashing of the vehicle's hazard lights. The two men inside had been waiting by the side of the road for nearly an hour. There was no need to speak. Each man knew exactly what needed to be done.

Planning the perfect hit had always presented a challenge for Billy Walker. Each situation offered a unique combination of circumstances and constraints. Just like snowflakes, no two murders were quite alike.

But if there were such a thing as classic murder-for-hire, this was it. "Make it look like an accident," the wife had directed, "and make it quick. I want my life back."

Done properly, murder was much faster than divorce and the return on investment was off the charts. The wife, in this case, got the life insurance payout and all the joint assets, with no attorney's fees. To top it off, she could play the role of the grieving widow afterwards, earning everyone's sympathy. Ignoring the ethical issues, there was only one downside. And if they were careful enough, that would never have to happen.

Their plan was straightforward. They borrow the wife's car, and have her call her husband and tell him she was stranded on a remote stretch of road. Husband rushes over; they grab him and one unfortunate auto accident later, the job was complete.

Headlights suddenly illuminated the car's interior. Billy switched off the radio.

Here he is. Right on schedule.

They heard a car door slam and the crunching of footsteps on the loose gravel.

Billy jerked open the door and shoved his gun into the man's face.

"Who are you?" Wallace Andrews stammered, his feet skidding to a sudden stop, his body recoiling reflexively at the sight of the weapon just inches away.

Billy forced the husband back into his car.

"You try anything, you're a dead man. Now drive."

The frightened and bewildered man finally summoned up his courage and spoke. "My wife. What have you done with her?"

Billy smiled at the man's misplaced concern.

"Carolyn... sends her regards."

Tuesday was the first of my two days off, and, as fortune would have it, Darby was free as well. The fact that she had agreed to play a round of golf with me bode well for our budding relationship, at least in my mind. This was a chance to reestablish my role as the alpha male, one which had been severely tarnished by her show of superiority in both running and tennis.

Darby also lived on course No. 5, in the "townhomes," which was the way most of the other residents of Chesapeake Bluffs referred to the only section of their development not occupied by single-family houses. They spoke the name in hushed tones, as if the townhomes were some sort of government subsidized housing project that brought blight upon their village.

In truth, these were upscale homes that integrated beautifully into the overall look and feel of the development. Not inexpensive by any means, they did provide the lowest-cost approach to taking up residence in the Bluffs, and were probably the only housing here that was affordable on a tennis pro's salary.

Since we both resided on course No. 5, we planned to tackle our home course. It didn't hurt that I was the pro for this course; I had an edge.

I parked my golf cart and found number 1612. Ringing the

bell, I pondered what Darby's place might look like inside. I'm very much the minimalist, happily satisfied with little or no clutter and knickknacks. From what I'd seen of Darby, it didn't appear as if she was an aficionado of country craft décor, but one couldn't always tell.

She opened the door decked out in a sleeveless top and matching shorts, capped off with a University of Virginia visor. So far, her décor was top notch.

"You didn't play golf for Virginia, too, did you?" I asked.

"No, but I have played a few rounds. My dad taught me."

"Your middle name wouldn't happen to be Nicklaus, Palmer, or Player, would it?" I asked, somewhat in jest.

"No. It's Didrikson, actually," she said.

"You don't mean...." I stumbled.

"She was my grandfather's sister," she said, matter-of-factly. *Babe Didrikson.*

Only the greatest female athlete of all-time. A track star, basketball player, baseball player and of course, championship golfer. She was so skilled and respected that she often competed in the men's tournaments. This was Darby's DNA?

"I'm very impressed. Now I'm starting to get a little worried. Golf was supposed to be my game."

"You should be ok. I haven't practiced in a while."

Somehow, she managed to pull off the difficult task of being simultaneously condescending and charming. I'd been working on that for years, without much success.

"Are you ready to go right now?" she asked, "or do you want to come in for a minute?"

"You don't have to ask me twice," I said, stepping through the doorway.

Before I could utter a word, she wrapped her arms around me and caught me by surprise with a most pleasant slip of the tongue. Assertive—*check.* Good kisser—*check.*

Coming up for air, she disclosed, "I've been wanting to get that out of the way."

"You read my mind," I replied. "If there's anything else I can help you with...."

"I'm good. For now."

Now, that's how I liked to start a round of golf. I took a

deep breath and took in my surroundings.

Her home was modern, mostly black and white, and totally uncluttered. What a relief. The occasional splash of orange and navy blue, the Virginia school colors, provided a colorful contrast.

She might be a keeper.

After a quick tour, we loaded up and headed to the Clubhouse. I was anxious to see how Darby's tennis skills, along with her athletic pedigree, translated to golf.

At the first tee, we stretched. While Darby took her practice swings, I checked out her form. No complaints there. And her swing wasn't too bad either.

Since I hit from the blue tees, the farthest back, I teed off first, hitting a solid 275 yard drive, ending up in the right rough. Not a bad shot, and just a short pitch to the green.

From the ladies tee, without even a practice stroke, Darby knocked the ball 200 yards down the center of the fairway. She had a textbook swing, smooth and seemingly effortless. Given the relative tee locations, our shots were not that far apart, and she had the better lie.

Is there anything this woman doesn't do well?

We both pitched onto the green, mine about twenty feet away, hers about fifteen feet short of the cup. I lined up my putt while she tended the flag. The putt was downhill, and broke slightly to the left, toward the water on that side of the green.

Not wanting to come up short, I gave the putt a little extra and watched as my ball traced its arc toward the hole. It rimmed the cup, ending up two feet away.

Darby's putt was uphill, with barely any break. Again, with no practice strokes, she took aim and tapped the ball. It followed a straight line, dropping into the cup for a birdie three on her first hole, putting her ahead of me by one shot.

"Nice putt," I said, shaking my head incredulously.

There's no way she's that good.

Yet here I was, getting spanked again. Kink on the course.

"Beginner's luck," she said graciously.

Beginners luck, my blistered butt.

Over the next eight holes, Darby played a steady game, but No. 5 was a long course and she was only able to hit four greens in regulation, and she managed to catch a couple of bunkers when her approach shots fell short of the mark. I had played my usual game, and came in at one under par, five shots ahead.

As we pulled up to the Clubhouse after the ninth hole, we had the distinct displeasure of running across Rodney Collingsworth.

"Oh, no," Darby groaned when she saw Rodney, "of all the people."

He spotted us and quickly navigated his cart next to ours.

"Whoa!" he said. "Are you two an item now? Isn't that sweet."

"I'm just showing her the ropes," I said.

"Didn't she tell you?" Rodney sneered. "I already showed her quite a few ropes." He turned to Darby. "We almost had enough ropes to tie a person up. Two people, even, didn't we, Darby?"

Darby's face turned to stone. She stared straight ahead, refusing to acknowledge his presence. She was fuming.

"We've got to get going," I said amiably, in an attempt to dissipate the tension. "We've got nine more holes to get in."

"Hey," Rodney yelled as we sped away, "maybe you'll get lucky and get a hole-in-one tonight. Me, I got tired of playing the same hole, over and over."

"Go crawl back in your own hole," Darby muttered under her breath.

I couldn't have said it better myself.

After we finished our golf outing, I was careful not to gloat after my twelve shot victory. Well, not too careful.

We stopped by my place, since Bertha needed her walk. Of course, she was overjoyed to see Darby, and as such, she allowed Darby the privilege of escorting her outside. I opened a bottle of wine and retrieved the glasses.

I was getting a little hungry. No, make that famished.

"How 'bout dinner?" I asked when they returned. "I'll cook. I can make you some of my world famous Chicken Parmigiana."

"I'm sorry to have to tell you," Darby said, "but I don't eat meat."

"How did I not know this already?" I said. "No worries, I can make you some of my world famous Eggplant Parmigiana."

"I don't eat cheese either. I'm a vegan."

"Now you're just being mean," I said. She laughed.

"You really don't eat any meat, fish, cheese, or milk?" I asked.

"Not for the last ten years or so."

"No bacon?"

"Sorry."

"How do you keep yourself from wasting away to nothing?"

"Do I look wasted away to you?" She arched her back, accenting her features, then ran her hand down her side, striking a model's pose.

Definitely not wasted.

Her move took me somewhat by surprise, and I was, momentarily, a man without words, reduced to simply staring.

She smiled and grabbed a towel off the counter.

"Here, let me wipe that drool off for you," she said, dotting my chin.

"Was I that obvious?" I asked.

"Let's just say, you're definitely a carnivore."

"I am kind of hungry. Actually I'm starving. I haven't eaten in quite some time."

"And you're looking to find some fresh game."

"You might put it that way."

"I hate to tell you, but out on the tennis courts they call me the gazelle. For your information, that's one of the swiftest creatures in the world. They're extremely hard to catch."

"I hate to tell you," I said, "but out on the golf course they call me a cheetah, because I win so much."

"What do they call you when you lose?

"I wouldn't know."

"There's always a first time."

Touché.

"I'll tell you what," she said, "I'll make you some vegetarian curry. First, let's see what you've got in this place." With that, she opened my refrigerator and rummaged through the bins.

"Do you have any potatoes?"

"I don't think so."

"Any onions?"

"No."

"Peas, carrots, garlic, cauliflower, ginger?" she asked.

"That would probably be a no."

"So you're telling me that you have no vegetables, whatsoever?"

"No, not true, hold on a minute."

Quickly searching through the pantry, I found what I was looking for. I proudly held up the box.

"Crackers?" she said. "That's not a vegetable."

"I don't see any meat on the label," I said.

"So tell me, exactly, how is it you were planning on making me your world famous Chicken Parmigiana, with no ingredients?"

"It was actually mock Chicken Parmigiana, made with the crackers. It's right here on the back of the box."

She just shook her head.

"We'll have to go to my place," she said. "I keep vegetables in stock."

"That sounds great," I said. "Can Bertha come too?"

At the mention of her name, Bertha trotted over. Her sad eyes looked directly into Darby's.

"How could I say no to a face like that," Darby said. "But I will need to take a shower before we eat. I'm all sweaty."

"Me too. Just how big is your shower?" I asked.

"It's plenty big enough for both you and Bertha to get yourselves wet."

"Well, I was envisioning something a little more cozy."

"Oh, you guys are welcome to use my tub then. It's got a Jacuzzi."

I wasn't going to win this game.

Bertha and I waited in the living room while Darby showered. Both of us were somewhat disappointed that we had to wait for our respective turns in the shower, but Bertha was taking it better than I was.

I could have showered at my house and then come over afterwards, but there's just something about using a woman's shower that makes the whole experience a little more exhilarating. It's kind of like how hot dogs always taste better at the ballpark, although I doubt

I'd find any hot dogs in Darby's house, unless they were of the tofu variety.

Darby emerged from her bedroom wrapped in a body-length towel to "check" on us. That was just wrong, definitely cheating. If I were a football referee, I'd have given her multiple penalties, starting with unsportsmanlike conduct, backfield in motion, a neutral zone infraction, and possibly even a delay of game.

"Do you need some assistance getting dressed?" I asked in my most innocent of tones.

"Now that's a new one," she said in an exaggerated tone.

"How so?"

"That's the first time a guy ever tried to get me *into* my clothes."

"Clearly, you don't know me that well. I'm a gentleman."

Her scoff told me that she hadn't completely bought into my story, and she retreated back to her bedroom. She returned dressed in form-fitting t-shirt and jeans, a simple, but pleasing ensemble.

It was my turn to hit the shower. And even though Bertha probably could have used a shower too, I thought it best to leave her to help Darby prepare dinner.

Kneeling down for maximum impact, I gave her strict instructions. "Now Bertha, you need to keep an eye on Darby. I want you to warn me if she tries to sneak in while I'm showering. If she tries anything, bark three times, and I'll unlock the door."

Darby prepared dinner while I cleaned up. I was starting to run out of hot water by the end of my shower, but that actually suited my situation quite well. When I finally made it back to the kitchen, dinner appeared to be almost ready. It smelled fantastic.

"How hot do you like your curry?" she asked.

"What are my choices?"

"You can have napalm, or volcano. I'm afraid I don't have enough chili pepper to get to nuclear fusion."

"That's too bad. I was so looking forward to having nuclear fusion with you. I guess I'll have to settle for napalm. Would that be chicken or beef?"

"Tempeh actually, it's made from fermented soybeans. I think you'll like it."

"And you base this on…"

"The fact that you want to make a good impression on me by appearing to be open-minded and adventuresome."

"I will do my best to appear that way."

By now, I was famished. Luckily, I had brought over the wine from my place and we polished off the bottle as we made quick work of her meatless cuisine.

"That was wonderful," I said. "My compliments to the chef. I didn't think I was going to be satisfied with a meatless meal, but I didn't miss it at all. You see, I can be open-minded when I need to be."

Having plied her with wine, I now felt free to ask Darby some personal questions.

"After seeing you play tennis," I said, "I'm guessing that at some point you must have thought about going on tour. I mean, I could practice for eight hours a day for the rest of my life and I'd never beat you. Not that I'm that great, but I'm really not half bad. You toyed with me out there like a cat with a mouse."

"I can't argue with that. In high school, I was ranked number one in the state. I was seventeenth in the country. I was signed up to go to the Bollettieri Tennis Academy in Florida."

"You didn't go?"

"No, my mom got sick and I didn't want to leave her. With all of her medical bills, I wouldn't have been able to go the academy, anyway. I took care of her until she passed away. It was about two years."

"I'm sorry to hear that."

"Thanks. I'm just glad I was able to be there for her. I wouldn't trade it for anything."

"How'd you end up at UVa?"

"I was twenty years old, and still had a chance at the tour, even though that's getting kind of old. I started the training regimen, the practices, you know, the tournament circuit. I got all the way back up to the finals in the Regionals.

"I was up by one set, and ahead in the second one. In the middle of a point, some kids were apparently playing catch with a ball in the stands. The ball got away and rolled into our court behind me. My opponent never called a let. While I was running back to retrieve a lob, I stepped on it and rolled my ankle. I had to stop right there and concede the match. It was a pretty bad sprain. It took me three months to recuperate.

"In the meantime, Virginia offered me a full scholarship, and since I wasn't getting any younger, I accepted. I played at number-one all four years. After I graduated, I stuck around as assistant coach for another two years while I got my master's degree. Then, I got a full-time job as coach of the women's team at McKean University.

"A friend told me about the opening here. I came down since I'd heard so much about this place. I never really expected to work here, but they offered me nearly double what I was getting at McKean. That was pretty hard to refuse. So far, it's been great, except..."

"Yes?" I said, waiting for full disclosure.

"You probably figured it out when we met Rodney this afternoon. We had a thing going for a while. That was before I found out he was sleeping with two other women at the same time he was seeing me. Of course, when I found out, he accused *me* of cheating on *him*. Typical Rodney. After we broke up, I thought about just getting out of here, far away from the bad memories, but I decided that I wasn't going to let one jerk decide my fate. I love my job, and I get to do what I do best. I just pretend he doesn't exist."

"If it makes any difference," I said, "he's my boss and I do the same thing."

"I'm glad we have that in common," she replied, her smile returning.

"Do you ever play tennis just for fun?" I asked. "I mean, before *I* came along, was there anyone who could even give you a run for your money?"

She just laughed.

"It's frowned upon if I beat up the clientele. But I play a couple of tournaments each year to give me a chance to go for blood. I have no qualms about crushing opponents who appear to be serious about beating me."

"I'm shocked, *shocked*. Well not that shocked."

"Don't tell me you didn't enjoy every minute of your thrashing. I bet you found it extremely exciting to find a woman who could dominate you so thoroughly, who kept giving it to you again and again, over and over, until you couldn't take it any longer."

All of a sudden, it was starting to get very warm in here. This woman definitely had a naughty side.

"More wine?" she asked, holding the bottle over my glass.

I nodded. She'd put on that devilish grin again. I guess she thought she had my number.

"You know I also practice archery," she volunteered. "I was pretty good at college. I went to the Olympic trials in 2000. I just missed making the US team. Would you like to see my equipment?"

I thought you'd never ask.

Before I had a chance to respond, she made her way over the closet, reappearing with an unstrung bow. It looked remarkably primitive, unlike the modern contraptions I've seen recently that look as though they could be used against imperial storm troopers in a Star Wars movie. She strung it in one swift motion and grabbed an arrow.

"It's called a recurve bow," she said, anticipating my question. "Compound bows aren't allowed in the Olympics."

"Where do you practice around here?" I asked.

"I actually haven't in quite a while," she said.

"I know just the place where you could go," I said, recalling Van Avery's humble abode. "It's at a mansion, the attorney at the Bluffs who's retiring. He's got his own private archery range."

"You mean Van Avery? Sweet."

"Maybe you could teach me," I said.

"I could show you a few things right now," she said coming around behind me.

"Now hold the bow up, and aim." She placed a surprisingly strong hand on mine as she reached around me and guided my hand in pulling an arrow back against the taught string, pressing her body against mine in the process. I really liked her hands-on teaching style.

"Now just remember that in this position, you're in possession of a deadly weapon. If you want to have any chance at all of getting to the target, you're going to have to be steady and strong. You're going to have to maintain absolute control at all times. Releasing too early would prove disastrous." As she spoke, she relaxed our pull on the string, and then placed the archery equipment aside, sliding around now to face me from the front, lips just inches away from mine. "Do I make myself clear?"

"Absolutely."

I woke up the next morning, sore in new ways. But it was all good.

No pain, no gain.

I'd taken pity on Darby after her trouncing during our golf match, deciding to let her have the upper hand in whatever events transpired later that evening. But I'd neglected to consider her extreme athleticism. And it hadn't taken long for her to remind me. Just to make sure that I didn't forget again, she had given me a full semester's course on the topic, condensed into a single evening, complete with pop quizzes, in-class participation grade, and one seriously hard final. I was actually hoping I'd failed, so I'd have to repeat. Next time, I'd be better prepared.

But this morning, my focus was on the greens, specifically, those on course No. 2 that had been ravaged by our weed control company. Bertha and I took the golf cart directly from Darby's place to the third green.

George Robinson had hooked me up with my new ride, one of just four demo units of the new Korean golf carts that we'd adopted at the Club. Just a few days ago, we'd seen the unveiling of the very first cart.

There had been quite a few oohs and aahs in the crowd when George pulled off the cover. And as soon as I saw it, I was hooked. Sleek and stylish, filled with electronic gadgetry, it was all a man could ask for in a cart, unless, of course, it came with its own personal beverage assistant.

As we tooled down the path, I decided to give it the old "Thomas performance test," so I hit the accelerator and ramped up to max speed, booking down the cart path as fast as I could make it go. When we came to the sharp turn at the hole-two green, I pressed hard on the brakes to slow to a safe speed.

Only, for a half-second or so, nothing seemed to happen. A half-second may not seem like a long time, but at our speed, that put us about ten feet past where I wanted to be, sending us into the turn at full speed. We screamed around the tight corner, Bertha sliding against me, her little doggy-mind most likely now in a full-blown canine-panic.

When the brakes finally kicked in, I had my foot down as hard as I could on the pedal, and the tires screeched to a stop as I struggled with all my strength to keep man, dog, and machine in one piece.

Holy shit.

I had barely managed to keep Bertha from crashing into the dash, but this could've been serious. Maybe we needed seat belts.

When I started breathing again, I looked over to make sure Bertha was ok. She responded with a strange whimper, which either meant "Thanks, bro'," or "What the hell, dude?"

Had someone tampered with my brakes?

Tom Jones had told me to watch my back, but now Bertha had been dragged into this. It's not cool to mess with a man's dog. I needed to have George inspect my cart posthaste.

We drove the rest of the way at a much more genteel pace, which seemed to be very pleasing to Bertha, now securely situated on my lap, her paws holding on as tightly as any canine's could.

Finally making it to the third green, we hopped from the cart and looked out over... a disaster.

After one particularly horrid job of cutting the lawn during my youth, where somehow I had managed to raise one side of the mower wheels higher than the other, leaving the yard in a crazy patchwork of slanted rows and columns, my brother had pronounced my work as a "cut-grass-trophe." Professional golf course greenskeepers tend to be more fastidious about their work.

And they have to be, especially when it comes to the greens. Ask a hundred people about the signature characteristic of any golf course they've ever played, and ninety-nine will tell you about a green. Those smooth carpets of short bentgrass command attention and respect.

And it's no wonder. On no other part of a golf course does the maintenance staff lavish so much time, attention, care, devotion and expense. Elegant and costly mowing equipment vacuum and cut the grass in the early morning hours to impossibly short lengths that allow the struck ball to roll with precisely defined and predictable movement and control.

And thus it was with considerable trepidation that Bertha and I approached the green at hole number three.

I didn't have to be the head greenskeeper to deduce that something had gone drastically wrong. Maybe not quite a "cut-grass-trophe," more like a "dead-grass-trophe." The once immaculate green was now almost completely brown. I knelt to examine the damage at close range, plucking a sample, only to have the dry blades crumble in my fingers. The dark brown soil usually covered by the grass was now exposed, the dirt now becoming the green's most dominant feature.

Apparently five other greens on the course were in similar condition, the result of some horrible accident of weed eradication gone wrong just a few weeks ago. Already, the prestigious Virginia Juniors' Championship tournament scheduled for the No. 2 course had been canceled. The state golf association had moved it to a competing course, a serious public relations blow for us.

Once at the office, Evan and I got right down to business with the head greenskeeper, Dennis Johnson.

"We have an existing contract with the TurfLove Company," Dennis began, "to completely handle fertilization, and weed and pest control on all six courses. We were having a problem with one particular type of weed, it's called the Spotted Spurge, around several of our fairways. It's particularly hard to eradicate and it makes the fairways look like crap. The TurfLove rep said they could do a special spraying to get rid of the Spurge. I gave her the ok. Two days after the spraying, we noticed the large brown patches on the six greens. In another three days, the grass was nearly dead. Apparently, the wind carried the spray."

Evan, who had been sitting patiently, could contain himself no longer.

"We've lost over one thousand rounds on No. 2 already due to the incompetence of this company. Our losses just for greens fees are going to be in the hundreds of thousands, and that doesn't include cart fees, food and beverage or merchandise. We need to hold these guys responsible. I say sue them if that's what it takes."

I looked over the TurfLove contract, and realized Evan would not be thrilled with the terms. I was glad that this contract pre-dated my tenure here.

"How about insurance?" I asked. "Do we have business loss coverage?"

"No," Evan said. "We waived the coverage. It's very expensive, and we've never needed it."

That coverage would have allowed us to make a claim for lost revenues as well as direct damages.

"So we decided to self-insure," I said. "Clearly, you win some, you lose some." I made a note to review all of the Bluffs' insurance policies to make sure we had adequate coverage.

"Have we ever had a problem like this before?" I asked. "Haven't we dealt with Spotted Spurge in the past?"

Dennis paused before finally replying. "Yes, we have. But it never went wrong like this."

"Let me read over the contract in detail," I said. "That will give me a better idea about how to proceed."

Something seemed odd in Dennis' response. If I hadn't known better, I would have thought he was hiding something.

"George," I asked, trying not to appear paranoid, "Bertha and I just about bit the dust in that new cart. Has anybody else had any problems?"

George Robinson seemed nonplussed by my near-death experience.

"Well," he said in his usual soft-spoken manner, "I saw a little bit of lag with the regenerative braking mode turned on. I turned it off in my cart, and now everything's back to normal.

That would have been nice to know. Yesterday.

Maybe I was being paranoid.

"The regenerative braking option uses the motor as the brake when you're not trying to slow down too quickly," he continued. "The motor charges the batteries while it brakes. You can almost double the range of the cart that way. It's the same thing that the hybrid cars do. That's why they get such good mileage in the city."

We were in George's wheelhouse now. He must have loved this stuff, judging by the pictures and décor in his office. He had somehow managed to get an entire antique golf cart in here. He must have had to take it apart, bring in the pieces and then reassemble it inside. If you sat in it, you could see right out his picture window onto the course.

"But," he continued, "there's software on the cart to figure out how much regenerative braking, and how much of the regular friction brakes to use. I talked to KG about it, and they said they're still tweaking that software now."

"Yeah, well it almost tweaked me right into the bunker on hole two," I said. "We need to turn that off on all the carts until we get the ok from the manufacturer that all the bugs are gone. And even after that, we need to test it thoroughly. If the only benefit is better cart mileage, it's not worth the increased liability exposure."

"There's a configuration option that turns off the regen braking completely," he said. "I'll make sure it's disabled on all four of our demo units. And, when the fleet arrives next week, we'll make sure it's disabled before they go into service."

"Well you can start with mine, right after we're done talking here. Who has the other two demo carts?"

"Well Evan said he didn't want one, so Alan in Finance has one, and of course Rodney has the fourth."

I was tempted to tell him to leave the braking untouched on Rodney's cart. I was already fantasizing about challenging him to a cart race.

Oh, didn't anyone tell you about the brake lag, Big R? Sorry about that.

My fantasy life was starting to get extremely violent.

By the next morning's meeting, I was prepared to dig a little deeper into this "sod" story. It was time for some tough love.

I'd found out some interesting information during a phone call with TurfLove's attorney. As I'd suspected, Dennis hadn't told us everything.

"Dennis," I said, "this special spraying that TurfLove did, was the chemical they used different from the ones they had been using routinely to control other weeds on our courses?"

"Well," he said, looking glumly down at his hands.

It was come to Jesus time.

"Their rep told me that they had an herbicide they used to control the Spurge, but that it had been banned since the EPA found it in some well water in Florida. But she said her company still had a big supply in storage. Since everybody around here has city water, I didn't see the problem. She said they could use up their stock, kill the spurge and everybody's happy."

"You let them use *what?*" Evan exclaimed, his face turning a bright shade of red. His lips continued to move, but no more sounds were coming out.

It was time for me to get legal. "I've read our contract with TurfLove," I said, "and it contains the standard language for liability."

I read aloud:

"TurfLove is liable only for direct damages, not for indirect, consequential, or punitive damages, or for lost profits.

"Now, that's the normal situation. Obviously, the spraying of an illegal chemical may give us a foot in the door to sue for more. But the fact that we authorized it pretty much negates that."

"Well, what about the direct damages?" Evan asked, finally regaining his voice.

"It's capped at no more than what we paid TurfLove in the preceding six months for services."

"How much have we been paying them?" I asked Dennis.

"We pay twelve thousand a month."

"So that's seventy-two thousand," Evan said. "That's a drop in the bucket compared to what we've lost."

"Our best bet right now is to find another contractor to replace TurfLove," I said.

"We've got a two year contract," Dennis said. "That's how we got the rates down. We can't get out without paying the remaining thirteen months."

"I know that's what it says, but I'm pretty sure we won't have any problems getting out of the contract early, considering everything."

"Is there anything else on this, Desmond?" Evan asked.

"Not right now." I shook my head.

"Well, then, I think we're done here. Dez, could you stick around for a few more minutes?"

That didn't bode well for Dennis.

After Dennis left, Evan got right to the point.

"The Board is going to want blood," Evan said. "Dennis is going to have to go. This is inexcusable."

I nodded.

"Do you think there are going to be any legal issues if we fire him?"

"Does he have a contract?"

"It's just our standard employment contract. Either party can terminate it."

"Well, Virginia is an 'at-will' state, and I think the grounds for termination are valid. He screwed up, big time."

"What if we ask him to resign?" Evan said.

"He wouldn't be eligible for unemployment in that case," I said. "You'd probably have to offer a severance package of some sort to get him to agree to that."

"I think a termination would appease the board more than a resignation anyway," Evan concluded. "It sends a clear message. What about the EPA? I assume we're obligated to report this."

That was a good question.

"Since it was TurfLove that applied the chemical," I said, "they should report the violation. But we should probably report it too, since it was applied on our land. If we don't, we may be liable for some additional penalties, that is, if there are any penalties. I'll give the EPA a call. While I'm at it, I'll notify the State Department of Environmental Quality. That'd be the safest thing to do."

After this fiasco, I was beginning to think a little spotted spurge wasn't such a bad thing after all.

Chapter 9

On my way to the driving range, I ducked into the men's room off the long basement hallway that headed outside. The hallway was a short-cut used mainly by workers and maintenance staff.

I intended to make a quick pit stop before the long afternoon of non-stop lessons. Settling in, I heard a sound.

Footsteps.

It suddenly occurred to me that I was defenseless. I had no weapon, no gun, not even a pocket knife. I hadn't done a very thorough job of watching my back.

The footsteps were getting closer. I was hardly in a position to defend myself, except perhaps to temporarily blind an attacker with a jet stream.

The door burst open. I froze.

"Dez!" It was Paul Owens, my best caddy bud. He looked down. "Hey, no need to stop for me. Glad I caught you. I have a quick legal question."

I exhaled and tried to resume where I'd left off. That had been a little too scary. If there was something behind Tom Jones' threats, I needed to be prepared with an equalizer. But for the time being, I was relieved it was only Paul, even if he did want free advice.

Sometimes, as an attorney, you can't even take a quick piss without being solicited for free information. The situation reminded me of the old story about the physician who was talking with his attorney friend at a dinner. The physician asked the attorney if people also pestered him for free counsel.

"Yes," the attorney said, "but I solved it. After someone asks me for advice, I just drop a bill in the mail with an invoice for my time. That put a stop to it pretty quickly."

"Great idea," the doctor said. "I'll try it."

Two days later, the doctor got a bill in the mail from the attorney. And people wonder why lawyers have such a bad reputation.

"What's up?" I said, doing my best to appear accommodating, while praying Paul would leave at least one urinal between us during this consultation.

He didn't.

"We're thinking about starting a new business to compete with the "Fore" Play girls. They're cutting into our income."

The Bluffs had permitted "Fore" Play to caddy on some of our courses, although not on our premier course, until their one-year contact expired. I assumed Paul had something similar in mind.

"Are you going to hire your own girls?" I asked.

"Oh no. Our service is going to provide sexy *male* caddies. What do you think of 'Steel Shafts' or maybe 'Fairway Woods?'"

Urinatious interruptis.

I was not prepared for this particular take on entrepreneurship. It took me a few seconds before I could resume.

"That's interesting," I said, trying to remain upbeat. "Where're you going to get your guys? Are you aiming for a Chippendales look?"

"We may have to hire a few younger guys, but we've got some pretty serious beefcake in our ranks already. We've started a workout program to get everyone into top shape. We've already scheduled the calendar shoot."

I stopped again.

This was going to be the longest piss of all time.

The Bluffs' caddies included middle-aged guys with receding hairlines, some turning gray, and most with serious beer guts. Paul could have been their spokesmodel. Perhaps he would be. As far as I could tell, they didn't meet anyone's expectation of beefcake. More like meatloaf.

"I'm sorry, but I've forgotten, what exactly was the question?"

Clearly oblivious to my discomfort, Paul pressed on.

"Right now we're organizing. We're not sure how to set up the company. Should we go public right away and sell stock, or maybe do one of those 'limited' things?"

Right now, I'd say, prospects look very limited.

"There are some ramifications depending upon how you structure your business, specifically regarding tax consequences and management. The LLC is popular, but it would be best if you set up a meeting in my office to review this. Give Sharon a call."

It was time to get out of the men's room.

"That sounds good," he said. "I told the guys we need to decide this before the photo shoot next week."

"Next week?"

So much for getting into top shape.

"Who all's in the shoot?" I asked.

"Most of the regular guys: Phil, Pinky, Tyler, Junior, you know, the guys you see around here. I'm Mr. CaddyMan for July. That's the hottest month, you know. It's gonna be nothing but me and the flagpole on No. 18." He beamed.

Oh the horror, the horror.

Carolyn McClelland Andrews was in serious trouble.

It's all because of that stupid squirrel.

She'd received quite a tidy sum from her father's sale of Chesapeake Bluffs to FirstResorts. But her fondness for the "first-class" lifestyle led her to blow through nearly half of her money in less than a decade.

It was her husband's fault, really, or she should say, her late-husband's fault. Wallace. She was glad to be rid of that deadbeat leech.

Carolyn had first learned of the plans for the expansion of Chesapeake Bluffs at a Board of Directors meeting almost ten years ago. The ambitious plan would require FirstResorts to acquire nearly 500 acres, some of it waterfront, which bordered the current property. When she had mentioned this to Wallace, he'd thrown out a suggestion. "Why not buy the property before they do? We could flip it back to the corporation at a huge markup."

The more she thought about the idea, the more she liked it. She would have to move fast, though, before word of the plans went public, and before the FirstResorts' buyers could beat her to the punch.

For the first time in her life, some of her college courses had provided her with training she needed for real life. The accounting fraud class she'd taken for her business degree had exposed her to several clever tricks she was able to utilize for her scheme.

First, she'd formed a dummy company in the Grand Caymans, then hired an attorney under the company's name to facilitate the land purchases. She'd done the same thing with three other attorneys. Nowhere was her name associated with any of the companies.

She was surprised how easily the plan had fallen into place. Although the land hadn't come cheaply, especially the waterfront parcels, she had been able to acquire all of the property for about $10 million, of which she had only been required to put up twenty percent as a down payment. And within a few years, the real-estate boom had almost doubled her properties' value. The new appraisals on the land had enabled her to take out very sizable additional loans backed by the property. The loans gave her access to some well-needed cash to fuel her lifestyle.

If only I'd sold it then.

But she'd known that FirstResorts would have paid double that price for the right to develop their two new courses and Mediterranean-style village.

She practically had the money in her hands five years ago. All the prices and terms were agreed upon. The sales documents had just needed signatures. It was only the discovery of that squirrel habitat at the last minute that had thrown a monkey-wrench into the plans.

The properties were unsellable now. The real-estate crash that had inevitably followed the boom had lowered the values below what she had paid for them.

She had spent hundreds of thousands on lobbyists and attorneys trying to reclassify the property or relocate the squirrels, all to no avail.

Through her dummy companies, she was still on the hook to pay hundreds of thousands of dollars more in property taxes for the land, and of course, she still had to make payments on her mortgages and the additional property loans she had taken out. She was now down to less than $100,000. At this rate, she would be penniless in a few months.

Her lover at the Club had been patient, but unless Carolyn could get the money out of this property, she knew it would eventually come out that her "rich and famous" lifestyle was just a façade. Without money, a woman her age might not be quite so desirable. But wealth could buy its own youth.

She had a plan, one that she'd tried to set into motion a few months back, but that idiot golfer Brooks had spotted the people she'd hired, and reported them. The police had nearly caught them.

That's what I get for using amateurs.

She wouldn't make that mistake again. It was still hard to believe Brooks had been out playing golf so early in the morning. She was glad he was now out of the picture, for good.

To top it off, the new Bluffs' attorney had been snooping into her real-estate transactions. After she'd met him at the reception, she'd hoped he'd get the expansion process back on track. Instead, he seemed to have zeroed in on her LLCs' land purchases. Her LLC attorneys had notified her that Desmond Thomas was inquiring into oddly-timed acquisitions. They hadn't given up her name, thankfully, she'd made sure of that. But she needed to nip this whole thing in the bud, before anything could be traced back to her.

She polished off the last of her 1937 single malt.

There might just be a way to make this guy go away.

In fact, it would require nothing more than a phone call. The longer she thought about her plan, the better it seemed. Desmond Thomas would be history.

Like a proud parent, George watched as the crew unloaded another set of KG golf carts from the large transport vehicle.

One hundred down, three hundred to go.

These were busy times for the maintenance staff, whose responsibility it was to prep the carts for eager Bluffs' golfers.

George was thrilled with the new ride, and even more so

now that his "education fund" had been activated by KG Limited. Though his employment contract specifically prohibited gifts from vendors, he rationalized that this wasn't really a gift; it was just part of KG's corporate philosophy. Even so, he wasn't about to report this charity to his bosses at the Bluffs, or the IRS for that matter.

The new carts had given the Bluffs a legitimate excuse to bump up cart fees by an additional $10 per round. But even at the inflated prices, the carts were a bargain for many of the members. Being the first American users of the most advanced production golf cart ever made gave them serious bragging rights over their less fortunate peers. Some members had already approached George about buying one.

George had tasked Dan Waters and his maintenance team to prep the carts. George had devised a checklist for each cart, which included road test, mechanical systems check, detailed diagnostics on electrical and software systems, and activation of the password system to prevent unauthorized changes.

Each of Dan's crew was assigned eight carts to check each day. That would consume their entire workday, assuming no glitches. Fixing any problems that were found would mean working overtime, as would taking care of any serious maintenance issues that occurred elsewhere on the course. It would be a busy week.

At least my men get paid time-and-a-half, Dan thought, *which is more than I can say for myself.* Even though he did as much hands-on work as his men, Dan was classified as exempt, which meant he didn't receive overtime, or even any extra pay over forty hours. It wasn't uncommon for his men to earn more than he did during the busy season, sometimes much more.

His brother-in-law, Charlie Peterson, who also happened to be on his maintenance staff, was quick to point out the inequity, and routinely showed Dan news articles about employees who had successfully sued to recover back overtime pay. Dan listened patiently, but never failed to remind Charlie that he should be worrying first and foremost about doing his own job well.

He'll be out of here before summer if he doesn't start to step it up.

As Charlie Peterson pondered the herculean cart checkout task that awaited him, beads of sweat began to break out on his forehead. Charlie almost always had something up his sleeve, and it rarely involved honest labor. But honest labor was what it would take for him to keep up with this aggressive schedule.

As it turned out, the first cart wasn't too bad, especially the road test, which was kind of fun, but the detailed checking of the electrical and software systems quickly became tedious, such tasks not necessarily being a good fit for Charlie's mechanical aptitude.

By lunch-time, Charlie had only finished two and a half carts. At the rate he was going, he didn't see being finished before seven.

That would be a problem, for Charlie had already worked up quite a thirst. The kind of thirst that required a beer, or maybe six, to quench. The thought of waiting another seven hours for his first cold one was unbearable. He had to do something.

He took his next cart out a little bit farther than usual, and then pulled it around the corner, out of sight. In just five minutes, he managed to check off half the items on his list.

It's just electronics shit anyway. They check that at the factory.

Of course, whenever he was back in the facility, within sight of any managers, Charlie worked as hard and as fast as he could. He was a man on a mission.

He finished up his fifth cart by two o'clock. He was now on a pace to be done before five, utilizing his revised testing procedure.

As Charlie began work on his eighth and final cart of the day, the thought of that ice-cold six-pack awaiting him at home spurred him to even greater levels of productivity.

Dan had taken notice, commenting to himself about Charlie's newfound work ethic.

Maybe Charlie's turning over a new leaf.

I finally heard from the Chapman County Sheriff's Office regarding the laptop complaint against Lucas Bennett, aka Tom Jones. According to Detective Reed, Bennett denied knowing anything about the laptop, or any phone calls made to my office.

"It's your word against his, and without any evidence, there's no case," Reed told me over the phone.

I got the impression that this case wasn't Reed's top priority. All told, he was not my favorite law enforcement officer, yet unfortunately, he seemed to be the point man for all cases at the

Bluffs.

"Well," I said, "I didn't really expect him to admit anything, but now at least the complaint is on the record. If we start seeing illegal activity on the credit cards, we'll know where to look."

"That'd still be tough to trace through to him. Your best bet is to notify the members of the theft, and have them cancel their cards." Reed sounded sanctimonious.

"We did that as soon as we found out," I said. "What about the threats?"

"Until he does something specific, our hands are tied. We can't investigate a reported threat, especially one that's not been corroborated. And we're not even sure that there was a real threat, maybe it was just advice."

"What if I were the President, and someone threatened me?"

"You probably wouldn't be talking to the Chapman County Sheriff's Office on the phone, now would you, Mr. President, *sir*?"

You got that right.

At least I'd done one thing. Kevin had installed a recording device on my office phone, along with an app for my cell phone. Fortunately, Virginia is a one-party consent state. If either party in a phone conversation agrees to record the call, it can be legally recorded. Since I always consented to record my own conversations, I was home free. If Bennett called again, I'd nail him to the wall.

Before I had a chance to lean back in my chair, the phone rang again.

One of those days.

"Desmond Thomas, Chesapeake Bluffs Golf and Country Club."

"Is this the lawyer?" the shrill female voice demanded.

Just what I need.

I started my new phone recorder, just in case.

"I'm the attorney for Chesapeake Bluffs, if that's what you're asking."

"I want to know what you're going to do about my smashed window. My four year old daughter was playing in her room when a golf ball came flying in. She could've been hurt or even killed by the glass. She's hysterical!"

I wonder where she gets that from.

"Do you know who hit the ball that broke your window?" I asked, already knowing the answer.

"No, those cowards took off. I do have his ball though. I think the guy might own a restaurant, maybe a Chinese one."

"What makes you say that?"

"His ball says 'noodle' on it."

I snorted. Very unprofessional, but still, this was the funniest thing I'd heard in a while.

"A 'noodle' ball," I explained, "is a type of low-compression golf ball. Anybody can buy it. I'm afraid what you've got is not a personalized ball."

"Well, anyway, are you going to pay to get my window fixed? That's the least you can do, after all we've been through."

"Do you live on the course?" I asked.

"We're on the seventh fairway of course No. 6."

My bet was that she lived in one of the dreaded "slice zones." Her house was probably about 180 yards from the tee, perfect distance for errant slices by right handed golfers.

The slice was so common that it had multiple names. It was sometimes called a banana ball, for the shape approximated by the ball's trajectory. A bad banana ball was often accompanied, as in this case, by the sound of breaking glass, immediately followed by the sound of four golfers madly stuffing themselves into their golf carts and driving like hell to get away from the area before an enraged homeowner came running out, demanding reparations. This shot was also known as the "shirt changer," since the golfer who hit it must change his shirt to avoid later recognition and retribution. No doubt, this lady's window breaker had done just that.

"I'm afraid it's the policy of our Club, and almost every other club, that it's the players' responsibility to pay for damages created by their shots. Also, you've assumed the risk of damage by living on the course, which was here before your house was constructed. Your real-estate agent should have informed you of that when you purchased your home."

"I can't believe this. I might have my husband come down to see you in person. Maybe he can talk some sense into you people."

Lucky me.

"Let me get your name and number, and we'll send you a

letter explaining your options."

"Well, alright then."

That calmed her down a little bit, as I'd hoped. Of course, our standard letter just reiterated that we were not liable, but it did include helpful suggestions like checking with the homeowner's insurance policy for reimbursement, and installing shatterproof windows, especially on the side of the house that faced the tee box. We could have summed it up in a single sentence:

If you live on a golf course, don't be surprised when your house gets hit by a golf ball.

As Caitlyn pulled the cans from her cooler, she felt flushed—and nauseated. The sweltering heat only intensified her discomfort—and it was only 11 a.m.

Plus, the smell of beer had suddenly become repulsive to her, and nearly all of her customers ordered beer. She found little humor in the irony.

Caitlyn tried valiantly to be pleasant and flirty with the golfers. But now, as she struggled to finish serving this foursome, all her focus was on keeping her restless insides together. The golfers, oblivious to her situation, sat passively in their carts while she brought their beverages.

Please don't open them right now.

The driver of the second cart added crackers to his order. She smiled gamely and fetched the snack, returning at the precise moment he opened his can, sending a stream of beer mist directly into her face.

Unfortunately for all, she was powerless to stop the reflex reaction now set into motion. The sudden and uncontrollable expulsion of her stomach contents occurred with an intensity that astonished Caitlyn, not to mention the two golfers who were quickly and totally covered with the partially digested contents of this morning's breakfast, and what even looked to be a few bits of last night's dinner.

As she surveyed the train wreck that was now the fifth tee, a sudden burst of insight came over her.

So this is morning sickness.

 *Chapter 10*

The Virginia Field Office of the US Fish and Wildlife Service happened to be located just a short drive away in Gloucester, near the coast. My meeting today was with Brian Landrow, who carried the impressive title of Assistant Field Office Supervisor for Endangered Species & Conservation Planning Assistance.

Entering his office, I scouted the room for any animal heads hanging on the walls. I'm not sure if this would have been a good sign or not, but in any event, I noticed that the walls were almost bare.

"I'm the new in-house legal guy," I began, "and I'm just getting up to speed. I wanted to see if there is any hope of being able to work out a solution for the property in question."

"There have been a number of policy changes in recent years that may be relevant to your petition to change classification," he said. "But I'll spare you the gory details, and just give you the executive summary, if that's ok with you."

"Sure."

I was beginning to like this guy.

"There's been a lot of pressure in Congress in past years to revise the Endangered Species Act. The Environmental Protection Agency, along with Fish and Wildlife, are aware of the need to be more flexible and creative in working with property owners."

"So far, so good," I said.

"In addition, recent appointments to the EPA have shifted interpretations of existing policies in ways that tend to favor property owners. These are all positive developments for you.

"I've reviewed your case under the new guidelines. I believe that you stand a good chance of continuing your development plans if you can do the following three things."

I almost jumped out of my chair. Positioning my notepad on the table, I grabbed my pen and held it, quivering. I nodded.

Yes, go on, please.

"One," he continued, "find a nearby alternative habitat for the squirrel, of the same size as the land to be developed."

That sounded plausible.

"Two, procure this alternative habitat and set aside the location permanently as a designated habitat for the northern flying squirrel.

"And three, fund the effort for the relocation."

"How much would such an effort cost?" I asked.

"It's hard to say exactly, but similar efforts have cost on the order of $5,000 an acre. It requires trapping, identifying current nesting areas, transplanting these areas to the new habitat, and monitoring the success of the relocation."

A quick, back of the envelope calculation told me the relocation and procurement of the additional land might cost us around four to five million dollars. That was doable.

"Any ideas on an alternative habitat?" I asked.

Landrow appeared ready for this question. "I've already had my biologists identify two or three possible areas. The good news for you is that the new area doesn't have to be totally contiguous. It can be comprised of several smaller chunks, as long as each chunk is permanently designated."

I felt like giving Landrow a big hug. Now I had the makings of a plan, and some degree of assurance that we could go ahead with the northern expansion.

Brian highlighted the potential areas on his map; he even had a copy already made for me.

Remind me to send him a Christmas card.

All that remained was to write up the report, and for Evan to present it at the next board of directors meeting. The project was back on.

Maybe they'd give me one of those new waterfront villas, as a bonus for my exemplary efforts.

Somehow, I kind of doubted that.

The dockmaster sat in his chair inside the new twenty-one million dollar Command and Control Center. As he glanced over the displays, he could instantly see the status of each and every container vessel in port. He could retrieve a detailed report of every ship's cargo.

He was intimately familiar with the workings of the Port of Long Beach, California, having been employed there for nearly twenty years. The Port was vast and busy, processing over seven million containers during the past year.

He still marveled at how the invention of that simple steel box had sped up the process of loading and unloading cargo by more than twenty times. It was now not uncommon for him to be able to unload an entire ship containing cargo worth upwards of $300 million in a single day.

Of course, with every improvement came a downside. The sheer volume of goods passing through the port made it impossible for him to inspect any but a small fraction of the cargo. It was his job to select which containers were inspected and screened. On an average shift, his staff of forty could inspect nearly 100 containers, only about two percent of the total passing through the port.

Following 9/11, his primary focus was shifted toward monitoring cargo for security concerns, which included screening for potential terrorist weapons. Of those containers that weren't designated by security or customs, he selected ones at random for physical inspection. Their contents were cross-checked against the computerized listing on the container manifest.

The physical inspections served to find contraband material, counterfeits, and mislabeled cargo that a party may be using to circumvent tariffs and taxes. Occasionally, he found something completely unexpected. His men once opened a container and discovered twenty young women, participants in an international sex-trafficking ring. The young ladies were sent back to their country, this time, via airplane.

He selected a container. The crane operator lifted the nearly fifteen ton container high in the air and swung the boom around, placing it in inspection area three.

On the ground, the five members of the team quickly went to work on the contents, using their allotted thirty minutes inspection time.

Ben Shuller picked a box near the middle, labeled MacKenna Golf clubs. The description on the box matched the manifest description. He scanned the barcode, and a picture of a golf driver appeared, indicating the location of the product's serial number inside.

Opening the box, he located the driver, and entered its serial number into his scanner. In seconds, his display beeped, indicating a valid number. MacKenna was one of the many companies that had worked with customs to interface their product database to allow on-site verification.

The two other team members duplicated Ben's procedure on other pallets. Forklift drivers worked in tandem with the inspectors, moving unselected and completed pallets back into the container.

Unfortunately for the MacKenna company, container R451C599 was not strictly on the up-and-up. Like many of the shipments from the Kan-shoo factory, it contained a mix of third-shift and legitimate clubs. The counterfeit clubs duplicated the serial numbers of the authorized products in the container, so any serial number check on any box selected would show up in the database as valid.

Only if they happened to select two that contained the same serial number would anything be flagged as out of the ordinary. And the odds of that happening were less than one percent. And given that only two percent of containers were even searched at all, this meant that the chance of a shipment being flagged by customs was less than two out of ten-thousand.

The accountants at Kan-shoo had, of course, already figured out these odds, and were quite content with such a loss rate. To them, this was simply another "cost of doing business."

As he waited for the foursome ahead to tee off, Bluffs' member Jim Hoffman experimented with the touch screen on the brand-new KG golf cart.

On previous holes, he had been able to surf the web, call home, send email, and most importantly, order beer and refreshments right from the golf cart, which were delivered engagingly by the smoking-hot beverage girl. She was quite the ticket, he recalled pleasantly. So much so that he had already made three separate orders today, and was pondering a fourth.

Jim entered the setup menu. *The whole world's driven by software these days*, he was fond of saying to anyone within earshot. Luckily, as a computer engineer, he had a few more insights into this subject than most people. He was pretty sure that the cart's settings would be password protected, so no one could alter the basic operation of the cart. But, you never knew.

He navigated down four levels until he hit the "Drivetrain Performance Setup" menu, after which he selected "Power Options."

The next page listed four separate options: "Economy," "Normal," "Sport" and "High Performance." "Economy" was currently selected.

"Let's see if it lets us change it," he said, to no one in particular. He tapped the "High Performance" box, and, much to his surprise, a green circle filled the box and the new option appeared to be enabled.

Jim looked up and saw the golfers ahead had finally cleared the fairway. It was time for his foursome to tee off. Hurriedly, he hit "Save." A new popup appeared, with a prompt:

Turn off regen braking in High Performance Mode?

Jim wasn't sure about this, but he certainly didn't want to reduce the braking capability, so he selected "No," before returning to the main screen. It was his turn to hit.

After teeing off, they returned to the cart. Jim hadn't told his partner about his tweaks to the system.

As soon as his foot tapped the accelerator, the KG cart surged forward, pressing the two golfers against their seats.

"Holy shit," Jim exclaimed, "this is a Ferrari." He put his foot to the floor. The cart accelerated rapidly along the narrow cart path. "I guess there's no speed governor in High Performance mode," he said as they flew over a small hill, car, men and clubs, temporarily airborne.

"I think that's fast enough, Jim," his increasingly alarmed passenger advised.

Jim maintained control as the cart landed, clubs clanging loudly in the rear. Turning his head to look back at the other two members of their foursome, he noted that they were still 100 yards behind.

Bet they wish they had my cart.

The cart was quickly approaching the dogleg for the par four, and was traveling at such a high rate of speed that they had already raced by their balls lying on the fairway. As soon as Jim looked ahead again, he realized that he'd overshot his destination.

An ordinary golfer driving an ordinary golf cart might have just slowed down and circled back, but in this case, ordinary described neither. Jim was working on his sixth beer of the day, and was driving the fastest production golf cart known to man. In full NASCAR mode, he stomped on the brakes before his turn.

But nothing happened immediately, and with the cart still at full speed, Jim yanked the wheel hard to the left, directing the cart sharply onto the fairway. The slight ridge on the fairway bordering the cart path posed no problem to a cart at normal speeds, but at nearly 40 mph, the physics were completely different. As the first tire hit the bump at full speed, the entire front and left side of the cart shot into the air.

Jim tried to correct by making a hard right, but with wheels in the air, no change in direction was possible. When the back right tire hit the ridge a few tenths of a second later, the front end came down hard, like a monster truck at a rally. Cranked all the way to the right, the small cart wheels dug deeply into the soft turf, preventing any further movement of the cart in a forward direction. This left only one outlet for the accumulated momentum of 1,400 hundred pounds of cart and contents. It flipped.

The cart completed three revolutions, finally coming to rest on its side, leaving in its wake a fifty-yard stream of golf balls, tees, expensive titanium and graphite clubs, beer, and, at the very tail end, two bodies sprawled on the grass, one groaning, the other not moving at all.

 *Chapter 11*

Evan and I exchanged glances, neither one wanting to show any sign of the tremendous stress we were under at the moment. *"Ladies and gentleman of the jury, have you reached a verdict?"* After months of preparation, followed by weeks of courtroom theatrics, we had at last arrived at this moment, where the results of thousands of hours of intense effort culminated in a single sentence.

"We have, your honor. In the case of Bristol Estate vs. Chesapeake Bluffs Golf and Country Club, we find the defendants guilty of negligence, and award the plaintiffs compensatory damages in the sum of twenty million dollars, plus punitive damages of ten million dollars."

Despite my best efforts to remain stoic, I gasped. Evan held his head in his hands. We'd failed, and with this crushing defeat, our jobs were on the line, not to mention the viability of the Bluffs.

Evan raised his head, and turned to speak. He had a woman's voice.

"Mr. Thomas. *Mr. Thomas.* Are you here? *Hellooo.*"

It was Sharon.

"Glad to have you back. Did you enjoy your nap?"

I must have dozed off, though it couldn't have been more than a few seconds.

"You said you wanted me to schedule a meeting with Evan on the Bristol case. He'll be available at eleven, assuming you can stay awake that long."

"Thanks Sharon, I was just resting my eyes."

She smirked, already chalking up another victory.

Prior to my brief respite, I'd been summarizing my suggestions regarding the Bristol drowning. Going to trial on a civil action was the last thing we needed. The risks were too high.

When most people think of an attorney, they picture the courtroom scene—judge, jury, a defense lawyer making impassioned pleas during a final argument, and witnesses on the stand being grilled by solemn-faced prosecutors. Generations had grown up with images of Perry Mason or Matlock as the archetypical attorney.

The truth was that only a small fraction of attorneys handled courtroom trials. These were the litigators, legal specialists who seemingly possessed an innate ability to persuade twelve jurors to see things their way.

I had tried a few small cases during my first years as an attorney. Despite my preparation, practice and a good deal of advance role-playing, I had come across in the courtroom as inexperienced, fumbling, unsure, and mostly ineffective, or at least that's the way it felt.

"I knew Perry Mason, and you sir, are no Perry Mason."

At the Bluffs, we utilized an outside law firm to handle any litigation needs that arose. It wasn't feasible or desirable for most businesses to keep a litigator on salary. If the need arose for their services, I'd be an interface between the Bluffs and the hired guns who'd actually try the case.

The vast majority of legal disputes never made it to the trial stage. The trial usually only exists as a looming threat, one that spurs negotiations. If you believe that your side will prevail in the hypothetical courtroom drama, you have the upper hand in negotiations, and you can force a more advantageous settlement. Alternate dispute resolution was generally far preferable to putting your company's coffers in the hands of unpredictable, and sometimes seemingly irrational, judges and jurors.

Negotiations often fail initially, and as part of the aggressive legal posturing that usually accompanies this waltz, the parties prepare for trial. Discovery ensues, whereby documents and information are requested by the parties. Depositions, motions and hearings of all types soon follow, at a not inconsiderable expense. This reality check is often enough to force parties to resume talks, resulting in many cases settled "on the courthouse steps."

In the Bristol case, in theory, we had the upper hand. The deceased, Peter Bristol, claimed that he had permission to dive for balls on our property after asking a maintenance worker employed by one of our contractors. Even the average Joe on the street knows that this sounds pretty suspect.

There was no record of this permission, since the worker was purportedly an illegal immigrant who had subsequently disappeared. The only record of this conversation was in Bristol's partner's head. The fact that they snuck onto the property via back roads did not lend credibility to their case.

Conversely, they had the sunken lawn tractor, and a grieving widow with small children. I was never one to discount the effect that a weeping woman and her wailing tykes could have on a jury.

The Bluffs' liability insurance covered us for up to $2,000,000 for any single claim. If we went to court and lost, and the damages exceeded this amount, we'd have to pay the difference ourselves.

After extensive talks with our insurance company attorneys, we had agreed that if we had to, we'd offer the Bristol estate up to a $750,000 settlement.

This amount more than covered Peter Bristol's projected future earnings in his chosen profession of golf ball diving.

First, however, we'd try our luck at getting this thing thrown out of court completely.

My afternoon was dedicated to golf lessons, that staple of every golf pro's existence. I was never quite sure what I was going to encounter when I gave a lesson. Sometimes I had to teach true golf neophytes. Alternatively, I'd been summoned by tour pros to examine their games for glitches. That was intimidating, but often another pair of eyes really did help.

Most of the time, I taught somewhere in between these two extremes. Most students take lessons just to improve their game. There was almost always something I could find that could improve a person's score by four or five shots a round, with practice.

I liked to explain it to people this way: If you can save one stroke a round on your drives, one stroke on your fairway shots, one stroke on your approach shots, one stroke on your chips and sand shots, and one stroke on your putts, you've improved your total score by five shots.

The first lesson I ever gave was during my initial internship, teaching absolute beginners. This was a couple on their honeymoon, who'd signed up for the golf package, which included complimentary lessons.

What their brochure hadn't told them was that their complimentary golf lessons would be with an extremely young student intern who was scared out of his wits at having to teach "real" people for the first time.

We started out on the driving range, and I handed the husband a five-iron to try out first. The irons are generally a little easier than the woods for beginners. Most real beginners, at least the males, always want to start out with the big drivers right away. They envision blasting 300-yard drives after a swing or two. It doesn't work that way.

I watched the guy take a few practice swings, tried to straighten out a few of his glaring faults, then set the ball on the tee and stood back—way back. He settled over the ball, took a ferocious swing, and hit a shot that went between his legs, almost hitting another golfer three tee-boxes over. Shank city.

A shanked shot, also known as a hosel rocket, occurred when a player hit the ball with the end of the shaft, or hosel, thus sending it shooting off in a seemingly impossible direction, generally sideways from the intended path. Shanks were the most common shot seen on those "funny home video" clips where the camera person gets smacked with the ball. I always made sure to follow rule number one in golf: always make sure to stand well behind a bad golfer when he swings.

The shank shot should not be confused with the skank shot, which was the term a golfer's ex-wife used for any shot hit by his current wife.

In my student's second attempt, he got more of the ball, this time hitting it off his left shin. Hopping around in pain, he handed back the club while giving this young "pro" the dirtiest of looks. His wife tried valiantly to suppress her laugh, but ultimately gave in to her giggles.

His better half managed to eventually hit some decent shots during her lesson. As I've learned over time, beginning woman golfers generally pick it up a little faster, being concerned initially with just making contact, rather than trying to demonstrate their power by taking their biggest rip right away.

I wasn't sure how the remainder of their golf vacation would go, but the wife seemed savvy enough to know that, to smooth things over, she probably needed to save her best strokes for their honeymoon suite.

But that was many years and many lessons ago. My first lesson this afternoon was with an employee of Chesapeake Bluffs, Ms. Beverly Sargent. One perk of working at the Club was discounted golf lessons.

Ms. Sargent arrived on time. She appeared to be in her early forties, and was in reasonably good shape for her age. Some might even call her voluptuous, as her plunging neckline revealed acres of cleavage, not all of which appeared to be one-hundred percent natural. Her too-short golf skirt completed the look.

She had the leathery appearance of someone who had spent entirely too many years out in the sun. The deep tan she now sported bore a slightly orange hue, indicating that it had most likely come in liquid form.

We exchanged pleasantries as we moved to the driving range. She had an impressive set of clubs, which probably had cost her, or someone else, well over a grand. I noticed a very large diamond on her finger, a huge solitaire that must have been three carats or more.

"I work over at Mulligan's," she said, which was the name of the Club's Irish Pub. "My fiancé is a member here. I'd like to learn to play better so that we can golf together."

That explained the rock.

"I've only played a little before," she said. One look at her pristine clubs had already told me that.

"Let's start with the irons," I said. Some things hadn't changed from my very first lesson. "Why don't you try your five-iron and I'll take a look at your form."

"I'd have thought you'd have noticed my form already," she

said, grinning impishly. "I've been working on it for months."

I wasn't sure how to respond to that line, so I chose, for once, to remain silent. After a brief pause, she pulled the club out of her bag.

I teed up her ball for her, and she took a typical beginner's hack at the ball, which she hit off the toe of the iron, sending the ball shooting to the right. We'd start with the basics.

I began with the grip, the most important factor in the swing. She appeared to be having problems duplicating mine.

"Let me try it out on your club," she said, putting her club down and grabbing mine. "Oh, much better," she said, "I like your shaft." She looked up to gauge my response.

I tried not to have one.

"I'm not getting this," she said, "can you show me how to hold it?"

I moved her hands into the proper position on the club. As I did, she leaned into me, pressing her large breasts into my side.

"That feels better," she said. "How does it look from there?" She had positioned herself so that I had a direct view of her greatest assets.

Ordinarily, I wouldn't mind if an attractive woman flirted with me. But this lady had already mentioned that she was engaged, and I had a budding relationship with Darby. Plus, her skin was like a baseball glove.

"Your grip looks great," I said, "let's try some swings."

"Oh, I like to swing," she said.

I'm afraid I didn't give her exactly what she was looking for. But it wasn't for lack of effort on her part. The remainder of our one-hour lesson was filled with enough flirtation and sexual innuendo to populate an entire TV season. I was a little surprised that she didn't try to jump me right at the driving range tee.

"I need to get your number so I can schedule my next lesson," she said after our hour was completed. "Can you call my cell?"

"Sure," I said, not really thrilled at giving her my number. I called her phone and she answered, then she proceeded to type vigorously, punching button after button.

"Oh dear," she said after one final push. "I think I've deleted it. Can you call again, please?"

I hit the number on my phone again, prompting a second call. Nothing seemed to happen on her end.

"It didn't go through for some reason," she said. "Let's try it again. Maybe I hit the wrong button last time." She punched a few more keys. "Sorry, one more time."

The third time seemed to be the charm, and she managed at last to enter in the information she needed.

Next time she called for lessons, I knew just who I could refer her to. My pal Rodney always had an opening he needed to fill.

Once a year I returned to my alma mater to give a talk to the PGA Golf Management majors, or PGMers, as we were called. PGMers are golf-loving fiends, and almost every single one of them, at some time, has dreamed about going on tour. Since there are only about 200 PGA touring pros in the world, it's a long shot. I was very fortunate. To qualify for the tour, you must finish in the top 25 in the annual qualifying tournament or "Q-School" as it is affectionately known.

Even though the odds of making the tour are extraordinarily slim, I never discouraged anyone from trying. One of the best things about tour golf is that it is a true meritocracy. If you're talented enough to get to the tour, you'll be able to qualify.

And if you don't, there are still thousands of careers a graduate can pursue to get paid while enjoying his or her passion for golf. I'm living proof of that, too.

The majority of PGM graduates go on to become successful club and teaching professionals. Besides teaching, graduates are involved in every aspect of the golf industry, running golf courses and resorts, managing all of the business aspects of golf operations including merchandising, running tournaments, fleet management, turfgrass management, and food and beverage operations. It's no accident that the PGM program is located solidly in the business school.

On this year's visit, I had a secondary agenda, visiting Cody Corrigan, my prospective summer intern. I needed to assess whether he was still a viable candidate for this summer's program. I had played against Cody the year before in the mini-tournament that was held at the end of my campus visit. From what I remembered, he'd been a fine player. As a matter of fact, he'd almost beaten me.

I'd done a little research into the accessibility of the facilities at the Bluffs, and I'd been happy to discover that our main stores, clubhouse and office complex were built just ten years ago, after the passage of the Americans with Disabilities Act. This meant that all facilities had wheelchair ramps and handicapped restrooms and that our retail outlets had at least one cash register and sales counter which could be operated from wheelchair height. This removed any impediments to Cody taking his turn working in the pro-shop. But, there was still the question about his ability to handle the golf side of things.

I got an early start and drove the two hours to Val-U's campus to make my eleven o'clock appointment with Cody and the director of the golf program, Kerry Boggs. Kerry had been the director since I was a student. He was a character, but he knew his stuff. He'd built the PGM program at Val-U, and his advice, experience and professionalism had made a huge impact on my career, as well as countless others. He was revered at the University, and the excellence of the PGM program brought many a student to Val-U.

When I arrived, I found Kerry and Cody at the driving range. Cody was seated on something that looked like a cross between a wheelchair and a golf cart. As I approached, Cody stood up.

How is this possible?

Moving closer, I realized that he was strapped into this hybrid chair/cart, man and machine working in tandem. I was beginning to understand Kerry's insistence that I see Cody in person.

We shook hands all around. I had forgotten how tall Cody was; he had a good five inches on me.

"That is one cool machine," I observed as I circled the chair.

"It's called the Handygolfer," Cody said. "It just came out last year. And you're right, it is pretty cool. Watch this."

He lowered the chair and steered to the tee box. Setting up a tee and ball, he pulled a driver out of the attached bag, positioned the cart, and using the hand controls, stood once again.

He lined up with his ball, and without a practice stroke, took a solid swing and drove it a good 225 yards.

I was speechless. Kerry had a big grin on his face; I could see he was enjoying this immensely.

"This thing'll go into the bunkers and on the greens," Cody said proudly. "I can play the whole course."

"How long have you been using it?" I asked.

"About a month. At first, I could only hit about a hundred yards with my driver. But after I got the hang of it, and my muscles started getting stronger, I'm hitting about twenty-five yards longer each week."

"That's phenomenal," I said. "How much do you practice?"

"I work on it about four hours a day."

"This kid's already beating some of our other PGMers," Kerry said, "and he's only improving."

Once again, Kerry had me pegged. There was no need for any long-winded meeting after this demonstration. Seeing how much effort he had already put into his recovery, I was sure he'd have no problems doing whatever we needed at the Bluffs. This kid was dedicated.

"If you still want that internship, it's yours," I said.

"Let me think about it," Cody replied.

What?

"Just kidding," he said. "I'll be there."

So that was that. We had forty-five minutes to kill before my lecture, so we took turns on the driving range, just like old times.

Kerry had a story or joke for every situation, many of which you probably couldn't repeat in polite company. But he had a method for conveying important information in a timeless fashion that even today's impatient generation of college students could grasp and remember. They listened to Kerry.

Focused on Cody, he said, "When somebody's taking a lesson, you want to make it entertaining, as well as instructive. That way they'll remember what you're trying to teach. Let's say you've got a guy who's lifting his head up before he hits the ball."

"You tell him about the young guy who was playing with a priest. They got to the first par 3 hole, and the priest asked 'What are you using, son?'

"'An eight-iron, Father, how about you?'

"'I'm going to hit a soft seven and pray.'

"The young man hits a strong shot, landing perfectly on the green. The priest tops the ball and it dribbles twenty yards out in front.

"'I don't know about you, Father,' the young man says, 'but in my church when we pray, we keep our head down.'"

Cody had apparently never heard this one before, and laughed appreciatively.

"You have my permission to file that away and use it as necessary in the future, son," Kerry said to him. "I'll give you the address where you can send the royalty checks."

After giving my lecture to a packed house, I stayed to answer questions and chat one-on-one with students who had time to linger. These PGMers seemed to be getting younger with each passing year. One of them actually called me "Sir." That hurt.

I must admit, I did feel a lot better after I smoked them in the annual tournament. You can take your "sir" and shove it down your 18th hole.

Still, it had felt good to be back in my old stomping grounds, although I certainly didn't miss the papers and exams. I was more than a little anxious to get back home. Tonight was going to be special. I was going to be personally evaluating a bevy of smoking-hot beauties.

Bull Durham had agreed to meet me at the gun range in the evening after I got back from the University. When I spotted him, he was toting a huge gun case, which I could only assume was a small part of his total arsenal.

When I had spoken with him yesterday, I'd just asked him for some advice on getting a gun for personal protection. Frankie's suspicious death, coupled with Tom Jones' threat, had left me a little rattled, as I'd experienced firsthand with my initial reaction during the restroom stalking incident. As luck would have it, Bull was somewhat of an expert on firearms.

"Have you ever handled a gun before?" was his first question.

"No, not really," I said.

"The first rule of firearms is that if you don't know what you're doing, you're just as likely to get yourself killed with it than to use it to successfully defend yourself. You're going to need to get some practice at the range, and then you're going to have to get a concealed weapons permit."

Once inside, he led me to a small classroom. "This is where they do the concealed weapons training," he said. "We better go over a few things before we actually try the shooting range."

On the table, he opened the case and showed me the goods. I wasn't tremendously well versed in firearms—in fact, the last gun I'd shot had used caps, back when I was about eight.

"I was thinking of a pretty small weapon that'd be easy to carry around. Maybe a .22," I said, trying to sound knowledgeable despite my pathetic lack of experience in the area.

Bull shot me a pitying look. "Yeah, that'll be guaranteed to stop any chipmunk that attacks you, provided you hit it at least three times."

So much for sounding knowledgeable.

"You want something with some knockdown power. You're not going to get many second chances when your life's on the line, so make every shot count. We'll probably want to go with at least a 9mm or a .38 Special, but we'll try a few different types."

"Can I carry it at work?"

"If you have a concealed weapons permit, and your club allows employees to carry weapons to work, then, yes."

"Who would know if our club allows it?"

"You'd probably want to check with legal."

Ouch.

"If not, the Club might allow employees to keep a weapon in their cars in the parking lot, provided it's in a secured container or in the glove box. Again, you'll want to—"

"I know, check with legal,"

"Now that I think about it," he said, "attorneys and police officers in Virginia are exempt from having to get concealed weapons permits. You, my friend, are in luck."

I was feeling a little bit better about myself now.

Once inside the range, I tried out the 9mm pistols, the .357s, and the .38 Special revolvers. I hadn't done too badly. Most of my shots were somewhere on the body of the target.

Then Bull showed me how it was supposed to be done,

putting all of his shots in the center circle.

Showoff.

I liked the compact .38 Special revolver the best, for combination of size and feel. I also really liked the laser sight option. That red dot made it pretty easy.

We got out and they ran an instant background check using the NICS system, and I was cleared to get my weapon. A few hundred bucks later, I had my .38 with holster, gun safe and several boxes of extra rounds.

I was already feeling more secure in dealing with any threats, real or imagined.

Chapter 12

The lawsuits on my desk came as no surprise, their presence preordained from the exact moment of the disaster. Preventing a personal injury lawsuit following a golf cart rollover accident would have required divine intervention.

Considering our country's current litigious climate, there are very few "victims" who can resist the siren song of today's legal temptresses, promising huge rewards with little risk.

We saw our share of cart "incidents" on the six courses at the Bluffs, but in general our clientele were somewhat older and more conservative than at many other clubs, so we didn't typically get large numbers of young, rowdy and macho golfers who liked to turn courses into mini versions of the Indianapolis 500, generally after enjoying substantial quantities of adult beverages. A rollover was rare.

Thankfully for us, but not so much for their attorneys, neither of the two golfers in the cart rollover accident on No. 1 suffered life-threatening injuries. The driver, Jim Hoffman, had been knocked unconscious. His hysterical partners called 911 and reported that he was dead. Fortunately, he revived a few moments later. Although the injured pair were on their way to recovery, concussions, broken bones and various other serious injuries could lower their future quality of life.

Both plaintiffs had retained the same agency, the renowned law firm of Gaines & Associates. The founder of this large personal injury factory was none other than the omnipresent Hugh Gaines, who had parlayed his given name into his signature slogan, "See Hugh Gaines for 'Huge Gains.'"

Of course the slogan could also have applied to his body mass index. From the looks of him, the senior Gaines never saw a fast food restaurant that he didn't like. Gaines' likeness was everywhere, on billboards, buses, benches, but most of all, on those nauseatingly recurring television commercials. His puffy face appeared on the screen multiple times each day, imploring potential victims to trust in the baby-faced goober who always looked perilously close to bursting out of his latest designer suit, apparently purposely tailored to be three sizes too small, demonstrating a serious, self-delusional, gravitational denial.

His son, and current partner, Hugh Gaines Jr., had been tagged at an early age with the unfortunate nickname of "Little Gaines," which, having been once associated with his likeness, could never be retracted, no matter how hard he or the ad agencies tried. Little Gaines often appeared on the TV commercials with senior, and without exception, the gaunt man in his late twenties would be the one to end the ad with their signature phrase, a clear attempt to transfer brand loyalty onto the next generation.

In actuality, neither man spent much time doing legal work. They occupied their days making commercials and managing their legal empire, and presumably, at least for the elder Gaines, enjoying the fruit of their success. Their lawsuits were filed by one of hundreds of associates, who signed their names to the documents under the famous letterhead, giving them instant credibility, if not respect.

In my legal fantasy life, I continually pondered the initiation of a class-action lawsuit against Gaines for multiple counts of intentional infliction of emotional distress, having been subjected to hundreds of hours of bombardment by that accursed figure and his slogan in every walk of my life.

The two golfers' lawsuits were essentially carbon copies. They brought suit against both Chesapeake Bluffs Golf and Country Club and KG Limited, the Korean manufacturer of the golf cart.

The first claim against us boiled down to four essentials:

1. Chesapeake Bluffs has a responsibility to provide safe carts that can be reasonably driven in a safe manner by all users;

2. We instead provided unsafe carts with potential to exceed the state speed limit of 20 mph for golf carts, such speeds being hazardous on the golf course. We failed to prevent operators of the cart from changing the operational characteristics of the cart to allow speeds in excess of 20mph to be achieved;

3. These unsafe carts were the cause of the rollover;

4. The rollover resulted in harm and injury to the plaintiffs.

A second claim accused us of continuing to serve alcoholic beverages to the driver of the vehicle with full knowledge of his inebriation, thus facilitating his impairment and contributing to the accident.

It was interesting to note that the passenger, Thomas Fields, did not sue the cart's driver. To do so would have meant using a separate law firm, obviously, but also would have weakened or nullified his case against both us and KG Limited, since it would have implied that the driver was partially or totally at fault. It probably didn't take Fields, or his attorney, very long to figure out which of these entities had the deeper pockets.

Each of the plaintiffs filed suit against us for $1,000,000 for injuries, pain and suffering, and lifelong rehabilitation.

I was doubtful that we would end up going to court on either of these cases, considering we had a pretty strong case for operator error. The driver had already been charged after this accident with a DUI under Virginia law, which governed a variety of vehicle types, including golf carts. In addition, three of the beers that Hoffman had consumed had been brought on the course by another golfer in his foursome, which, aside from being against our course rules, meant that the consumption of this beer was unknown to the beverage cart attendant, who had served him only three beers over the course of the four hour round.

Hoffman had also intentionally and willfully bypassed the

operational characteristics of the cart by switching from economy to high performance mode. In economy mode, the carts are limited to a top speed of 15 mph, clearly within safe limits.

Plus, the state of Virginia is one of the few states that follow a pure contributory negligence system. If the victims were found to have contributed in any way to the accident, they recovered nothing. And there were at least three areas where Hoffman contributed to his accident: his DUI, tampering with the cart, and reckless driving.

Most other states use what is known as a comparative negligence system, where victims may still recover something even if partially to blame for the accident, though their financial recovery may be reduced.

And finally, all renters of golf carts at the Bluffs are required to sign a liability waiver. For members using carts, the waiver must be signed as part of their annual membership agreement. The waiver contains an exculpatory clause that explicitly absolves the Club from liability in the case of a golf cart accident.

This case was dead on arrival. It wasn't going far. Under the circumstances, maybe I'd even accuse Gaines of filing a frivolous lawsuit.

His loss is my "Gain."

"Evan wants to talk with you," Sharon said, the perplexed look on her face indicating that she had no idea of the subject of this urgency. "Right now. In his office."

I dropped what I was doing, and headed down the hall.

"Shut the door," he said.

"We've had a complaint. Sexual harassment," he continued.

I nodded. That didn't really shock me. In my times spent around various country clubs, I'd seen, or heard about, plenty of behavior that some might consider over the line.

"It's against you."

My heart skipped a beat. *Me.* There are things in life you never expect to hear. This was one of them. I struggled to think about who my accuser could be. Not a single person came to mind.

"I'm afraid I have no idea what this could be about," I said, "or even who would say such a thing."

"We take these things very seriously," he said. "We have to.

If we don't, the corporation can be fined or even sued. Every employee here goes through our HR program, which incorporates training to prevent these kinds of matters."

"I just took those courses, Evan," I said, chafing at his parental tone, "and I'm an attorney, if you haven't forgotten."

"*Then*, as you know, the EEOC will perform the preliminary investigation. We have to take each and every complaint seriously. We're required to, by law."

I was very familiar with the Equal Employment Opportunity Commission. My old law firm had represented clients on both sides of harassment claims.

"Can you tell me who the complainant is, and what's the nature of the complaint?"

"It's Beverly Sargent, one of our hospitality workers."

Beverly. From the golf lessons.

"I'll read you the complaint."

> Complainant states that she made the acquaintance of Mr. Thomas during golf lessons. At that time, Mr. Thomas made repeated lewd and sexually suggestive remarks, which she attempted to ignore.

> Complainant states that Mr. Thomas obtained her number and made repeated calls in which he pressured her for sexual favors, promising to use his influence to help Ms. Sargent obtain a better position in the Club. Complainant stated that she told Mr. Thomas to cease calling or that she would report him.

> Complainant states that Mr. Thomas appeared the next day at her place of employment and tried to pressure her into performing sexual favors in return for said employment help.

Clearly, the flirting and odd behavior at the driving range were part of some kind of bizarre setup for these charges.

I was familiar with the plight of the falsely accused. Even if there was no basis for the charges, the EEOC would have to investigate to make such a determination. If word of this leaked out, I might become a pariah within the Club.

There was no real recourse on the part of the "harasser." I could always file a counter-suit, but the real damage was done by the negative publicity and the stigma attached to the charges, real or manufactured.

It was possible that this was strictly a money ploy. She might be looking for a quick settlement. But why me?

"Evan," I said, "the charges are totally baseless. I met the woman for the first time just last week in lessons, that much is true. The rest are lies."

"I can't comment one way or another," he said. "As I said, we are required to take these matters very seriously. We expect your full cooperation with any investigation."

"Of course," I said. "But this is bullshit, and you know it."

I knew the drill. The initial investigation by the EEOC would determine if the case had any teeth. If they found that the accusations were warranted, they could assist the complainant in taking action against me or the Club. If not, the EEOC would drop the case. The complainant could always continue to pursue a civil action with a private attorney, but it would be a considerably weaker case without EEOC backing.

"It would be understandable," Evan said, "if after taking a while to think about these charges, you decided to offer your resignation. There would still be an investigation, but you wouldn't have to deal with the ramifications of all that while you were here."

That was where I drew the line.

"I have nothing to be sorry for concerning this woman or my work at this Club. If you want to get rid of me, you'll have to fire me. But I'm not going down without a fight."

Determined not to let the harassment charges affect my job or my personal life, I intended to continue in my role as in-house legal counsel and golf pro as if nothing had happened.

Much to my own surprise, I had found that I was enjoying the legal part of my job almost as much as the golfing side. There had been enough legal work for a full-time job, and I was finding that my allotted twenty hours a week was insufficient to make a dent in the backlog. But it had been challenging, and had required research into a surprisingly wide array of legal issues.

As a new attorney, I'd found that emotional intelligence could often trump legal acumen. Many cases could be resolved by letting folks air out their differences.

On the golf course, people skills were just as valuable. I had a full slate of afternoon lessons, including four back-to-back sessions. I had become the "go-to" pro at the Bluffs.

First up was Bob Powell, a gregarious giant. Imagine Shrek with normal ears, and not quite so green. He wanted to work on his drives. Bob had developed a pretty nasty slice. As he described it, "The more I try to fix it, the worse it gets."

A slice was caused by sidespin imparted to the ball upon impact. Almost all novice golfers have had to deal with a slice at some time or another. Many golfers tried to correct it by aiming more to the left. Drawing their club back to the right of the ball, this technique ensured that they imparted even more sidespin to the ball, compounding the problem.

This "slice spiral-of-death," in its completed form, often resulted in a very expensive driver being thrown into the closest available body of water. Hopefully Bob had not already resorted to such drastic measures.

In order to evaluate his mechanics, I asked Bob to go through the motions of the swing, without actually hitting a ball.

"I'm already an expert at that," he shot back.

And a smart-aleck, too.

After his warm-up, he took his first swing, just catching the top of the ball, sending it only a few inches forward. I had to admit, it was always great fun to watch a big, muscular type step up to the tee-box, peel back and rip a tremendous swing, only to see the ball dribble two feet off the tee. One could almost see the testosterone draining into the grass.

According to golfing tradition, if a male golfer's shot didn't make it past the ladies' tees, the golfer had to hit his next shot with his pants down, to "prove" he's not a woman. Of course, it was even better if a cart girl was watching. She'd be sure to explain the rules regarding the "dick-out" shot. I figured it was prudent to skip this bit of instructional lore for Bob.

He finally settled in and began to make solid contact. I watched as he muscled a few drives, and true to form, his shots veered to the right, some with frightening speed.

How many windows had Bob shattered with that shot? I wonder if he uses noodle balls.

For Bob's benefit, I replicated his swing, peeling off a banana ball or two in the process. Next, I demonstrated how a slight change in grip and stance could allow him to hit the ball with the club face square and with a straight swing path.

As directed, he began hitting drives with the improved technique, under medium power. We immediately noticed a difference. His new drives were straight, and some even had a very slight right-to-left draw. Bob was psyched. I could see he wanted to pulverize one.

"Go for it," I said.

With a backswing to complement his size, he wound up and let it rip.

A loud crack slightly preceded the sight of Bob's $500 club-head rolling along the turf in front of us.

"That was a brand new driver," he whined, suddenly reminding me of a child who had just broken his favorite toy.

Bob had chunked his shot, hitting the ground before the ball. It's also called hitting it fat. When done with an iron, the shot was sometimes called a pooper-scooper or a chili dipper, named for the visual image presented as an iron scoops up a gigantic strip of turf which peels up over the ball, giving rise to yet another name for this shot, laying the sod.

But in any case, I had never seen a driver snap in two like that just from a simple fat hit.

"Where'd you get that club, Bob?" I asked.

"I got it here, at the pro shop. Just a few months ago."

"Then it'll still be under warranty. I'll get you a replacement. We can have it tomorrow."

One of the advantages of buying clubs from Chesapeake Bluffs was the promise of instant replacement for clubs under warranty. We kept extra stock for that very reason. Of course, that level of service didn't come cheaply. Members paid list price for the equipment.

It was my job now to make sure Bob didn't get "the shaft."

The extended weather forecast never varied—warm and sunny. Many people would be rather pleased at such news, but Carolyn Andrews was not among them. At first, the long spring drought had been a godsend. She had needed dry weather for her scheme to succeed, but now she would have given up half her fortune for one good, old-fashioned thunderstorm.

The plan had been set for months. In fact, her men had been on standby for nine straight weeks. She only needed them for a single night. And that one night's work would cost her plenty. Half up front, and half when the job was done, like countless movies she'd seen.

But this time, she was the villain, the one hiring the goons and planning the job. Of course, she didn't see it quite that way, but then, people like her rarely do. They are experts in rationalization. They're only remorseful *after* they get caught.

In Carolyn's case, she justified it as necessary for her survival. She had run out of options. Circumstances had left her no choice.

It had taken her time to find a capable arsonist. At first, she had absolutely no idea how to find one. She was sure they didn't advertise on Craigslist. Then she remembered the principle of degrees-of-separation. You may not know an arsonist, but more than likely someone you know, knows someone else, who knows one.

She had hired a slightly less-than-reputable-sounding handyman from a business card tacked on the wall at a home store. She'd hinted to him regarding various "things" she needed done, some of which might not be strictly legal. He knew another guy who "might" be able to handle something like that. At each stage, she became more explicit, until finally, she found someone purported to have the perfect credentials.

But $50,000? How much skill did it take to start a fire in the woods? In the beginning, she'd even thought about doing it herself. But she was savvy enough to know better. The men she ultimately hired were supposedly the "best" arsonists in the area.

How does one measure that? It's not exactly like they're certified.

Their modus operandi, she had been told by her contact, was to imitate the origins of a naturally occurring fire. They employed a portable spark generator of their own design, which left no traces of gasoline, diesel fuel or any other substance that could possibly be detected by fire investigators. Supposedly, they already had three successful burns on their resumes, with no suspicions of arson.

The intention was to wait for an evening electrical storm, then watch until lightning struck somewhere within the targeted forest area, after which they would move in and light the fire in the vicinity of the strike. Smart-phones made it easy enough to track the strikes. No one would ever suspect that the fire was due to anything other than lighting. And the pièce de résistance was the Forest Service policy—let natural fires burn their way out.

But to her continued dismay, there were no electrical storms in the forecast, and she was almost out of money. She couldn't afford to wait two more weeks, let alone another month. She needed to get the squirrels off that land. If she could do that with a blaze of glory, so much the better.

She finished off her last pack of cigarettes. Chain-smoking once again, her wastebasket, now overflowing with empty packs, testified to the power of the resurrected addiction. Pouring herself another whiskey, she picked up the phone, then hesitated, and finally placed it gently back down.

Calling the number would start a sequence of events from which there would be no return. She was certain the fire couldn't be traced back to her, even if for some reason her contractors got caught. They'd never met her, didn't know her name, and couldn't track her disposable phone.

With no lightning in the forecast, the arsonists would have to use a second, less desirable option. The men would pitch a small pup-tent and build a campfire in the woods, which would just happen to grow out-of-control. The investigators would come across the tent and the fire ring, and chalk it up to careless campers.

But for any of this to happen, she first had to make the call. One last shot of scotch helped dull her defenses. With trembling hands, she dialed the number on the back of the card. A gruff voice answered.

"Yeah."

She uttered the agreed-upon words.

"Smokey Bear is a go."

Chapter 13

In the morning, I set off to the pro-shop to deliver Bob's newly decommissioned driver. When I'd called Trevor Dunne, the pro-shop manager, to let him know I'd be coming over, he'd suggested we use the time to do some training in the "sack." I considered referring him to Darby, whom I felt confident would attest to my proficiency in that arena.

The sack was the informal term for the Bluffs' Swing Analysis Center, the new state-of-the-art computerized golf swing analyzer, housed completely within the pro-shop. I'd heard it was a pretty slick toy.

The pro shop, a golf megastore, included huge sections devoted to men's and women's clothing. The apparel was embroidered with the magical Chesapeake Bluffs' logo, which served to increase its retail value by some 200 percent.

Trevor was at his desk, deeply engrossed in some sort of trade journal. Only... it wasn't a journal. I'd seen that ball retriever somewhere before.

Busted.

Trevor was passing the time contemplating the contents of "Cart Girls Gone Crazy." I cleared my throat, and watched as he quickly buried Miss September and her bosomy buddies under a pile of documents.

That's no way to treat a lady.

He stood up as if nothing had happened.

"Desmond, good to see you. That's a nasty break, isn't it?" he said, admiring Bob's handiwork.

"He chunked a drive. The club head went farther than the ball."

"After you called yesterday, I found Bob's purchase record in the system. We have an exact replacement in stock." He pointed to the shiny new club sitting in the corner of his office.

"What happens if we don't have the club in stock?"

"We try to keep duplicates of the most common sizes and brands we sell. On the odd occasion when we don't have one, we can get them from our distributer the next day. They're only an hour away."

Next, Trevor showed me the swing analysis center, his pride and joy. The room was impressively high-tech, with a rack of computer equipment along one wall, and several large video cameras pointing toward the spacious tee area in the center. It was a techie's wet dream.

"Let's get started," he said. "You can be my guinea pig. Grab a driver and tee up."

When the green light flashed, I gave it my all, a 300-yarder, at least. After all that effort, the ball thumped into the large canvas screen a few yards ahead.

A few swings later, and we were done. The whole process took less than five minutes.

The lights in the room dimmed, and my larger-than-life visage appeared on the oversized flat screen display. Unlike the fuzzy videos I'd seen in the past, this image was super clear, sharp enough to count each individual nose hair.

Time to trim those suckers.

My backswing began in super-slow motion.

"You can freeze the video at any time, and capture an image with just a click." He demonstrated by stopping the video at the top of my backswing.

Looking good.

"The instructor can then point out any problem areas with the student's swing."

At this moment, a comely young woman appeared at the doorway. A closer look revealed it to be Miss Cart Girl of September, in the flesh, sadly, sans ball retriever.

"Hey Trev. Caitlyn said if I came by to sign your calendar and get my picture taken, I could pick out a free shirt." She glanced my way. "Oh, is this a bad time?"

"I don't know what you're talking about," he said. "Caitlyn must have made a mistake. I'm busy right now, can't you see?"

"Sorry," she said, retreating with a perplexed expression.

What kind of operation is "Trev" running here?

At first glance, he appeared to be swapping company merchandise in return for a private photo shoot. I might have to look into this a little more. An interview with Miss September may be merited.

"Where were we?" he said, doing his best to refocus my attention. "Oh yeah, the report. A lot of good stuff in here, but the most important is the last section, the golf club recommendations. This is where we suggest the type of equipment best suited to help the student's game. We sell all of the recommended brands, of course."

Of course.

"We offer free demos on all our clubs. You should schedule a lesson with the student, and have them use the demo clubs. Kind of like a test drive. During the lesson, make sure to ask him how the clubs feel. We want the student to buy into his selection."

All of a sudden, I was beginning to feel a lot like a car salesman.

"Now, as an added incentive for the student to buy the new set, if he purchases within thirty days of getting the analysis, the SAC charge is applied to the purchase price of the clubs."

And we'll throw in free floor mats.

"You earn ten percent commission on any set sold to a customer with whom you've worked. Anything over five sets in a month, add another five percent onto your commission."

"How many sets a month do we sell?" I asked, wondering if such a feat was even remotely achievable.

"You'd be surprised. We've seen our purchase numbers take off since we started the SAC. We've doubled our monthly sales. It's been a great investment."

Then, Trevor and I reversed roles. I operated the system while Trevor swung the clubs. He had a few problem areas in his swing, which I felt obligated to point out. Fortunately, I had just the solution for him. A brand new set of top-of-the-line clubs that would take his game to the next level, in addition to impressing his friends and neighbors. We just happened to have a set *right here.*

Financing available.

I had always wanted to see a meteor shower, but for some reason, they always planned those things for 3:00 a.m.

But, what a guy will do for love. My alarm went off as scheduled. I reached over to the night stand and finally managed to turn off the irritating warble.

Rolling over, I saw that she was still sleeping, her tenderness and vitality evident even in her deep slumber, her slow and steady breathing the only sounds audible in the quiet of the early morning. She looked so lovely that I almost didn't have the heart to wake her. But I had no choice. The meteors weren't going to wait for us.

"Bertha, time to get your butt up," I said as I picked up the snoozing, slobbering canine and moved her to the foot of the bed. She grumbled and farted.

Darby mumbled and rolled over.

"You too, sleepyhead," I said in a somewhat softer tone. "This was your idea, remember. Don't bail on me now."

"What time is it?" she murmured.

"Time to get dressed. We've got a shower to see."

She turned over and reached her arms around my neck. "You could shower me with some affection now, if you want."

Well, when you put it that way.

It had been nice having Darby stay over at my place on a regular basis. I was amazed that someone so beautiful, talented and intelligent hadn't been swept off her feet long ago, but I guess her bad experience with Rodney had soured her on men for a time. Perhaps he'd done me a favor. Still, after all my dealings with that turd of a man, I had vowed to be the complete opposite of him.

I am the anti-Rodney.

After a brief, but thoroughly enjoyable delay, we hopped out of bed, quickly threw on some clothes and headed to the garage.

Bertha was finally awake, but just barely. Slightly grumpy, she was used to getting a few more hours of beauty sleep, as was I.

We climbed into the golf cart, eagerly anticipating what promised to be the most spectacular celestial display of the new millennium, or so we'd been told.

We hummed silently along the cart path, Darby's long hair gently blowing in the breeze, Bertha's long tongue doing the same. This wasn't such a bad idea, after all, despite the early morning hour.

It was a cloudless night, perfect for viewing. But the problem with viewing on course No. 5, the one in which our houses were situated, was that the streetlights and porch lights tended to wash out stars and other dim objects, exactly the things we hoped to see.

What we needed to find was a dark, isolated area away from any lights. I knew the perfect spot. Course No. 1 was the most isolated course on the Bluffs, especially the area farthest from the Clubhouse at hole 15. So, off we went.

Driving on the golf course at night was somewhat trickier than in the daytime. Even with the headlights on the golf cart, the hills, dips and curves of the cart path made for an eventful ride. Darby held onto Bertha with one hand and onto me with the other, while I held onto the steering wheel with both hands and hoped we didn't veer off the path by too much.

A few times I had to stop altogether when I couldn't see where the path was going, and a couple of times I ended up going around one of these circular loops at a tee-box when I took the wrong turn.

But eventually we arrived at our chosen destination. We spread our blanket in the center of the fairway, and lay down on our backs. Once our eyes adapted to the dark, we began to see more and more celestial objects. And then, for the first time in my life, I saw a shower of shooting stars.

As we lay there, nearly drifting off to sleep, Bertha suddenly jumped up and growled.

"What is it girl?" I said, my heart now pumping as my adrenaline kicked in. I envisioned a huge black bear charging us.

Bertha was focused on the woods that bordered the fairway. Except for the first ten or twenty feet, these woods were part of the so-called "North Property," the infamous acres of which I had spent so much time pondering of late. As I strained my eyes, Bertha's concern became apparent.

There was a light in the woods, maybe more than one. I could hear faint voices.

Hunters?

I wasn't familiar with anyone who hunted in the middle of the night, except maybe for those innocents that had been set out to find the elusive snipe.

As I watched, more lights appeared, only to merge together a few seconds later. It finally hit me. Somebody was lighting a fire.

I had seen the red-flags on the weather channel. The three-month-long drought had created tinderbox conditions in the whole area. The pine straw that covered the forest floor could create a wildfire in a matter of minutes.

I reached for my phone, and came up empty.

Damn.

Neither of us had bothered to bring our phones, seeing no particular need for such devices while viewing meteors.

As remote as we were, it would take a good twenty minutes to get to the closest phone if we took the cart path. But I knew a shortcut through the woods that could get us to the guardhouse in five.

We jumped in the cart and I blasted down the fairway at full speed, narrowly missing a bunker hidden in the darkness. After a few seconds, I found the shortcut.

We reached the road in less than a minute. I was set to turn toward the Clubhouse when headlights approached from the opposite direction.

"Maybe they have a phone," I said. I turned the golf cart toward the oncoming vehicle, signaling with my headlights.

"What if..." Darby began, but the vehicle, a pickup truck, was now upon us, its tires grinding to a halt. The headlights from our cart cast an eerie glow over the scene.

"There's a fire over—," I started to yell to the driver, stopping as soon as I saw his gun, aimed squarely at my head.

"What the hell are ya doing, Darrell?" his passenger yelled. "Keep going, we gotta get out of here!" The driver hesitated for one long, uncomfortable moment.

Then the truck's tires spun, showering us with dust and pebbles as it sped away into the dark.

"Those had to be the guys that started the fire," I said, heart now hammering in my chest. "I saw the driver's face. The guy said a name."

"His name was Darrell," Darby said. "He had a mustache and an eagle tattoo on his neck. He was driving a tan Dodge Ram 1500 quad cab with an aluminum toolbox in the back. The license plate was DKP-0418."

Damn!

Furious over his colossal blunder, Darrell lashed out. "Why the hell'd ya say my name?"

"Why the hell'd ya stop for a golf cart?" came the reply. "And then you showed 'em your gun. No way they won't go to the cops, now. We're done."

"I woulda taken care of it right there, bam, if you hadn't a wussed out. *'Drive Darrell, drive,'*" he said in mocking falsetto. "This ain't no picnic. You gotta take care of things."

"Like you're gonna shoot them right there." Mike said. You never shot nobody in your life, and you know it, and you ain't about to start now. We don't shoot people, we burn shit. I ain't gonna sit here and let you send my ass to fry in the chair just cause you're a damn stupid dumbass who can't just keep drivin'. You gonna stop for every cart we pass by? Smile at 'em, wave your gun, and hand 'em your drivers license? Stupid dumb shit."

Darrell could take it no longer. The massive quantities of adrenaline coursing through his body completed his transition from flight to fight. His rage now overwhelmed any logic. Unconsciously, he floored the accelerator.

He grabbed at the pistol sitting on the bench seat next to him. His mind, fueled by fury, had room for only a single thought.

Shut this guy up.

Finger on the trigger, he aimed the gun at Mike's head. Even in his frenzied state, he wasn't planning on shooting his partner, just scaring him into silence.

"What the fuck!" Mike yelled in response to this unexpected threat. He grabbed for the gun while simultaneously ducking to avoid a head shot. The additional pressure on the sensitive trigger was enough to set it off. The bullet grazed the top of Mike's scalp before smashing through the passenger window.

The truck swerved violently as Darrell tried to drive with his left hand while wrestling for control of the gun with his right. He jammed on the brakes, skidding the truck to a stop, and sending Mike sliding off the bench seat, crashing into the dash with a sickly thud. Blood spurting from his head wound, Mike's death grip on the weapon hardened, as he fought to turn the gun around.

For a split second, Darrell managed to gain an advantage, pointing the gun at Mike. It was kill or be killed. Darrell squeezed hard. Mike screamed and let go.

"My leg," he yelled. "You shot me in the fuckin' leg!"

Darrell was stunned.

What the hell just happened?

Mike reached for the door handle and in a last, desperate attempt at self preservation, yanked hard and launched himself into the darkness.

Darrell raced away. Moments later, he realized his predicament.

What if they find him alive?

He knew without a doubt what would transpire, and it began and ended with the metallic clang of a prison door.

Darrell had never killed a man before, but he had never before had such a pressing need. He knew exactly what had to be done.

He stomped on the brakes, shifting the truck in reverse before it had time to fully stop, transmission complaining noisily but finally complying as he punched the throttle, sending the truck weaving and whining wildly backwards along the dark road.

He got back to the spot.

Where is he?

He crept down the road, trying to aim the headlights toward the place where Mike's bloody body should be.

He leaped out of the truck, gun in hand, and scanned the nearby area. He ran down the road, following the headlight's path. Nothing. Mike was gone.

He's crawled into the woods.

There was no hope of finding him in there at night.

Chills ran up his spine as Darrell heard a distant wail. Police or fire, he didn't know, or really care at this point. He just knew he had to get out of there, fast.

Cursing his luck, his fate, his partner, and most of all, himself, Darrell jumped back in his truck and sped off into the night.

We easily identified Darrell in the police lineup. It was hard to forget the mental picture of that raging redneck wildly brandishing a .44 Magnum. The tattoo on his neck sealed the deal.

They'd picked him up based on Darby's description of his truck. He'd been doing over a hundred on a two-lane road. They'd found his buddy lying next to Old Fort Road. He'd almost bled out by the time they arrived. Apparently, they'd had some sort of altercation. The police said that in another fifteen minutes he wouldn't have made it. He still wasn't in any shape for a lineup, although chances were pretty good he'd have cut a deal by now. He certainly couldn't be feeling too much love for his former partner.

It took days to finally contain the fire. The dry conditions had helped it spread with unbelievable speed, sometimes at more than fifteen miles-per-hour, faster than a man can run. It was estimated that the blaze consumed roughly 10,000 acres, including nearly all of the Bluffs' planned expansion. Several homes adjacent to the woods were destroyed, although the occupants managed to escape unharmed.

Both my house and Darby's townhome bordered parts of the forest, but fortunately, the golf course fairway served as a buffer between the woods and our property. It had taken a few hours before we could see the first flames from our houses, then just another hour before they began to reach the edges of the fairway.

Bertha was fascinated by the fire, barking incessantly at the flames. When this failed to repel the blaze, she settled down to a routine of sleeping, waking, pacing and, growling, all in an apparent attempt to keep the fire at bay with sheer Bulldog bravado.

Of course, the fire threw a huge monkey wrench into the plans for the squirrel relocation. A call to Fish and Wildlife confirmed as much.

"The owner of the land can't profit from the eradication of

the protected species," Landrow said, substantiating my assumption.

It would be impossible to buy the land until this mess was sorted out. We'd need to determine whether the owner was involved in the arson, which frankly, seemed likely. Who else but the owner/seller of a property that contained endangered species would have a motive to start a forest fire?

Maybe there *was* someone else.

The buyer.

In my few available hours, I'd made some headway on Lisa's insurance lawsuit. It wasn't Shakespeare, by any means, but it did have all the pertinent information. The insurance company had the burden, in court, to prove that Frankie committed suicide. Frankie's use of anti-depressants, his gambling debts and poor financial situation would be used by their attorneys as circumstantial evidence to bolster their claims of suicide.

On the flip side, there was no note or statement by Frankie to friends or family that he was contemplating suicide. He had a loving wife and kids. These were big points in our favor.

I was hoping for a quick settlement, banking on the belief that the insurance company would not want to spend more in legal fees than the policy payout. At least this was my hope. In actuality, they had far more resources to wage this battle than I.

Along these lines, I hadn't forgotten about breaking into Frankie's email. The first step in that effort was figuring out the two lost password questions. I started with golf.

When had Frankie made his first hole-in-one?

My best recollection was that it was in the spring of our sophomore year.

Armed with this memory, I called on Val-U's Kerry Boggs to see if he still had the records. According to Kerry, the university didn't keep individual score cards, just the total scores. Seeing that this was over ten years ago, he suggested it might be somewhat challenging to find the records.

"It was in the student paper," he said, "and it was probably online too, on the university web page. Is there any way you can pull up a page from that long ago?"

I had no idea, but I knew somebody who just might. After

finishing with Kerry, I immediately called my brother.

"Hello," the groggy voice responded, reminding me of the fact that Kevin was an habitually late sleeper, rarely awake before ten.

"Do you know of a way to pull up a web page from ten years ago?" I asked.

"Good morning to you, too."

"Sorry Kevin, it's Dez," I said. "Good morning. Now about my question?"

"Ever hear of the wayback machine?"

"From Rocky and Bullwinkle, right?"

"Right," he said. "There's a web archive site named after the machine from the cartoon. It lets you go back in time, at least on the web. It crawls the web every day and archives the pages. If you know the URL, you might be able to find what you're looking for. Ten years is quite a while back, however."

"How do you use it?" I asked.

"Search for 'wayback machine' and you'll find the site. What are you looking for, anyway?"

"The Virginia Lutheran golf team page," I said.

"You trying to relive your glory days?" he chuckled.

"At least I had some," I said, thankful for his easy setup. With a few clicks, I located the wayback machine web page. That was easy enough. I had thought at first that he might be kidding, but, it was indeed a real site.

"Ok," Kevin continued, "in another window, bring up the current university golf web page."

I located the Val-U page and navigated to the golf news.

"Got it," I said.

"Now copy the address at the top, and paste it into the search box for the wayback machine."

After a few tries, I managed to cut-and-paste the address into the right place. An hourglass appeared.

"It's thinking," I said.

After a few more seconds, a list of dates appeared. They went back for almost 15 years.

"Well, I think it's working," I said. I clicked on a date from what I thought was approximately the right timeframe. After another wait, a page appeared from out of the past. I had traveled back in time!

I wonder if Baywatch is on tonight.

I recognized the names of some of my former teammates. My name was even mentioned in one article.

"Anything else you need help on?" Kevin asked.

"I think that's it," I said. "Thanks."

"I'm going back to sleep then."

"I won't call so early next time. Promise."

The archived page had no mention of a hole-in-one. Neither did any of the other nearby dates. I finally tried every date available from my sophomore year. Nothing about Frankie's hole-in-one.

I was pretty sure that I had the right year, but I had to admit that the wayback machine's recollection might be a little more accurate than mine. I tried the links for our junior year. On the third date, I found it.

> Junior Frankie Brooks aced the par-three third hole, the first hole-in-one of his career, en route to a one over par 73 to lead the Wildcats to their fifth victory of the year.

So much for my bulletproof memory.

This happened on a Saturday, according to the article. Frankie had made his hole-in-one on Saturday, April 25th, 2000. Sweet. I needed to send a thank-you letter to those wayback guys.

Going back to the email site, I brought up the "lost password" page. I was poised to crack this baby.

When did I make my first hole-in-one?

Crap, what format is the date in?

According to Kevin, I'd be locked out if I answered wrong too many times.

I typed "4/25/00," and hit enter.

Incorrect entry.

Next, I tried "4-25-00."

Incorrect entry.

I didn't know how many chances I'd get.

I tried "4/25/2000."

Bingo.

The screen came back with a new response.

What was your first pet's name?

Shoot me now.

Kevin hadn't told me there would be a follow-up question. How long would this go on?

I was due to call Lisa with a status update, so I figured I'd ask her about Frankie's pet, too. Maybe she also knew the answer to the other lost password question, his favorite movie character.

"Lisa," I said, "I need to answer some questions in order to get into Frankie's email accounts. I thought you might be able to help."

"I've got a minute," she said, "then I'm picking the kids up."

"Ok. What was Frankie's first pet's name?"

"That's an easy one. He talked about the first cat he had all the time. Its name was Ben Purr."

I had to chuckle at that. No wonder she remembered.

"How about his favorite movie actor?"

"I really have no idea on that one. Sorry to rush, Dez, but I've got to run."

"No problem. I'll fill you in later on the lawsuit and the email accounts."

I went back to the laptop and typed "Ben Purr" into the box. After a brief moment, the system asked me to set a new password. I wrote everything down. I wouldn't want to have to do this all over again.

After that, I was in, and a list of emails showed up. They were all from the same sender.

Clicking on the last message in the list, I didn't have to read between the lines to get the drift. But it was the signature that hit me. You could have knocked me over with a feather.

sargentb12@sjpmail.com

Had a great time last night, lover boy. Too bad you couldn't
stay all night.
Miss you already – in all the right places.

Luv,
Bev

Frankie had been having an affair with Beverly Sargent!

My head was still spinning over the ramifications of the
Frankie and Beverly connection. Was she a spurned lover, who did
him in? Then it hit me.

Lisa.

What if Lisa had found out? Maybe she'd uncovered
Frankie's gambling debts, too. She might've hired somebody to have
Frankie whacked for the insurance money, double indemnity. But
what if they'd done their job a little too cleanly? Instead of Frankie's
death looking like an accident, the coroner's suicide determination
had put Lisa between a rock and a hard place, knowing the truth but
unable to tell anyone, lost in limbo.

But what did any of this have to do with the bogus sexual
harassment charges against me? Other than Lisa, I wasn't sure anyone
even knew that I was investigating Frankie's death. What made me a
target?

As difficult as it was, at the moment I had to put aside such
questions and deal with more pressing issues. Interns. More
specifically, there was one moving into my house right now.

The summer golf interns at Chesapeake Bluffs always arrived
during the third weekend in May. Each year, the Club put out a call
for Bluffs' residents with spare rooms to host an intern for the
summer. With lots of room in my new crib, not to mention the fact
that I was Cody's supervising pro, it just made sense to offer up my
place.

In anticipation of the move-in, I transferred most of my stuff
to the guest bedroom, leaving the master bedroom for Cody. The

extra space and accessibility of the master bathroom would be perfect, according to the Bluffs' housing office. This was hardly a sacrifice, as the guest bedroom was luxurious by any reasonable standard.

It did involve a little bit of work to get things ready. Luckily, Darby was happy to assist. Naturally, once everything was settled, we had to test out my new room to make sure it was totally satisfactory. We gave it five stars.

Darby had gone back to her place to whip up some eats for the moving team, as my kitchen's inventory remained woefully inadequate for her culinary needs.

The moving crew consisted of the three summer interns who'd moved in already. As was customary, all interns pitched in to help each other move. And this Sunday morning, they were more than a little curious to meet this "guy in the wheelchair who plays killer golf," as one of them put it. They seemed like nice guys, a little on the cocky side, but that was to be expected. The Bluffs attracted only the best interns, and they almost always tended to be pretty confident.

Bertha was thrilled at the company, and did her Bulldog best to beguile the boys.

I loaded them up with hot coffee. Darby, carrying an enormous plastic container, strolled in minutes later and introduced herself.

The guys were pleasant and polite, but, boys will be boys. I could tell they were checking her out. When Darby turned away, one of them gave me the thumbs up.

Glad to see you approve.

"What did you bring?" I asked.

"Vegan cupcakes," she announced triumphantly.

The boys gave each other skeptical looks, but their desire for sugar overcame their initial suspicions. After their first bites, they nodded affirmatively, pronouncing them wholly acceptable.

Cody's caravan of three vehicles arrived a few minutes later. We met him outside. He was piloting the lead vehicle. He parked, then deftly maneuvered from SUV to wheelchair in less than a minute.

That boy has been practicing.

Mother and stepdad, father and brother occupied the two cars that followed Cody. After introductions, I gave them the grand tour of the house. Cody's mom took me aside after I had finished to let me know how grateful she was for this opportunity for her son.

I glanced out the window into the back yard and saw Cody, now driving the Handygolfer, along with the other interns. As always, they were competing, this time in a chipping contest, trying to land balls into a metal pail that they had appropriated from my garage. From what I saw, Cody was holding his own.

Bertha chased down any missed shots and brought them back. She would unfailingly return the ball to whichever boy had hit it. After a while, the interns began to change places while she was chasing the ball, seeing if they could fool her, but she would always bring it back to the hitter. I finally let them in on the secret. She was just bringing it back to the one who was still holding the club.

Outwitted by a dog.

After a little while, Cody moved into his regular wheelchair. As I suspected, the other boys had wanted to try out his mechanical marvel.

Chipping a shot into a bucket was one thing, but reaching the green in regulation on a 500-yard par-five was another. I'm sure many of them doubted Cody's ability to compete. They'd know soon enough, as their first tournament was slated for this afternoon, the winner claiming bragging rights for the next month.

I was anxious to hit the course myself. Someone needed to show these young whippersnappers how golf was really meant to be played.

Chapter 14

Every Monday, Sharon's report contained a section which had become known as "The Week's Top Hits." This was a list of all the "hit-by-golf ball" incidents that had been reported during the past seven days. In many weeks, there were several such happenings.

In general, the golf course cannot be held liable for incidents in which one player strikes another with a ball. In addition, the unfortunate target normally cannot collect from the hitter, either. To recover damages from such an injury, there has to be a deliberate or negligent action. Golfers assume a certain risk when they step onto the course. In other words, it's a war zone out there.

There have been cases, however, where a golfer known to be in the habit of shanking shots has been found liable for hitting someone in an adjacent fairway, given that he possessed the knowledge that there was a high probability of an errant shot.

In other words, if you really stink at golf, look carefully before you hit.

This week there were three incidents. The second one had the potential to become a real ball-buster for the Bluffs.

The report read:

> Course 2, Hole 4 - Player Steven Fullman was struck by the tee-shot of golfer Phil Cooper while on the fairway of hole

4, approximately 250 yards from the tee. Fullman suffered a mild concussion and was taken to the hospital for observation. He was released a short while later. According to witnesses in Cooper's group, Bluffs' ranger Ted Counsel had joined the foursome temporarily as they waited for Fullman's group to hit their second shots and clear the fairway area ahead.

The ranger assessed the scene and determined that there was no risk in having the players in Cooper's group tee off. Cooper hit first, and hit the shot that struck Fullman on the temple. He yelled out 'fore' after he saw his shot heading toward the group. Cooper was quoted as saying that this was "the longest drive he had ever hit in his life."

I groaned. Seemed like he should have yelled "forehead" instead of "fore." Our rangers should never encourage a player to hit into another group, no matter how far away they seem to be. The players have to decide this on their own. Once a representative from the Club gives them authority to hit, we could become liable for damages should their ball strike one of the players. According to the legal doctrine known as respondeat superior, an employer is responsible for the actions of employees performed within the course of their employment. This put us on the hook for the ranger's actions.

Rangers have a few jobs, but their primary goal is to monitor the pace of play and to keep slow golfers from clogging the course. Our rangers should have been instructed, however, never to speed up play by having golfers hit into the group ahead.

The quote about "hitting the longest drive of his life" was not that unusual. When golfers are concerned that their shot may possibly hit someone in the group ahead, they tend to ease up and not hit with their hardest swing. The result, quite often, is a better struck shot, which many times goes farther than they would have believed. It's something we try to teach golfers when we give lessons. It's not how hard you swing; it's how well.

I called our head ranger.

"It's about Ted Counsel, isn't it?" he said. "I've been expecting you to call."

Why not just call me, then?

"I thought we'd instructed the rangers not to tell players when to hit," I said. "There's a significant liability issue here."

"I know, I know. I've told him. He screwed up."

"That mistake may end up costing us," I said. "As it is, we may be on the hook to pay medical costs for the struck golfer, or at least our insurance company might be. This can't happen again."

"Do you want to let him go?"

"That's up to you, but regardless, we need to train everybody so that they understand not to give safety assurances, solicited or not."

"I got it. I'll get all the rangers together and do some role-playing."

"Really?" I said. "You have some rangerettes, too?"

"Sheesh," he said. "You know what I mean. I'll do my best to make sure this doesn't happen again, and each ranger understands the consequences."

Next time, heads were going to roll.

The TV was turned to the movie channel when I heard it. The distinctive whistling intro from the classic western "The Good, The Bad and The Ugly." It was also Frankie's trademark ringtone.

The lost password question!

Entering "Clint Eastwood" at the prompt, I was optimistic that Clint indeed was Frankie's favorite actor. The second question appeared.

What is the last name of the best man at your wedding?

I had to laugh. I should know this one. After entering "Thomas," I was asked to reset the password.

Almost there.

I set the new password to match Frankie's other account. I finally had access.

Just as before, all of the messages were from a single sender. It didn't sound like another mistress this time.

All the messages had a return address of:

Evan316@rlymail.com

Evan? I read the most recent message.

Evan316
RE:

Nothing's changed. We won't go over $75K.

On Fri, Mar 19, 2010 at 7:20 AM, <fjb18.barlmail.com
> wrote:
> Important! Must increase next payment to $150K

I'd found the money trail.
I read through the entire list of nine messages, including the
ones in Frankie's "sent" folder. All together, they painted a rather
disturbing portrait, one indicative of extortion or even blackmail.
Frankie had been receiving regular payments from Evan316. At one
point, he demanded an increase from $50K to $75K. But most
disturbing was the final message, occurring just three weeks before
Frankie's death.

Why would Frankie blackmail my boss? Maybe Evan had
been having an affair of his own and Frankie had caught wind of it.
But still, those were awfully large amounts for hush money. And what
was up with the 316? Was it some sort of religious reference?

I went through the messages again, this time writing them
down in chronological order, and cross-referencing against Frankie's
bank records. Everything seemed to match.

Oct 3 – Frankie sent his account information to Evan316.

Oct 5 – First wire transfer of $50,000 deposited to
Frankie's account.

Oct 6 – Frankie acknowledged.

Apr 4 – Second wire transfer of $50,000.

Apr 4 – Frankie acknowledged the same day.

Sep 15 – Frankie demanded $100,000.

Sep 15 – Evan countered with $75,000.

Sep 16 – Frankie agreed to $75,000, "for now."

Oct 4 – Third wire transfer into bank account of $75,000.

Mar 19 – Frankie demanded $150,000.

Mar 19 – Evan responded – Won't go over $75,000.

Mar 19 – Frankie requested meeting to "straighten out" differences.

It was time to go back to the police. But first, I needed advice.

"Kevin, you busy?" I said over the phone.

"Just updating my blog," he said. "I'm thinking deep thoughts."

"Good. I need some deep thinking on this."

I brought him up to speed on the email and money trail I'd just discovered, plus the news on Frankie's affair.

"I'm planning on going to the police with this," I said. "It looks like there was some kind of extortion scheme going on."

"Makes sense," he said. "But if the police reopen the investigation, they're going to confiscate Frankie's laptop and then get into the email accounts. I've already got a copy of the laptop disk here, but you'd better print out hardcopies of the emails, in case they lock us out.

"I'll set up POP3 accounts on my email client to pull copies of the messages off of Frankie's two webmail accounts."

"That sounds great," I said, not understanding a word of his technobabble.

"What do you make of Frankie's affair?" I asked.

"Isn't she the one with the rawhide rack?" he said. "What was Frankie thinking?"

Helpful, not.

"I mean," I said, "do you think the affair ties in with Frankie's murder, the extortion scheme, or Sargent's complaints against me?'"

"Hell if I know. I'm no detective. Unless you can interrogate her personally, I'm not sure how you'd find out."

So much for his brilliant mind.

"Are you going to tell Lisa about the affair?" he asked.

"I don't know. She said she wanted to know everything, but I don't see how telling her would help matters at all. I'm leaning toward no."

"That's 'affair'-ly reasonable argument." Kevin injected.

Ignoring him, I pressed on. "Let me know when you've saved the emails. In the meantime, I'll get this ready for the police."

Maybe I'll bring some donuts.

I found myself, for the second time, sitting down in front of Detective Reed's desk. The décor hadn't improved since my last visit. Unfortunately, all matters related to Frankie's death had to go through Reed.

He glanced over the pages I had printed out, and then the bank account statements.

"It's all circumstantial," he said dismissively.

This wasn't off to a good start.

"But look at the dates. They match up," I pointed out.

"Didn't I tell you before not to get involved in this? Last time, if I remember, you thought it was the bookie. Now you've got some new theory. Next month, you'll be telling me the butler did it. Like I said, stay out of our business."

"I'm trying to. That's why I came to you with this evidence. So you could do something with it."

"And what exactly do you want me to do with it? Right now, all of our detectives are already working overtime trying to handle the cases we've got open. You want me to reopen a closed case just to satisfy your curiosity? Who's going to pay for that? Who's going to work the extra hours?"

"The evidence looks pretty compelling to me," I said.

"Let me ask you," Reed said, "how many homicide cases have you been involved in?"

Cleary, he wasn't expecting an answer.

"That's what I thought," he said. "People have a hard time

accepting a suicide. Friends, family, everybody, they come here for months afterward with information, trying to prove that the death wasn't self-inflicted. But ninety-nine percent of the time, their information leads nowhere."

"There's always that one percent."

"I'll let you know if there are any developments," Reed spat out.

Like that was going to happen.

I could see that our discussion was officially over. The detective had started straightening papers and cleaning up his desk, not-so-subtle hints that it was time for him to get back to work, and for me to get going.

"It was a pleasure, detective," I said, not making any attempt to disguise the sarcasm.

"Likewise," he said, returning the favor.

I stopped in mid-gulp as the first item in Sharon's report seized my attention. Identity theft. A Bluffs' member, Cecil Raines, had filed suit against the Club, claiming that,

> … as a result of Chesapeake Bluffs' negligence in their admitted loss of confidential and personal membership financial data, the plaintiff's debit-card information was appropriated by unknown persons who fraudulently used the lost data to steal $21,541 from plaintiff's account.

Tom Jones.

He'd threatened to leak the laptop contents. This might be the first in a wave of complaints.

"Sharon," I said, "can you come in here, please?"

She strode in, folders piled high in her arms.

"I'm assuming you'd like to know if we contacted Mr. Raines in regard to the laptop data theft. Yes, we did, by phone and letter. I'm also assuming that you'd like to know if any other members have reported improper use of their financial data. No, they haven't."

That was good news. Maybe this had nothing to do with the bookie at all.

"Thanks, but what I really wanted to know was—how was

your weekend?"

She chuckled, confident in her victory.

"I'm assuming," I said, "that those folders contain the results of our efforts to contact our affected account holders."

"We have detailed records on the date and time we called each person. We also have the return receipts for the certified letters we sent out to each account holder, ensuring that each one received written notification of the possible breach of data. I've got the Raines file right here. The records indicate that he acknowledged, online, the possibility of financial data compromise, along with our recommendation to cancel his existing card."

"Has Raines changed the card attached to his account since the incident?"

"Nope."

"So let me see if I've got everything straight. Mr. Raines was contacted by phone, by certified letter, and signed off on his web account that he understood our recommendation to cancel his card, and that the Club assumed no liability in the event that the member declined to do so."

"Correct."

"We also offered each member an online coupon good for fifty dollars off purchases at our online store, as a good-faith effort to compensate them for their inconvenience, plus a six-month free subscription to a credit-monitoring service. Did Raines utilize either of those?"

She had to look down at the report this time to find the answer. It was a small victory for me. Temporary, I was sure.

"It appears that he used the coupon, but as yet he hasn't signed up for the service."

That was all the ammunition I needed. I could now call Raines' attorney, holding the legal equivalent of a double-barreled shotgun at point-blank range. I could already smell the testosterone in the air. Either Raines had withheld this information from his attorney, or his attorney knew about it and just wasn't too on-the-ball.

"Thanks Sharon. Great work."

"No problem," she said. "And by the way, I win."

I couldn't argue with that. There was always another day.

Raines attorney was one D. Joseph Riggleman, Esquire.

"Riggleman, this is Desmond Thomas at Chesapeake Bluffs."

"I've been expecting your call," he said eagerly, the voice sounding surprisingly young. In the next few minutes, I unloaded all my information on the newbie. When I was done, I gave him a chance to speak.

"Well," he said, a little less eagerly now, "perhaps we could arrive at a settlement that would please both parties. Going to court could get expensive."

"Listen, Riggleman, you sound like a nice guy," I lied. "So let me give you some advice. I will stomp you in court. It won't be pretty. I'm already hired by the Club so it's not going to cost *us* any more to litigate this. Do your client a favor and tell him to cut his losses. If you want to help him, tell him to use a credit card, not a debit card. Tell him that he needs to monitor his checking account and report any suspicious charges when they happen, not two months later. That way he'd be protected against this kind of fraud. He'd have saved himself the 21K, plus your fees, and we wouldn't be having this conversation.

"It was good talking to you, though," I continued, "but I've got to run. Think about what I said. I'm sure you'll do the smart thing." I ended the call. I envisioned Riggleman sitting on the other end, mouth flapping, no words coming out. I was hoping he'd take my advice and drop this turkey of a suit.

It was still only 10:30 in the morning, and I'd already owned Riggleman.

Isn't the law wonderful?

"Half of gettin' what you want is knowin' what you gotta give up to get it."

Our mediator, William "Wild Bill" Haycock, was kindly sharing his lifelong wisdom and experience prior to the start of our mediation with the Bristol estate.

The Bristol drowning lawsuit was my very first case at the Bluffs, and I would be thrilled to put it to bed today.

We had tried to get it dismissed completely, going before the judge with a motion for summary judgment, which had been denied.

The law now required us to attempt to mediate a dispute before going to court. This was where Wild Bill came into the picture.

I was here with the attorney for our insurance company. Whatever payout the Bluffs made would be coming out of our business liability coverage, so they had a big say in what we would be offering. Susan Bristol, the widow, was here on behalf of the estate, along with her attorney.

Reaching a settlement at mediation prevented the need for a full-blown jury trial, easing the burden on the busy court system, not to mention reducing everyone's legal costs. The key to a mediated settlement was for everyone to come away feeling like they got something. In order to do that, as Wild Bill so aptly put it, "you've got to give it up, too."

"Wild Bill" was a celebrity in his own right. His public persona had been burned into the nations' consciousness as a defense attorney in a series of high profile real-life courtroom dramas. Wild Bill was famous for his down-home "country" style of law, complete with gee-whizz, aw-shucks, and various other homespun affectations and sayings. When not participating in various legal defense dream-teams, or working as an analyst on courtroom TV, Bill worked as a mediator. He said it relaxed him.

"I'd like to welcome all y'all here today. I express my heartfelt condolences to the widow in the loss of her husband. There's no amount of money that can bring him back, but I understand that y'all have brought suit against the Chesapeake Bluffs Golf and Country Club for twenta' million dollahs. I'm hopin' we can all come to an agreement right quick, 'cuz I got two more of these here mediations to do after this. Lately, I've been busier than a one-legged man in an ass-kickin' contest.

"Now, I know the facts of this case, so you can spare me the details and get right to the good stuff. Y'all want twenta' million. Bluffs, are y'all prepared to offa' anything?"

I began. "We would, Mr. Haycock. Although we believe that Chesapeake Bluffs is in no way at fault, and the evidence of any negligence on our part is tenuous at best, we understand the expenses associated with a jury trial. We'd like to propose a settlement for one hundred twenty-five thousand dollars."

"Now we ah gettin' somewhere," Wild Bill said. He turned

toward the attorney for the Bristol estate.

"Now, y'all telling me that Peter Bristol was thirty sumpin' years old, making about twenta thousand a year divin' for golf balls. Let's say he worked for another forta' years, that's eight hunned thousand dollahs over his whole life. These folks over heah offered to give you one hunned and twenta-five thousand dollahs just 'cuz he happened to drown on their property. That seems pretty reasonable to me, in fact it's downright neighborly. 'Cuz it seems to me, he wasn't even s'pose to be on their property. Where'd you pull that twenta' million dollah number out of?"

The attorney for the Bristol estate appeared a little flustered.

"Chesapeake Bluffs," he began, "needs to compensate the widow and family for the loss of their husband and father beyond the mere loss of his lifetime income. Those three boys will go to bed each night hoping for a father who will never—"

"Hold on right there." Wild Bill turned to the widow. "Ma'am, pardon me for my language. No offense intended, but your attorney needs to save his bullshit for the cow chip throwin' contest. We got just two hours scheduled to work this out, and that argument was so bad that if I was a dog, I'd have to lick my butt just to get the bad taste outta' my mouth. Now it's your lil' red wagon, you can push it or pull it, but if I were y'all, I'd start gettin' real fast."

The widow spoke up. "Lord knows Pete wasn't necessarily the best husband in the world. He had drinking problems, and a temper, but he was my husband and I loved him, and I've got three little ones at home now without a father, and no way now to pay the rent. He didn't have any insurance, so we're going to be evicted unless something happens here. Chesapeake Bluffs gave him permission to dive for balls in their ponds. He wouldn't have died if he hadn't gotten tangled up in that equipment. That's not his fault."

"Thank you, Mrs. Bristol," Wild Bill said. "Now we all gonna go into our separate rooms, and I'm gonna come round and talk to each of y'all, and we'll see if we can't be a fair piece closer when we get back."

Nothing discussed at mediation could later be brought up in the trial. That was an iron-clad rule. It allowed parties to freely discuss issues to reach a settlement without fearing that what they said could be used against them. That being said, there was nothing that prevented us from doing our own investigation to find out about a possible drinking problem, now that we were aware of it. It could be that Bristol was drunk when he drowned.

We got up and followed Wild Bill into a small conference room.

"Do y'all need some time to talk alone?" he asked us.

The insurance attorney and I looked at each other.

"Not really," I said. "We're sticking with our offer of one hundred twenty-five thousand."

"Ok. Now twenta million. That's nuttier than a squirrel's turd. I'll go over and knock some sense into that feller, see if we can't get out of here sometime this century."

Fifteen minutes later, we were back in the big room.

"Chesapeake Bluffs has kept their offer for settlement at one hunned and twenta-five thousand dollahs. The Bristol estate has a new figure of two million dollahs. Now we are cookin' with gas. Call us butter, cuz' we 'ah on a roll."

We were prepared to go to $750,000, but beyond that, we would be looking at a jury trial. They didn't have much of a case, but it would still cost us a pretty penny to defend it, and there's always the risk. That submerged old tractor, the "Pond Deere," was a sticky issue. In their lawsuit, they claimed that we should have posted a warning sign about the possible danger. We'd had the tractor removed from the pond after the drowning, but that wouldn't help us in this case. It didn't hurt us either. Subsequent remedial measures couldn't be used against us to prove negligence. On our next go-round, we raised up our offer to $250,000. They came down to one million. The smell of a settlement was in the air.

After one more round, we both agreed on a figure of $500,000. We were satisfied, since this was considerably lower than our top figure.

"I'm as happy as a clam at high tide," Wild Bill said at the end of our ninety minute session. "We got that done faster than a knife fight in a phone booth. You know it's a good mediation if, at the end, both sides are grumpier than my wife after I forget to put the toilet seat down. That's my wish for all y'all."

Shucks, I couldn't have said it better myself.

Chapter 15

It had happened again during my afternoon lesson. Another broken golf shaft from one of my students. The state-of-the-art, carbon-fiber shaft snapped right above the hosel during a drive. I'd now seen four clubs break during my short stint at the Bluffs.

I'm no stranger to broken golf clubs. Many times, they're a result of careless, or even clueless, handling on the part of the owner. Tops among reasons given for broken clubs include being run over by a golf cart or automobile, being slammed by the lid of the car trunk, or simply being in a golf bag that fell the wrong way. Occasionally, they're the aftermath of an incensed golfer's misplaced rage.

But the vast majority of club damage occurs when golfers attempt to play balls that have come to rest within a few feet of a tree trunk. Anyone who has ever seen a picture of an auto accident where a car hits a tree knows which wins. The tree comes away with a small area of missing bark. The car is totaled.

Does the golfer really think that his fancy iron with the graphite shaft will end up victorious over a hundred-year-old oak, one that can stop an eighteen-wheeler without blinking? I doubt it. It's probably that such a golfer doesn't really think at all.

Faced with his ball behind a tree, the optimistic golfer believes that he can, instead of chipping the ball away from the tree, save that one lost stroke by altering his swing, missing the tree, and hitting the ball 150 yards or more toward the hole. Due to the awkwardness of it all, he takes little or no practice swings for this shot.

There are always repercussions with this approach, usually three sounds. The first is the crack of club impacting ball. The second is the crack of club hitting tree. The third is the crack of clubhead freeing itself from the tyranny of the shaft. The clubhead travels in one direction, while the golfer's ball dribbles a few inches away, if at all. Actually, there is almost always a fourth sound. Loud cursing by the player as he examines his broken equipment.

Graphite shafts usually snap. Steel shafts, being somewhat stronger, just bend. Either way, the shaft is ruined. The tree always wins.

I had, in my time, run across steel shafts that were broken cleanly in two. These breaks occurred directly in the center of the shaft, coincidentally, exactly where a golfer's knee might come in contact with the club. No tree was necessary.

But here at the Bluffs, the four clubs that shattered during my lessons had all broken during what appeared to be regular swings at the driving range. True, a couple had been "chunked" shots, but ordinarily hitting such a fat shot doesn't break the shaft, unless one is hitting off of a very hard surface like a dry hardened clay, or maybe off of an artificial grass mat at a driving range. But we had neither.

These were not your bargain basement clubs either. All were high-end clubs, purchased here at the pro shop. I was becoming a fixture in Trevor's office, now exchange central.

I sank into the oversized guest chair, wondering how many cart girls had been in this same spot.

Eww.

I handed Trevor the latest casualty from the front lines. He looked it over, and shook his head.

"These new graphite shafts are great," he said, "but they're not as strong as good old-fashioned steel."

"This is the fourth shaft I've had a student break on me during lessons in a little over a month. Do we keep any records on these? Do you think there's some sort of quality problem?"

Trevor turned serious. "No, like I said, the graphite shafts are more fragile. We send all of these back to the distributor, who returns them to the manufacturers to assess quality control. We give our customers guaranteed one-day replacement, *no questions asked.* It's hard to do much better than that."

"I understand that, but I've never seen a graphite shaft break before on a normal shot, even a chunked one. That's in over ten years of playing and teaching. Now I've got four broken in just a few weeks. Plus, I've been hearing of similar breaks from some of the other pros and players. It's not just my clients."

His serious tone turned testy. "Our policy is to replace any club within two years of purchase. It's a very generous policy and it's a big selling feature. We all benefit from these sales. Our pros can make a pretty good chunk of change if they participate. Going on about defective clubs is not going to help matters. Who have you been talking to about this, if I might ask?"

Obviously, I'd hit upon a sore spot. I backed off.

"No one in particular. Like I said, these aren't just my clients."

Trevor was clearly irritated. "The last thing we need is somebody *else* going off half-cocked on some sort of crusade against our equipment."

Somebody else?

"I'm not on any crusade, I just wanted to know if there might be a problem. Did you say there was somebody else who had concerns?"

"No...," he said, trying to recover. Clearly, lying wasn't his forte. "I meant that we don't need one of our own people going off and denigrating our product. The distributor returns all clubs to the manufacturer. They can assess if there's a quality lapse. I haven't got a single complaint from any of our customers. Like I said, we replace their club on-the-spot most of the time, and if not, we'll have a new one the next day. Even if the club was abused. You can't beat that anywhere."

From Trevor's verbal gaffe, it was obvious I wasn't the first person to bring this up.

"I think the Bluffs' policy is fantastic," I said, "I really do. The number of broken clubs just seemed odd, that's all."

"Why don't you stick to playing golf, and let me handle the equipment end. From what I hear, you've got enough *troubles* of your own right now."

I tried not to let my surprise register, but the hairs on the back of my neck were standing up. Obviously, this was a reference to the Beverly Sargent issue. How had this gotten out? Clearly, Trevor was trying to highlight my vulnerability. But all he was succeeding in doing was reinforcing the idea that he had something to hide. If there was a problem with the clubs, he should be the first to step in and figure out what was going on. Instead, he was throwing up some pretty serious roadblocks.

"Yeah, you're probably right," I said, in my best placating tone. "It's still a pretty small number. Could just be a coincidence."

"Leave the club replacement business to me," he said, calming down, "and everything will be ok. Sorry I got a little overzealous there. I didn't mean to comment on your situation."

"No harm done," I said, picking up the new club. "I'll get this replacement club back to its owner ASAP. Thanks for the fast service."

"No problem," he said, "my pleasure."

Whatever.

Trevor's implied threat meant that the sexual harassment complaint wasn't exactly the world's best kept secret. Someone was leaking the information, probably Ms. Sargent, but maybe someone else with an axe to grind. Maybe even my boss. If Evan was involved, maybe he wanted to just get rid of me, too. But why not just fire me?

I had to tell Darby. Now that the harassment charges were apparently public knowledge, it seemed inevitable that she would hear about this through the Bluffs' grapevine. This "dirty little secret" was simply too juicy to contain. Once Rodney Collingsworth got hold of this, not a single person associated with the Club would be spared this momentous news.

I wondered how my expanding golf lesson business would be affected if this news became widespread among the members. I might have a little more free time on my hands in the afternoons.

I pondered how to best bring up this unpleasantness with Darby. The direct approach seemed the least painful. I'd just tell her straight out at dinner tonight. But first, I'd make sure she was still coming over to my place.

I fired off a text to remind her. If she was on the courts, as she most often was this time of day, she'd get back to me between lessons.

Trevor's change of attitude over the broken clubs was grating on me. Intuition told me something was very wrong, but I needed someone who was a little distanced from the situation to give me some perspective.

Kevin answered on the first ring.

"For once it's not six am in the morning," he said. "I don't know whether to be pleased or alarmed. What's up?"

"I never call you at six. And it's not my fault you don't get up before noon. You got a minute?"

"You caught me at a good time. My internet went out this morning. I'm totally at the mercy of the cable company. All I've got is my phone to connect me to the web. I feel so alone."

"Well this won't require Google, at least I don't think so."

I brought him up to date on my recent meeting with Trevor.

"I'm going to tell Darby about the sexual harassment thing," I said. "I'm pretty sure she'll get wind of it anyway."

"When's the last time you talked with her?" Kevin asked.

I thought back. "It was yesterday morning. I spent the night at her place."

"So things are heating up between you two, huh?"

"We're getting to know each other better."

"Sounds like it. Well, I'd be shocked if she hadn't already heard something about this."

"I doubt it. She didn't say anything yesterday."

"Once news like this gets out of the can," Kevin said, "it travels at the speed of sound, or maybe I should say, at the speed of a golf ball. True or not, this is a really sensational piece of gossip about someone whom most everybody knows. You're high profile, dude. You should have come clean with her early on. Now it looks like you're hiding something."

Kevin didn't pull any punches, and didn't see the need to. Sometimes it helped to be totally devoid of any emotions. At any rate, it looked like I'd be doing some serious damage control soon.

"What about the rash of broken clubs I've been seeing? When I talked with him, Trevor let it slip that there had been someone else asking questions."

Kevin was silent for a while. This was usually a sign that he was in analysis mode. Or that we lost our phone connection.

"Are you still there?" I asked.

"Based on what you've told me, it sounds like there may be some kind of quality problem with the clubs, particularly the shafts. Trevor's response could be a normal defensive reaction to someone stomping on his turf, or it could be that he's hiding something. Since I wasn't there to read his body language, I can only go by what you've told me."

"Which is?"

"Which is, I can't really say. It sounds like you should quietly ask some of your colleagues to find who was on a crusade before you."

There were still a number of people at the Club I knew I could trust, including three or four of my fellow pros. One thing for sure, I would not be querying Rodney about this topic.

"Ok, what do I do if I find out something?" I asked.

"You can always call me back before you do anything...."

rash, ...stupid, ...that I would regret?

But he left it at that. Clearly, my brother had finally learned a little bit about tact.

It was about time.

I could almost hear Rod Serling's distinctive baritone:

"You have now entered into the 'The Banishment Zone.'"

Apparently, this was now my current residence, at least as far as my relationship with Darby was concerned. After calling her for the third or fourth time, I got tired of listening to her voice mail greeting.

"... at the sound of the beep, the ball's in your court."

If the ball was in my court, I had to figure out the most appropriate shot to hit back. I was leaning toward a defensive lob.

It was pretty clear that she had heard something, most likely from Rodney, who would have undoubtedly embellished any news with a generous helping of sleaze. I could just hear it.

"Darby, sorry to be the one to have to tell you this, but your lover-boy just got hit with a sex-suit. It's not like I couldn't see this coming, the way this guy gets around. He's always pressuring his lady clients for a few *extra* swings after hours. Your guy just can't keep his putter in his pants. I got it on good authority that quite a few of the beer girls stop their carts by his house at lunchtime. He's not just walking the dog, if you know what I mean."

Rodney was a smooth talking con man, prone to prevarication. He had crossed over the line from truth to lie so many times that he couldn't find it anymore. To Rodney, the truth was whatever served his needs at the moment.

But my problem now was Darby, or to be more exact, our relationship. I'd been an idiot to think that the perpetrator of the complaint would keep things discreet. As Kevin had reminded me, somebody wanted me out of the Club.

I pondered knocking on her door, demanding to talk. But for some odd reason, women didn't seem to care for that approach to reconciliation. I'd tried it once long ago, but after standing outside for ten minutes, yelling a "conversation" back and forth through the front door, I'd realized that there had to be a better way, presumably one that didn't make me look like a crazed stalker.

A hurt woman is a difficult animal. She doesn't want to talk, and will rebuff all attempts at reconciliation. But if you don't do anything, she'll come back later on and say that you "didn't even try." I was stuck between the proverbial rock and the hard place, banished, but not altogether forgotten. I needed to explain my side of the story.

I did have one thing going for me, in that I possessed a weapon of such strength and potency that any attempt at resistance would ultimately be futile. And no one yet, no matter how infuriated or incensed, had been known to be immune. I began to formulate a plan. It involved, among other things, a wagon, a snazzy outfit, cans of spray paint, and one truly irresistible canine.

The next few hours were spent planning the details, after which I rang up the first florist I found in the phone book.

"Hello," I said. "Do you happen to carry any flowers in orange and blue?"

The following morning, after more unanswered texts and another restless night of continued banishment, I dragged myself to work. I still wanted to talk to a few of the other Club pros to see if they had seen an increase in the number of equipment failures. I also hinted around to see if they knew of anyone else at the Club who might have carried the torch for this cause.

The first three pros I approached had all seen a rise in equipment failures over the past several years. None of them seemed particularly concerned about this, as they all believed that the "no questions asked" instant replacement policy of the Bluffs adequately covered the issue. No one recalled anyone getting too bent out of shape about it.

I tracked down Dave Arnold, the final pro on my list. Dave had been extremely grateful to me for resolving his "Tom Jones" issue. He was more than happy to answer my questions.

"Have you seen an increase in broken clubs lately," I asked him, "more so than in the past?"

"I've seen a lot of broken clubs, mostly shafts, in the last few years. I figured that maybe the new lightweight shafts were weaker than they used to be. The Bluffs replaces them for free, so I wasn't too worried about it."

This was pretty much what I'd heard from the others. I wasn't getting very far.

"But Frankie," Dave continued, "for a while there, he was getting hot about it."

"Really?" I said.

Now we're getting somewhere.

"He planned to talk to Trevor and Evan about it. He was upset. He thought we might be getting some fake clubs in here. 'You gotta be kidding me!' I told him. 'At Chesapeake Bluffs? That'd be the day.'"

"Do you recall what happened after that?"

I was in major interrogation mode.

"I think he talked to them. After that, I didn't hear anything more about it. I didn't even think about it, honestly, until the next time a club would break. I figured Frankie just dropped it."

"Do you recall when this happened?" I asked.

"It would have been a couple of years ago." He paused, thinking back. "I think what first got him going was that free set of clubs for his one year anniversary."

Dave's lesson had shown up, so we were done. For now.

I'd hit the jackpot. Frankie had been the one on the crusade. And for some reason, he'd suddenly gone quiet, just about the time the payouts started coming in to his bank account.

I had no idea what to do with this newly discovered information. For some reason, Frankie had deemed his new clubs so important that he had to keep them in storage.

Maybe it was time to take a closer look at these clubs. But, tonight I had other plans.

When my package arrived in the afternoon, I'd already assembled the other requisite components for my reconciliation remedy. I packed everything into the golf cart, and headed to Darby's, determined to win her back.

I was pretty sure that she was home. Before the banishment began, we had made plans for this evening.

"Ok, Bertha, time to work your magic."

Bertha, my wingman, or in this case, wingdog, was outfitted in an orange and blue skirt, the team colors of the Virginia Cavaliers, Darby's alma mater. A brand-new extra-large Cavaliers hat fit snugly on her giant head. I sat her down gently into the toy wagon, which now sported a custom two-toned paint job that complemented her outfit, a delightful ensemble, if I say so myself. I carefully placed the sign around her neck. The letters were painted in navy blue:

**If I had a tail,
It would be
"wagon"
for you.**

Bertha's paw print served as her signature.

I put my note and flowers on the wagon with Bertha, then wheeled the entire assemblage up to Darby's doorstep. This was my peace offering.

Bertha didn't know exactly what to do, never having been put in quite such a situation before. She paced around the wagon, anxious because she knew that she was at Darby's house. I sat her back down.

"Stay, Bertha, stay. Sit. Good girl."

I rang the doorbell and started to slowly back away. My goal was to be around the corner when Darby opened the door. But if I started doing the ding-dong ditch too quickly, Bertha might run after me.

"Good girl," I repeated from a distance, continuing my slow retreat.

Bertha suddenly turned toward the door. She must have heard a noise from inside. I quickly backed around the corner and peeked out from behind a bush. The front door opened.

"Awww."

Darby had fallen prey to my trap. Clearly, she had never encountered anything quite so fiendishly clever.

"Bertha, you're adorable. Did you bring me flowers? What a good girl! I've missed you."

Bertha was beside herself with joy.

So far so good.

"I've got a treat for you inside. Let's go."

Darby brought the entire wagon, dog and all, into the house, then closed the door. She hadn't even looked to see if I was around. This wasn't exactly how I had expected my restoration to unfurl.

Fifteen minutes later, it appeared that I was still banished. I was getting the feeling that I had been stood up, or stood out. Eventually, I reasoned, Darby would have to open the door to give me back my dog.

At least I hoped so.

Chapter 16

Rejected in love, I continued to channel my pent-up frustration into work. At ten the next morning, I was deep into a stack of service contracts that had been signed prior to my tenure. Presumably, these contracts had been reviewed by Van Avery, although it appeared from my vantage point that Van Avery's reviews almost always resulted in some sort of glaring legal oversight. As I perused our service agreement with Fairview Greenery Services, I became acutely aware that I was not alone.

Glancing up, I saw a group of people congregated in the hallway outside of the office. How long they had been staring at me, I hadn't a clue. In addition to Sharon and Evan, the usual suspects, a third figure graced the doorway, one whose face was, unfortunately, already familiar to me. Not, however, in this context.

"Desmond Thomas," Detective Reed said as he stepped inside the room, "is that your car in the parking lot, a silver BMW M3 convertible with tags that read 'PRO-SE?'"

My immediate thought was that something had happened to my car.

Was it stolen?

But he'd said it was in the parking lot.

"Yes, that's mine. Is everything ok?"

"We have uncovered illegal substances inside the vehicle."

What the hell?

"What does that mean?"

"We found three ounces of marijuana in your car."

Given that I didn't own any pot, nor had I in recent memory transported anyone that did, I was a little befuddled.

"We had permission from Chesapeake Bluffs to conduct a drug canvas using our dogs. We searched the grounds, including the parking lot. They zeroed right in on your vehicle, giving us reasonable suspicion to believe that there were controlled substances within."

"You mean you searched my car without my permission, without a warrant?"

He held up a fairly large clear bag containing some sort of dried brown material.

"Do you recognize this?" he asked me.

"You must have made some kind of mistake. I don't use illegal drugs, pot or otherwise, and I certainly don't have any in my car. And what are we doing running drug canvasses at our Club? Evan, what's going on?"

"Apparently," Evan answered stiffly, "the police received an anonymous tip about drug activity at the Bluffs. They asked for permission to search the grounds. George, in facilities, gave them the ok. I didn't find out until just now."

"George doesn't have the authority to do that. Didn't anybody think to consult legal about this?" I said.

Evan shot me an odd look, one which I could only interpret as, *"Looks like we just have."*

The detective went on, "I've requested permission from Mr. McDermott to conduct a search of your office for additional illegal substances."

This wasn't happening.

"There's no way I'm giving you permission to search my office," I said. "I have confidential client records that I cannot allow to be accessed. I don't know how any of these alleged drugs allegedly got into my car, but there's nothing to say that whoever put them there, if they were there at all, wouldn't plant them in here now. I'm within my rights to refuse your request to search."

Reed didn't look too thrilled at my insinuation.

Tough.

"I'll tell you about your rights," the detective said as he pulled out his handcuffs, clamping them down hard on my wrists, arms behind me. "You got a few, since you're now under arrest for possession of an illegal substance. You have the right to remain silent. Understand? Anything you say, can and will be used against you in a court of law. You have a right to an attorney. If you cannot afford an attorney, one will be appointed for you. You can decide at any time from this moment on to terminate this interview and exercise these rights. Now, do you understand each of these rights I have explained to you?"

"I got it," I said.

"Having these rights in mind," he went on, "do you wish to talk to me now?"

Fat chance.

I shook my head.

This whole thing was bullshit. There was no proof that the bag he was toting around was even within 200 yards of my car. For all I knew, it could have been Reed's own personal stash.

"Who's the tough guy now?" he whispered in my ear.

I decided to exercise my right to remain silent, at least to Reed. But I had to say something to Sharon.

"Sharon," I said, "if they let the police search my office, you need to stay with them, watch them. They may try to plant something here. For some reason, it looks like somebody's out to frame me. If you're watching these guys, they won't be able to get away with anything."

I didn't know entirely what was going on, but something was obviously very wrong. This whole thing reeked all right, but it wasn't from any smoking bag of weed. Apparently, someone was still seriously pissed at me.

I knew I could trust Sharon to watch my back. But right now, I wasn't too sure about anyone else. It was time to give my trusty private-eye a call.

I got out of jail by posting a $500 bond, which was, coincidentally, the same amount as the misdemeanor fine for first time possession of marijuana in Virginia. I was going to fight this setup, going all the way to trial if I had to. There was no way it was legal to search my car in the parking lot, at least the way I saw it. Nobody but Reed had claimed to see the drugs in the car. It was a sham.

First the sexual harassment charges, then the threats from Tom Jones, now the frame-up on pot charges. What was next?

One thing I was happy about was that I now owned a handgun, my trusty .38 Special.

I called Bull with my story.

"I've heard a lot about Reed," he said, "and none of it's any good."

"How so?"

"I mean I've heard he's been known to take a few liberties with the drugs in the evidence room. The rumor was that he was selling them for extra dough. He lives in a huge house outside of town. Hard to imagine paying for that on a detective's salary. I heard a while back that they made a drug raid and confiscated drugs that still had evidence tags on them from the last raid. Looks like somebody there was an early advocate of recycling."

"Why wasn't he arrested?"

"Apparently, for lack of evidence."

He paused, and it took me a moment before I realized Bull was actually attempting to be funny.

"Anyhow," he continued, "they did an internal investigation, but couldn't pin anything on him. Maybe he's a little more careful now."

"Any idea why he would be framing me?"

"Let's see, from what you've told me, you've been threatened by a bookie with police connections, you're continuing to look into Frankie's death even after Reed specifically warned you to stop, you've uncovered evidence of a conspiracy that may be tied into extortion and murder, of which your boss might be a ringleader, you've fingered the suspects in an arson case, and somebody set you up on bogus sexual harassment charges to try to force you out of your job. Nope, I can't think of a thing."

This guy was on a roll.

"I think I need some more protection," I said.

"Your love life's not really my area of expertise," he quipped.

"Funny. What can you do for me in terms of security systems?"

"First thing would be to set up the security perimeter around your home. I'm thinking hi-res surveillance cameras tied to motion sensors, maybe some infra-red, everything recorded on DVRs and streamed to the web. That way we can perform surveillance from any computer anywhere in real-time or pull it up for review later, even from your phone. There's a mobile version for your car. It sounds like a lot, but considering everything you're getting, it's really not that expensive."

I could tell Bull was getting excited just talking about this project. This would be a PI's dream system to install and tinker with. He gave me a rough idea of what this might set me back. Clearly, "not that expensive" meant something different to a private-eye than it did to most normal people. Still, I didn't have much of a choice, other than to pack up and move out.

My paranoia was not without merit.

I conferenced Kevin into the call. I figured he might have a few more ideas of what high-tech goodies we might want to include in the system. He and Bull hit it off right away as they each tried to one-up the other on the level of surveillance sophistication. Kevin had a few insights on some of the capabilities that the real spooks in DC were able to put together. When I told him my budget, he grumbled, realizing that he wouldn't be able to redirect spy satellites over my house, hide snipers in ghillie suits in my yard, or enact whatever other wild plans he was pondering.

The only thing I knew after this talk was that I'd have to sell quite a few more sets of high-end golf clubs to pay for these guys' dream system.

I lifted the storage unit door, carefully gauging Cody's reaction to its contents. Cody was a natural fit as my forensic golf club examination assistant, seeing as he was completely in the dark about my friendship with Frankie, the bank accounts, or my concerns about faulty golf equipment. I was hoping his lack of familiarity with these details would allow him to come up with some new ideas; ones that I could no longer see because I'd been looking at it for too long.

The storage unit was the smallest size available in this facility, but still, the lone set of golf clubs sitting there looked rather pathetic.

Cody chuckled. "Are these your clubs?"

"No, they belonged to a friend of mine."

"Why would someone rent a storage unit just to hold one set of golf clubs?"

"That's what we're here to figure out."

"Can't you just ask your friend?"

"He's dead."

"Oh. Sorry." His voice trailed off apologetically.

"No problem," I said. "There's no way you could've known. So what do you think? Why *would* someone rent a storage unit to hold a single set of clubs?"

"Maybe he didn't have room in his place. Like maybe he lived in a small apartment."

"Alright," I said, "but in this case, space was not the problem."

"Maybe he wanted to hide this from somebody, his wife. Or maybe he was afraid that someone might steal them."

"What if I were to tell you that this guy had four or five other sets of clubs in his garage?"

"Sounds like a golf pro," he said. "I've seen your garage. This set might be more valuable than the others. Maybe it had sentimental value. I don't know."

I brought the set out into the light where we could examine it.

"They're almost brand new," Cody said. "It doesn't look like these could have much sentimental value, they don't even look like they've ever been used. The tag's still hanging on the bag."

It read: "MacKenna Clubs, Elite Green Set."

"I have reason to believe," I said, "that these clubs belonged to Frankie Brooks, former golf pro at Chesapeake Bluffs. The Bluffs gives a set of clubs to all the pros after their one-year anniversary on the job."

"I remember reading about him," Cody said. "Wasn't he the one...?"

"That's right," I said. "Any more thoughts on what these clubs might be doing here?"

"They're the top-of-the-line MacKennas," he said, "but still, it seems odd to stick them here. He could be saving them to give to his kid. Did he have kids?"

"A seven and eight year old."

"They wouldn't be able to use these clubs anytime soon," Cody mused.

"Maybe he put them here so someone else could get in and use them, without his wife knowing. All they would need is the code and the key. A secret golf club affair. Here's a wild thought, maybe the clubs were used in a murder, and they have evidence, blood or something on them."

"Why would he keep the evidence around," I asked, "rather than destroy it? This could be incriminating."

"Unless it wasn't Frankie that used them," Cody surmised. "He might keep the set as evidence against somebody else. Maybe he was involved too, and this was his leverage, or maybe he was blackmailing them. If that's the case, he wouldn't want them in his house. Maybe we shouldn't be handling them. They could have evidence on them, like fingerprints or hair or something."

"Do you see any evidence on these clubs?" I asked.

Cody looked at the clubs, careful now to avoid contaminating them.

"What about right there?" I said, pointing to a spot on the heel of the driver.

He stared at the spot for a moment, and then leaned back, lost in thought.

Cody photographed the serial number from the driver and texted it to me. He pulled up the MacKenna website on his phone a moment later, and then followed the registration link. They provided both an online form, and a phone number to call.

I decided to go with the phone option, where I might be able to get a little more information if I asked the right questions. I put the phone on speaker for Cody's benefit.

"Hello, MacKenna product registration, how can I help you?" I was shocked. A real human had answered.

"Yes, I'd like to register my golf clubs."

"Certainly, sir. Can I get your name and address?"

"Actually, I may have already sent in the card. Could I just give you the serial number to see if I've already registered them?"

"We can do that. I will need your name, however, to verify the registration."

"It's Franklin Brooks." For some reason, I felt guilty giving out someone else's name. Guess I could never truly be comfortable as a private-eye.

I gave her the serial number, and we waited for a moment while she researched the data.

"Sir, I'm seeing that the clubs have already been registered, but not to a Franklin Brooks."

"Could you tell me who they are registered to?"

"I'm sorry, sir, we're not allowed to give that out. We can only verify your information. If you tell me where you purchased the clubs, I will contact the seller and try to clear this up. Did you buy from an authorized retailer of MacKenna equipment?"

Time to end this charade.

"Umm... let me get back to you on that. I appreciate your help. Thank you."

I turned to Cody.

"I really don't want them contacting Chesapeake Bluffs and telling them that a Franklin Brooks had been asking around about MacKenna clubs that he purchased there. That might rustle a few feathers."

"Do you know for sure that these were Frankie's clubs?" he asked. "This was his storage unit, but maybe the clubs were somebody else's."

I had assumed all along that these clubs belonged to Frankie, but Cody had a good point. They may have belonged to someone else, and that may have been to whom the clubs were registered.

"That's possible," I said. "How are we going to find out who really owns the clubs?"

"That should be pretty easy," Cody said. "I've seen a couple dozen sets of MacKenna clubs being toted around by our members. During a lesson, we'll take a picture of the serial number off their drivers, ask them in conversation how old their clubs are and where they got them, and then later check with the manufacturer to verify the registration. You could probably even talk some of them into getting a new set. Don't you make a commission on that?" He smiled.

The kid was a natural. He was exactly right. In a matter of a few days, we would probably have at least a dozen serial numbers that we could cross-reference against the owner registrations.

"One thing, though," Cody said, "why wouldn't the owners figure this out when they registered the clubs?"

"That assumes that they did register them. Most people never send in the registration cards, much less call the number."

"Yeah, but to get anything repaired under warranty, doesn't it need to be registered?"

"Not at the Bluffs," I said. "They have a no-questions-asked replacement policy. The owners never have to register the clubs because the Bluffs has a record of the purchase."

I was willing to bet that the Bluffs told buyers that they would take care of the registration for them. That way, the owners wouldn't even bother.

We put the clubs back in the storage unit and closed it up.

It was time to commence... Operation Licensed Drivers.

It had taken a while, but Lisa's insurance lawsuit was at last ready to file. I wanted to review it with her in person before filing. I drove over to her place in the morning.

As soon as she opened the door, I thought about backing up and rechecking the house number. Had I come to the wrong place? This wasn't the Lisa Brooks I was accustomed to. She was, for lack of a better term—a mess. Dressed in a frumpy terrycloth robe, no makeup and tangled hair, it looked as if it had taken all her effort just to get out of bed. And her soulless expression gave me reason to believe that her outward appearance might not be her biggest problem at the moment.

"Are you alright?" I said, the words coming out instinctively, before I had time to consider how awful they must have sounded.

"I've been better," she said in dull monotone. "I got laid off from work yesterday. They said that there weren't enough summer kids to justify my position. Just like that, I'm unemployed." She didn't seem upset, or even terribly concerned as she relayed the news. It just was.

"I'm sorry. How about I come in and we can talk about it," I said, trying to steer the conversation away from the front door.

I stepped inside into a disaster. It looked as if a tornado had touched down in her living room, making several unscheduled stops along the way; clothes were scattered on the floors and furniture, food wrappers and dishes littered every room.

What was going on?

It was dark. The blinds on every window were shut.

I stepped carefully to avoid tripping over any debris. Clearing off dishes, newspapers and mail from the table, I carved an oasis of clean space in which we could review the lawsuit.

The guilt was catching up to me now, as I realized that my preoccupation with work had led me to totally miss Lisa's recent deterioration. Being able to help her had been one of the big reasons I came to the Bluffs in the first place.

"I can't sell the house," she said, without inflection. "It's worth less than the mortgage, and even so, I can't afford to make the payments much longer. I've still got the payments on the SUV. I don't know what to do. Sometimes, I wish it were me at the bottom of that cliff instead of Frankie. He took the easy way out, and I'm stuck here clawing my way out of the bottomless pit."

I was pretty sure her current financial situation wasn't as dire as she was making it out to be. She was getting monthly Social Security survivors' benefits, plus she had the insurance payout from the Bluffs' policy on Frankie. But I'd neglected to take into consideration the emotional toll. She appeared to be, at least to my untrained eye, clinically depressed.

"Lisa, the good news is that the lawsuit is ready to file. We can go over it together now. If you give me the ok, I'll submit it."

"Does that mean we'll get the money soon?" she said, perking up slightly.

I knew that my next words were likely put a damper on that.

"The court sets the date for the trial. I'll try to schedule the settlement talks as soon as possible, but we don't control the timetable. These things take time. It could be months before we sit down at the table with them. But hopefully, we'll get there."

She slumped.

I still wasn't one hundred percent certain that Lisa was as entirely in the dark about Frankie's affair and gambling problems as she claimed to be. Maybe her current depression had something to do with repressed guilt. Her behavior just didn't seem normal for a widow in her situation.

"Lisa, I feel like you're keeping something back. What aren't you telling me?"

Her vacant stare vanished. "You're supposed to be helping
me, not interrogating me. Just get the lawsuit filed," she said
brusquely. "I'll take care of the rest of this mess myself."

Picking up the paperwork, she thrust it into my chest.

"I'll file it today," I said, somewhat taken aback by the turn
of events.

I retraced my steps, making my way back to the front door
through the debris without incident.

"I'll let you know when I have some news," I said as I
reached the front door, trying to end on a somewhat hopeful note.

Receiving no acknowledgement, I left, discouraged,
frustrated, and with more questions than answers.

All in all, a fairly typical day.

The local newspapers ran the story on page one, with the
headline "Golfer Sues to Recover Hole-In-One Prize." In this case,
the prize was a brand new pickup truck, retail value of approximately
$20,000. Unfortunately for Chesapeake Bluffs Golf and Country
Club, we were named as one of the three defendants in the lawsuit,
the other two being the Antelopes Club and the local auto dealer.

This explained the thick document on my desk. The suit
claimed that the plaintiff in this case, Chad DeBartolo, participated in
a charity golf tournament sponsored by the Antelopes, held at
Chesapeake Bluffs. The Antelopes advertised that the first person to
make a hole-in-one on the par three 13th hole would win the truck,
which had been proudly displayed there for all to see.

Mr. DeBartolo's tee shot had found the cup on the
designated hole, and after suitable celebration, he had gone to claim
his prize at the dealership, and was refused. Needless to say, the
winner was more than a little upset. Hence, the lawsuit.

In the entire history of the Antelopes' sponsorship of this
event, no one had ever made a hole-in-one on the prize hole, so there
was little anticipation that the dealership would have to dole out the
pickup.

I was very familiar with the way these things were supposed
to work. Typically, the dealership buys "hole-in-one insurance" from
a company specializing in such things. For a tournament with 100

players, a quick check on the web revealed that it would cost around $400 to insure the giveaway.

In this case, the Antelopes Club had talked to one of the salesmen at the dealership, and claimed to have worked out an oral agreement for them to give away the truck as the prize. As an attorney, I'm not a big fan of oral agreements. Such agreements can be binding, but it's pretty hard to prove who promised what when it's left up to people's memories. Always get it in writing. This lawsuit was case in point.

The dealership, which had participated in such giveaways in the past with the Antelopes Club, claimed not to have made any such agreement this time. As their proof, they pointed to the fact that they had not purchased any hole-in-one insurance for this event, unlike in prior years.

Dealers participate in these giveaways for the advertising. The dealership gets its shiny new vehicle seen by all the golfers, many of whom may be in the market for one. The sponsor attracts more participants by offering such a prize. Everybody wins—if it's done right.

The dealer claimed the truck was for display only. The Antelopes claimed that the dealer agreed to provide the hole-in-one prize. In addition to DeBartolo's lawsuit, the Antelopes and the dealership had filed cross-claims against each other. It was getting pretty nasty.

Our involvement in this whole fiasco was minimal. We were just the venue. We made no promises or statements in any fashion concerning the giveaway. More than likely, we were included in the lawsuit just because the plaintiff's lawyers decided that it might increase their chances of a settlement.

But it was bad publicity for our Club, even though we were faultless. And we still had to respond to this lawsuit, which would require time and expense on our part.

After thinking through all the issues, I came up with a plan that I thought would resolve the lawsuit for all parties, and prevent this from ever happening to us in the future. If I could get the dealership to agree, we would split the cost of the car with them. It would be great publicity for us. I could already see the fluff pieces in the newspaper and on the web, about how we "stepped up to right a wrong," and all that good stuff.

The real lesson was that we needed to be more careful in the future. We'd have to make sure that people holding events on our courses had all their "trucks in a row."

I was awakened from a sound sleep, the voice speaking in a strange staccato. "Possible ... intruder ... alert ... south ... side ... of ... house."

What the hell?

An eerie glow lit up my bedroom. It was my phone.

After a few more neurons began to fire, I realized that the new surveillance system was alerting my phone that something had been detected outside. Now, at two thirty-six in the morning, it was streaming video from the cameras outside the house.

Live.

I stared hard at the image on the display. It was dark, way too dark for me to make any sense out of it.

What was it that Bull had told me?

At night, use the infrared.

An instant after tapping the "IR" button, a ghostly white human figure appeared in the darkness, next to the garage.

Holy shit, somebody's trying to break in.

Adrenaline kicked in and paved the way for my rising anger to take over.

Enough is enough. How many more times is somebody going to try to screw with me?

I wasn't about to call the police, at least not the crew that had planted the drugs in my car just a few days ago. The only thing I was willing to put my trust in right now was my shiny new .38 Special. It was time to test a new kind of peacemaking skill. Clearly, this guy wasn't aware of how ticked off I was.

After extracting the weapon from the bedside gun safe, I crept out of the room, carefully closing the door to make sure Bertha, still snoring soundly, wouldn't be able to get out. The last thing I needed was to have her run outside and start barking while I was stalking my target. Darby's absence, at this moment, was a relief. At least she was safe.

According to the live feed, the intruder had reached the side garage door. From there, I knew he couldn't see the front of the house.

I got this sucker.

Quietly opening the front door, I stepped out into the humid air, checking the feed for a reaction. Nothing. I was holding all the cards now. I knew exactly where he was, and I had a gun.

With optional laser targeting system.

Keeping my eyes glued to the phone, I tiptoed down the front porch steps toward the perp. I needed to get to him before he could get inside the garage, where things would get much more complicated.

On the final step, my foot flew out from under me. An instant later my face hit hard against the ground, followed by a metallic crash, all this accompanied by a cascade of golf balls.

I had somehow managed to knock over a metal pail full of practice balls.

Damn those interns and their chip shots.

The clamor was enough to awaken or alert anyone within a three block radius. Even worse, my gun and phone were lost in the night. Now he knew exactly where I was. And I was pretty sure he had a gun. So much for holding the cards.

It was at that moment that I began to question my approach.

Maybe I had been a little rash.

Above the din of my pounding heart and ringing ears, I heard what sounded like footsteps approaching.

Oh my god.

Real or imagined, I wasn't about to stick around to find out. Pain or no pain, it was time to get back inside. At least now I knew enough to look out for any stray balls in the way.

I raced back up the stairs. Even so, it felt as if I was exposed for an eternity, a giant target painted on my back, lit up brightly by the porch lights.

Shoot here.

Once through the door, I heaved a giant sigh of relief. But there was still no telling where this guy was.

"Are you all right?" a voice asked.

Cody.

Awake from all the commotion, he was rolling out of his

room.

"Call 911!" I yelled. "There's someone trying to get in the house."

"Ok, ok. Where is he now?"

"I don't know, just call now so the police get here. I lost my phone outside."

In all the chaos, I'd forgotten about my housemate. I'd put him at risk by not calling the police.

What was I thinking?

I heard him talking to the 911 operator, calm and logical, no sign of panic.

A good man in an emergency.

I turned on my laptop, remembering that I could monitor the surveillance cameras from any computer on the web. Kevin had bookmarked the site.

Was that guy still out there?

We watched the computer screen, both of us now sporting large kitchen knives, staring intently at the feed, switching constantly between cameras, not seeing anything suspicious, until the flashing lights of the squad car made an appearance in the front driveway.

I was fairly convinced that the police would just chalk my story up to the delusions of a slightly paranoid homeowner. But, then I remembered.

This whole thing had been recorded.

We put the knives away before I answered the door.

Despite my previous difficulties with the Chapman County Sheriff's Department, all was forgotten now, at least for the moment. I was genuinely relieved to have uniformed officers on the scene, and even more so when I found out that Detective Reed wouldn't be joining us.

The officers searched the perimeter of the house, and, of course, they found no burglars still hanging around, waiting to be apprehended. I told them about my misadventures on the front porch, after which they managed to retrieve my phone and the loaded Smith & Wesson.

"It's generally not a good idea for the homeowner to take matters into his own hands, Mr. Thomas. You were lucky this time. It could have been much worse."

"You're right," I said. "It was stupid."

I actually meant it.

"You said you fell from the porch steps. Are you hurt?"

So concentrated had I been on the matters at hand that I hadn't even thought about my fall. I looked down to assess any injuries, and discovered, much to my embarrassment, that I had no pants on. I was still sporting my plaid boxers and t-shirt after having been abruptly roused from bed. Neither Cody nor the police had said a thing this whole time about my getup.

I had a couple of nasty looking scrapes on my thigh where I must have hit the stone walkway, but no major gashes or cuts. I was pretty lucky that my face had hit the grass.

"It looks like I'm ok," I said, "except for an extreme lack of attire."

"Next time," the officer said, "call us sooner, rather than later. We'd like to catch this guy. And we don't want anybody getting hurt."

As soon as they left, I put my pants on.

I hadn't told the police about my recording capability. I wanted to have Bull take a look at the videos first, before the police did something silly like try to "commandeer" them, which would be hard to do since they were stored on some web server in God only knows where.

At that moment, the phone rang. It was Bull.

"I waited to call until I saw the police leave on the surveillance video. I saw the whole thing," he said. "You remember we set it up so that I get all the alarms here, too. I couldn't call you before because I didn't want your phone to ring and give you away while you were outside in your BVDs stalking that guy. Look, when I got you that gun, I explained that it was for self defense. Next thing I know I'm watching you go all Dirty Harry and almost getting yourself killed. Was it worth it?"

"I made a mistake, alright."

"Damn right you made a mistake. There's a lot more that can go wrong than you might think when you're tracking somebody, at night, holding a loaded weapon. You could end up looking more like Barney Fife than Clint Eastwood, except when it's real, it's not funny.

Police officers train for these situations. They make their mistakes when they're practicing. You're doing it for the first time, when it's life or death."

"I got it, I understand. It won't happen again."

"Did you look at the videos?"

"Not yet, we were watching it live until the police came. I didn't tell them that we had it all taped."

"Good," he said, "I want to take a good hard look at them, see if we can figure out who that guy was. I got some buddies who can do some image enhancement on it, if we need to. I got a pretty good idea who that guy was, though."

"Well?" I asked.

"It looks like our old friend, Detective Reed. But let me review the tapes first before I officially accuse the scumbag. So tell me, would you have shot the perp, if you had gotten to him?"

"If he tried to shoot me."

"What if he just tried to run away?"

He was baiting me now. Bull knew that the state of Virginia had not approved a "Castle Doctrine," a law which provided a homeowner with immunity from prosecution when they were defending their home. If I shot an intruder in the yard while he was running away, I would most likely find myself charged with attempted manslaughter and on the wrong end of a very costly civil lawsuit.

"I know about the Castle Doctrine," I said.

"Then you must know what they say."

I knew exactly.

"'Dead men tell no tales, and they don't hire attorneys.' So Dez, unless you're prepared to shoot to kill, you have no reason being out there, and make sure you don't shoot him in the back."

The sun was coming up, and I had only gotten a few hours of sleep. Worst of all, in just about three hours, I was due to testify as the defendant in my sexual harassment hearing.

Some guys get all the fun.

Chapter 17

The whole new career thing hadn't worked out quite the way I'd expected. It had started well, with an unexpected romance with a beautiful and talented woman, and a chance to ponder and practice for a return to the pro tour. Then, just like that, everything evaporated.

In the past few months I'd been falsely accused, repeatedly threatened, had a gun pointed at my head, been dumped by my girlfriend, framed for possession of drugs, and to top it off, I'd alienated the one person I'd come here specifically to help. My bucket list had morphed into a fail pail. And that pail threatened to overflow with this morning's interrogation over the Beverly Sargent matter.

The EEOC investigator arrived at our facility a full hour before the hearings were due to start. I supposed he wanted to get warmed up before he started grilling. I was the first witness. Tuesdays were ordinarily an off day, so I was already perturbed about having to come in. The morning escapades at my house weren't helping my mood, either. I just wanted to go home and get some sleep.

I was intimately familiar with EEOC operations and procedures, having represented clients in several investigations in the past, only one of which was a sexual harassment case, the others falling into one of the many other types of workplace discrimination handled by the commission, such as race, age, and disability.

I knew all the steps of an investigation, including this meeting, the interview with the defendant. Almost certainly the investigator had already talked with representatives from the Bluffs. It felt odd, not to mention, uncomfortable, having to participate in one of these investigations as defendant rather than as counsel, even knowing, as I did, that this whole thing was a ruse.

The investigator's questions, of necessity, would no doubt involve detailed personal information about my life, most likely coming with unpleasant sexual accusations. I was the one who felt violated.

Ordinarily, in my role as counsel, I would have been representing the company. However in this case, that was an obvious conflict of interest. So the Bluffs had no choice but to drag Van Avery out of semi-retirement. I was pretty sure he wouldn't be too pleased.

"Thomas, what the devil did you get yourself into?" were his first words when I entered the conference room.

I remained silent, deciding that it was probably not wise to answer his query at this particular time. The room was occupied only by Van Avery and one other serious-looking fellow, whom I assumed was the investigator.

As an attorney, I recommend that a defendant facing a sexual harassment complaint hire legal counsel. However, in this case, I felt competent to represent myself, not only because I was an attorney, but because I knew the case was totally without merit. Clearly, I was ignoring that oldest piece of lawyerly advice, "The attorney who represents himself has a fool for a client."

The EEOC investigator, Aaron Samuels, introduced himself. He was capturing the proceedings electronically in addition to the old-fashioned way – with a notebook. He swore me in, and we began.

"Mr. Thomas, are you familiar with the complaint against you, filed by Beverly Sargent?"

"Yes, I am."

"When did you first become aware of these charges?"

I detailed the conversation in Evan's office.

"Since that time, have you had any contact with Ms. Sargent?"

"No, I have not."

"Are you, or were you ever in a supervisory position to Ms. Sargent at Chesapeake Bluffs?"

"No, never."

"Had you met Ms. Sargent prior to the events that transpired during her first golf lesson with you?"

"Never, at least not that I can recall."

"Please describe her first lesson with you."

I went over all the details of that first encounter, including her outfit, her flirtatious behavior, and especially the reasons for having to call her phone three times.

"What happened at Mulligan's restaurant?"

"Nothing. I never went there. That was a fabrication."

"Did you promise Ms. Sargent that you would attempt to get her a better position at the Club in return for sexual favors?"

"Never. I have no connection with any restaurant or other such positions at the Club."

"Did you report this incident to anyone?"

"I thought it was bizarre and strange, but didn't feel the need to report it. I thought she was just a lady who didn't want to take no for an answer."

"Did you discuss this with anyone at all?"

"No, I didn't."

"Not even Ms. Darby St. Claire?"

I wasn't aware that anyone really knew about Darby and me, that is, officially. Yet somehow, the investigator seemed to know about her. It was bad enough that this accusation had already damaged my professional life, my reputation and my love life. Were they now going to drag her into this witch-hunt too? I was not pleased.

"No, I didn't discuss it with Darby."

"Do you know of any reason why Ms. Sargent would lie about being harassed by you?"

Recent events had left me feeling frazzled. I told the investigator that I thought someone was trying to force me out of the Bluffs. At this point, I wasn't entirely certain of who that was. I even mentioned Beverly's affair with Frankie Brooks. Samuels politely listened and took notes, so everything I said was now on record.

I answered what seemed like an endless set of questions, but, at long last, the investigator exhausted his supply, and just like that, I was free to leave. On my way out, my heart sank.

There, seated in the lobby, across from Beverly, sat Darby.

Beverly Sargent sat down at the conference table, dressed in a conservative business suit and skirt. The thought of going through this ordeal repulsed her. She had been led to believe that her charges against Thomas would have long ago resulted in his resignation or dismissal. She had been led to believe wrong.

She had rehearsed for this moment all day yesterday, having a friend ask questions while she practiced her responses. Once she had the facts memorized, she'd worked on adding the appropriate emotional components. This would be her only chance to sell her harassment charges to the investigator.

But when the curtain rose, and she found herself sitting at the table, under oath, with the investigator looking at her, listening to her, and judging her, the knot in her stomach tightened considerably. She smiled in a feeble attempt to ward off her nervousness, but the end result came out looking something less than natural.

"Do you have an attorney, Ms. Sargent?" Samuels asked.

"No, I don't."

"Very well then, let's begin."

"Had you met Mr. Thomas prior to your golfing lesson with him?"

"No, I had not."

"What led you to choose Mr. Thomas for your lesson?"

She hadn't practiced for this question. She knew she had to answer quickly, or he would know she was making up her answers on the fly.

"I was told… I was told he was a good golf instructor."

"And do you recall who it was that recommended him to you?"

Shit. Think fast.

"I believe it was one of my friends at the restaurant. Yes, it was Deloris Whitfield, another waitress. She said he was a very good instructor."

"So then, if we look up the records for Mr. Thomas' past lessons, we should find Deloris Whitfield listed among his previous clients, should we not?"

For an instant, Beverly's face registered surprise and shock. Then she caught herself and forced another weak smile. Samuels was staring right at her.

This guy doesn't even blink.

"Well, I'm not a hundred percent sure it was her, now that I think about it. I'm not sure who recommended him."

"I see," Samuels said, as he began writing in his notepad.

Beverly watched the investigator's slow and deliberate penmanship.

He knows I'm lying.

She tried hard to hide her desperation. Her heart was pounding, her face getting hotter. Beads of sweat rolled down her temples. Her fingers fidgeted.

I hate this.

"Please describe that first lesson with Mr. Thomas."

Finally.

But her thoughts poured out in a jumble. She wanted to say everything she had practiced, but she couldn't think how to present it in a coherent fashion. The end result was a nonstop narrative.

"He made a pass at me while we were on the driving range. He grabbed my hands and wouldn't let go until I pulled away. He rubbed against my legs while he was showing me how to swing the club. He said he felt like taking me right there, but since we couldn't do that with all the people around, we could go back to his place. I told him no, I was engaged. I showed him my ring. He said he didn't care, he said he had connections with the Club, he could get me a promotion if I went back with him. And if I didn't, I'd regret it."

"How long into the lesson was it before the harassment began?"

Beverly thought for a moment. "I would say it was about ten, fifteen minutes."

Samuels took out a second pen, then slowly wrote again in his notebook. Beverly noticed the new notes were in red.

"And were you aware if there were any other people on the driving range at this time?"

She winced, and then watched as Samuels wrote in red again.

Oh my god, has he already talked to some witnesses? What if they've already testified? Then he knows for sure I'm lying.

"I think there were some other people there," she said, "I'm not sure."

Samuels nodded, his face impossible to read.

"Now I will remind you, Ms. Sargent, that you are under oath."

She tried to say yes, but couldn't get it out.

"Now, about the phone calls, could you describe where you were when these occurred?"

"I don't know, I don't remember. Why do you keep asking me all these things? I'm not the one who did this. I'm the victim. You treat me like I'm a criminal. He's the criminal." She began to cry.

The investigator came prepared. He handed her a tissue from his large box.

"Ms. Sargent. These are serious allegations that can ruin people's lives and careers. I'm asking questions to make sure that I understand exactly the events that transpired. Some people have been known, for whatever reasons, to make false harassment charges. If I determine that your charges are merited, the EEOC will stand behind you with all of our resources. But if I find that you have knowingly made false statements under oath, we will most certainly not support your case. You may end up being terminated by your employer, and perhaps even be subjected to a lawsuit for making false accusations.

"Is there anything you would like to tell me now, Ms. Sargent, before we continue any further?"

Defeated, Beverly put her face in her hands.

"That's enough," she said, her voice surprisingly calm and controlled. "I'm done. I'm not doing this.

"I made it up, none of it's true. Mr. Thomas did not harass me. It's all a lie. I had to do it, I was blackmailed. Someone threatened to tell my fiancé all about my past if I didn't do this, and then he wouldn't want to marry me, and I'd be stuck working in a dead-end job forever."

In the course of his job, Aaron Samuels had conducted a great many investigations, but Ms. Sargent's revelation surprised even him.

"Please don't let them fire me," she went on. "She made me

do it. I never wanted to do this. She's psychotic. I'm so sorry I ever met that crazy bitch."

"Who was blackmailing you?" Samuels asked.

"Carolyn Andrews. She's the only woman on the Bluffs' Board of Directors."

While she waited to testify, Darby pondered the advice she'd received in the past weeks on the subject of love and romance.

She recalled the day Rodney stopped by the tennis center. She'd been in the middle of a lesson, and had done her best to avoid looking anywhere near his direction.

Get lost, dirtbag.

But when he sat down at the nearby benches and waited, she knew she wouldn't be able to elude him for long, and sure enough, as soon as her student left, he approached.

She had looked at him without saying a word, but that hadn't prevented him from launching right into his revelation, telling her all manner of terrible things about Desmond, which included much more than just the sexual harassment complaint. She had done her best to remain stoic, not wanting to give him the satisfaction of showing any evidence that his disclosures bothered her.

Of course, she had known that with Rodney, whenever his lips were moving, he was certainly lying. She had found that out the hard way.

So she'd needed to verify the story, and her friend Amber, in HR, was by far her best source. Although Amber warned her that she wasn't allowed to divulge anything confidential about any employee, she did let it be known that if Darby asked the right questions, she would say "no," as appropriate.

"I've heard that someone at the Club made sexual harassment charges against Desmond Thomas, is that correct?"

The silence on the other end of the phone made Darby's heart sink.

"Are you aware of him seeing anyone other than me?"

"No," Amber said, "I don't know anything about that."

Still, people didn't get accused of a crime unless there was something to it, Darby thought. Even Desmond had told her that most of the defendants he had represented in the past had been guilty. Although the legal system presumed innocence until proven otherwise, her love life need not necessarily be held to the same standard.

After her devastating relationship with Rodney, Darby hadn't been very keen to jump back in the saddle, and it had been almost two years since she had begun dating again. When Desmond came along, he had seemed totally different, even if he was a golf pro.

She'd received lots of unsolicited advice from friends and relatives about her budding relationship with the hybrid golfer/attorney. They all liked Desmond well enough when they met him in person. But a few said to be wary of any handsome, athletic guy. One even wanted to steer her off men completely.

Desmond was charming and intelligent, but then, so had Rodney been, at first. But unlike Rodney, she hadn't seen any dark side emerge from Desmond, and she had almost gotten comfortable believing that none existed. Until this.

What had she done to be so unlucky in love? Perhaps she attracted the wrong kind of man. Maybe she needed to find a nice boring computer geek who was so unappealing that he would never be tempted by anyone else. She shuddered. That would be a tough pill to swallow.

It was almost enough to make her consider dabbling with lesbianism… almost. But after a moment's reflection, Darby knew that she just wasn't cut from the heteroflexible mold. She still preferred more rigid gender distinctions.

But most of her friends had urged her to wait it out, until the truth finally emerged from the accusations. They had told her things like, "If he cares about you, he'll still be there for you when this is over… assuming he didn't do anything. If not, then you're better off without him."

The whole episode had been hard, but perhaps her friends were right. But it had been a sad and lonely time for her and on more than one occasion she had nearly given in and called. When he'd sent Bertha in with those flowers, she'd almost caved completely.

Then the subpoena arrived, and she felt compelled to wait until the outcome of the hearing before talking to Desmond.

Still deep in thought, Darby was startled by an unfamiliar voice.

"Ms. St. Claire?"

"Yes?"

"I'm Aaron Samuels, with the EEOC. Your testimony is not going to be needed today, after all. I'm sorry to have inconvenienced you. The charges have been dropped. The complainant has recanted."

"What does that mean, exactly?"

"It appears that Mr. Thomas didn't do anything improper. Ms. Sargent has testified that the charges were fabricated. You're free to go. Thank you for taking the time to come in."

Samuels then headed back into the conference room.

Darby heard the muffled voices resume from inside. Apparently, there were still a few issues to resolve with the horrible orange-toned bitch who'd started all this. Maybe it was a good thing she hadn't come back out. Darby felt like she'd be completely within her rights in ripping her a new one.

As she thought about Desmond, she felt for him, first for the false charges and accusations he'd had to endure, by himself, and also for her part in not believing in him.

There was nothing she could do that would change the past, but the future hopefully still held promise. She had to do something to make it up to him.

Now, how to make up with a man....

Picking up the phone, I was surprised to find myself talking again with Investigator Samuels. Wasting no time, he informed me that the complaint against me had been withdrawn and the case dropped. For some reason, the mention of blackmail caught my interest.

Just like that, the whole harassment case was over. Now I was left with even more questions, such as, what had I done to piss off Carolyn Andrews?

I'd only met her once, during the reception dinner on my first day at work. If one were to believe Beverly Sargent now, Carolyn had blackmailed her in an attempt to drive me out of the Bluffs.

At the dinner, Carolyn had been anxious to find out if I was going to be revisiting the plans for the expansion of the Club. The first thing I'd done was to start probing into suspicious-looking real-estate transactions. Presumably, the LLC attorneys would have gotten word back to the owner that someone was fishing for information.

All of this made perfect sense, if Andrews were indeed the owner of the LLC properties. As a board member, she would have had early access to the plans for the expansion. She could've used her insider information to buy up property before the corporation had started their own purchasing effort. This was unethical, to say the least, and possibly illegal.

That explained why she wanted me out of the Bluffs. I was getting too close for comfort. She probably figured I'd get fired or maybe just resign for personal reasons.

And if Carolyn did own the properties, then I had a pretty good idea who had hired the arsonists. Desperate people take desperate measures.

According to what I'd heard, the arsonists never met the person who hired them, they'd only heard her voice over the phone.

Carolyn's voice.

If she was capable of arson, what else would she do? Was she involved in the extortion scheme with Frankie, or even responsible for his death? It was high time I went to the authorities with this new information. But my immediate question was—which authorities? I certainly wasn't about to play the role of Reed's punching bag again.

And of course, I'd be willing to bet, by this time, Carolyn Andrews would be long gone.

Chapter 18

This past week, I'd had a chance to evaluate Cody's teaching skills. It turns out, the kid wasn't half bad. Most adults were initially skeptical at taking lessons from someone who couldn't even walk. That was natural, I suppose, since they hadn't seen him drive ball after ball in practice like I had. As soon as they witnessed him smack a drive fifty yards farther than they could ever hope to, they became believers.

He had a good eye for picking out the problem in a golf swing. Not every pro can do it. Time after time, he'd make the same suggestions that I would have made. That right there was the sign of a great instructor.

Even with the best instructors, there are a few players who can't seem to master even the most basic elements of golf. It's not always the pro's fault.

I schooled Cody on one player's problems.

"He's got too much loft," I said.

"Really, you think he was hitting the ball too high?" Cody said.

"No. LOFT. Lack of fucking talent."

I was surprised Cody hadn't learned that one yet. I'd have to alert Kerry Boggs to this major deficiency in his curriculum.

I'd brought Cody up to speed at the Swing Analysis Center, and he'd already managed to sign up three members to have their swings analyzed. This kid was a golf-lesson machine.

Most importantly, in the course of the week's lessons, we'd snagged serial numbers from eight sets of MacKenna clubs purchased at the Bluffs' pro shop.

Out of the eight, five had not been registered at all, and three sets were registered to a different person other than the student. At least six had broken clubs exchanged in the past year.

This confirmed my initial belief regarding Frankie's clubs. Somehow, the serial numbers on some sets of clubs were getting registered to other people. It also meant that any exchanges hadn't gone through MacKenna's factory warranty repair service, since the clubs weren't registered to our players.

I needed to get my head around this issue. It was time, once again, to make supplication to a higher authority.

"We have a problem," I said as soon as Kevin answered his phone.

"What you mean 'we,' white man?"

"I mean, I think we've uncovered some kind of a scam going on in the sale of golf equipment, and it looks like Frankie had figured it out. He appeared to be using his knowledge about counterfeit golf equipment to extort money. That is until they finally shut him up."

"Let's see, counterfeiting, extortion, murder." he said, "I thought you said you were calling about something important. Maybe you ought to go to the police with all of this, ya think?"

"I tried a while back, but they blew me off. Plus, I think Reed's in on it."

I brought him up to speed on our latest research.

"You've got your summer intern involved in your detective work? A college student? Are you nuts?"

"I needed another set of eyes on the problem."

"That's not his job, Dez. You're putting him in a bad position; this could be dangerous. You're not even certain about this stuff, yet you've got him playing Watson to your Holmes. You need to stop that shit now, Sherlock."

"Why don't you really tell me what's on your mind?" I said. Kevin could be a pain in the ass when he wanted to be.

"Let *me* be your sounding board in the future. Got it? Not only am I extremely capable, but I'm also in a position to tell you if and when I don't want to get involved, unlike your subordinates at work."

He had a point.

"Alright. Clearly I screwed up. I won't do it again. But now what am I supposed to do?"

"Isn't it obvious? Talk to the culprits, get them to come clean about the counterfeit equipment, get them to admit to being the victims of extortion, and finally, get them to confess to having Frankie bumped off. You don't have to be a rocket scientist."

"Why didn't I think of that?" I said. "It's so simple."

"Really though, there is a way we can get in touch with them," Kevin said, leaving me hanging.

"I'm all ears."

I waited eagerly for the big reveal.

"It's elementary, my dear Dez," he said. "We just email Evan316."

Sleuthing was at the top of my to-do list this morning, but as soon as I arrived at my desk, Sharon dropped off a document and walked away.

"Let me know if you want me to get Milton."

Uh-oh, what had he done this time?

I had been extremely pleased when Milton Langford had finally seen the light about the "Cart Girls Gone Crazy" calendar, and had reigned in his desire to terminate the four offending beverage ladies. As I had imagined, we'd had a few isolated complaints from members who were morally outraged, but in general, I got the feeling that most people were either indifferent, or that they really, really liked the calendar.

And from what I'd heard, quite a few people were calling in to schedule tee-times asking if any of the "calendar girls" were working that day. The girls were mini-celebrities in their own right.

I read the first paragraph of the attorney's letter. Wrongful termination.

Oh joy.

The client was Caitlyn Ross. Speaking of calendar girls, she was one of our four. Miss Cart Girl of August, according to my best recollection. What had Ms. Ross done now to deserve Milton's wrath? I read on.

Pregnant. Milton had fired her after she became pregnant.

What the hell, Milton?

Clearly, Milton had never heard of the Pregnancy Discrimination Act.

I'd thought we had an understanding with our managers; they needed to contact HR before terminating any employee. Knowing Milton, he probably just told her not to show up for work any more. Problem solved, or at least that's what he thought from his end.

Of course, his solutions resurfaced on my end; and my end tended to be a lot more expensive.

I rang up Sharon.

"He's coming right up," she said, before I could utter even a syllable.

She's fast.

While he was on his way, I scanned the rest of the letter. I was shocked.

Rodney Collingsworth was alleged to be the father.

Milton arrived and sat down.

"We just got a letter from Caitlyn Ross's attorney. They're threatening to go to the EEOC. What happened?"

"She fainted out on the course about a month ago. Right at the seventeenth. She was bending over to grab some stuff out of her cart, got back up too fast and blacked out. We had to take her to the hospital. Then we found out she was knocked up."

"Ok?" I said.

"That was only a week after she threw up all over two of our members. Morning sickness, I understand. From what I heard, it was what they call pro-ject-ile vomiting."

For some reason, he enunciated each syllable of "projectile" in his slow, southern drawl.

"Completely covered those golfers. That projectile stream must have gone a good five feet."

I was starting to feel a little queasiness coming on myself. His vivid description was not helping. "I get the picture."

"It's not good for a pregnant woman to be out there. She might get hurt."

"Or hurt the business," I said.

"Well, when it comes down to it, yeah. Big baby bellies don't sell beer."

"Did you know Rodney Collingsworth was the father?"

The look on his face told me all I needed to know.

"She never mentioned that."

I had a sneaking suspicion that there was more to the story. Whenever Rodney was involved, there were usually a multitude of problems and ill-will.

"Did Rodney ever talk to you about Caitlyn?"

"Now that you mention it, he came into my office a few months before the incident. He wanted me to move Caitlyn to his course, No. 3."

"Did you do it?"

"Well, yeah. I shuffled around a few schedules, and moved her to weekends."

The weekend slot on No. 3 was the best slot any cart girl could hope for. I was pretty certain that beverage cart girls working that shift made more money than I did.

"What reason did he give for asking?"

Milton scratched his head. "I don't rightly recall. You know Rodney, he could talk a dog off a meat wagon. It must have sounded good at the time."

As far as I knew, Caitlyn hadn't filed a sexual harassment complaint. *Yet.* It was possible Rodney hadn't pressured her into sex with a promise of a better position. But this was Rodney we were talking about, so if you assumed the worst, you were rarely disappointed.

Clearly, Rodney had never heard of the Civil Rights Act, which prohibited any type of sexual harassment in the workplace. And if it was harassment, it would fall under quid pro quo, literally "this for that," which described the situation where job promotions were based on submission to sexual advances. Only in Rodney's case, we might have to call it quid "golf-pro" quo.

"Milton, reinstate her, now. You just can't fire someone for being pregnant. It's against the law."

"You don't see too many pregnant girls working at Hooters, now do you?"

I searched for "pregnant Hooters girls," and in about two seconds there appeared pictures of quite a few such ladies who seemed to be happily working in their restaurants. I turned the screen around so Milton could see.

"Well, I'll be dog-gone," he said, "what's next, pregnant lap dancers?"

"I wouldn't know," I said.

"We're going to have to offer her back pay, including estimated tips, and any legal costs she's incurred thus far. Hopefully, that will persuade her to drop any complaint."

"Well, you know, once the bread's toast, it can't be bread again."

"What exactly does that mean?" I said, trying to make sense out of another one of his mind-bending colloquialisms.

He shook his head. "It means you can't put the toothpaste back in the tube. How do we know she's going to take back her old job now, even if we give it to her?"

"She was making good money. It's hard to beat a job like that."

"You know, in the old days," he said, "we could pretty much run this business the way we wanted to. Everybody sues nowadays. It's getting to where you can't even take a piss outside without having some damn lawyer sue you for dumping toxic waste."

I tried hard to suppress the image in my head.

"I'm going to contact her attorney and tell them about our offer. If it's accepted, you need to put her back on No. 3 on weekends, just like she was. Do you have a problem with that? If you do, you need to let me know now."

"I can do that," he said. "But LeeAnne ain't gonna be too happy to lose that spot. Just letting you know."

"I got it," I said. "But those are the breaks."

"What if it gets too hot for her during the summer," he asked, "with her expecting and all?"

That brought up a good point. We'd have to accommodate her with another position if that happened.

"Milton, in your recollection, have we ever temporarily accommodated someone due to injury? Moved them to another position for a while?"

"Sure. One of the girls broke her leg last year. We moved her inside as a clerk until she could drive the cart again."

"In that case, we'll do the same for Caitlyn if she can't handle the heat in the summer. We've already established a precedent."

He looked like he was about to say something else, but I cut him off.

"Sharon's going to make an appointment for you with HR. You can't be going around firing people like that anymore. Look what happens. It could cost us big time."

"I understand. Sorry Dez." Milton, properly chastised, slouched out.

Now for the fun part. Since we had uncovered a potential incident of sexual harassment, we were obligated to start our own investigation on Rodney, which could result in his being disciplined or terminated. He may have been my boss on the golf course, but now I had the responsibility to diligently investigate his role in this incident, and I planned to be very, very diligent.

Couldn't happen to a nicer guy.

After a lengthy and somewhat heated discussion, Kevin and I eventually came to an understanding. We agreed that we didn't have the experience, knowledge or authority to track down the counterfeiters by ourselves.

We realized that we couldn't just try to trap Evan316 in our own bogus extortion scheme, because that would be a crime, and when all was said and done, who's to say we weren't actually extorting him, not just pretending? We could end up in jail ourselves.

Not to mention that if these people really were killers, we'd be risking the same fate as Frankie. And finally, even if our plan succeeded, we'd eventually have to go to the authorities with the details. So, why not just begin there? It sounded a whole lot safer.

After my resounding rejection by the local Chapman County authorities, I elected to go to the top of the investigatory food chain, the FBI. A cursory check on the internet revealed that they investigated "criminal counterfeiting, piracy, and other federal crimes." That sounded perfect.

When I phoned the FBI's Richmond office, I was directed to Special Agent Matthew Griffiths. I told him about the counterfeiting, and also mentioned a little about my blackmailing and murder hypothesis. I also told him about my "Carolyn Andrews as arsonist" theory. Poor guy. I dumped so much information on him that he must have thought he was talking to one of those conspiracy kooks. He was probably expecting to hear my thoughts on the 9/11 bombings. Since he didn't dismiss my story out-of-hand, I filled him in on the details about the serial number registration checks we'd done.

We opted to meet in Richmond, rather than having FBI agents descend upon Chesapeake Bluffs, since it seemed likely that someone in management here might be involved.

For purely selfish reasons, I'd asked Kevin to accompany me to the meeting. I knew that if he came, he'd feel compelled to organize all of our information into one master presentation, complete with spreadsheets, links, references and videos.

No dummy, me.

I supplied Kevin with all the documentation I had, including the golf club registration numbers and names of the owners, copies of the bank account records and the complete file from Bull Durham.

The next day, as I stood near the door to the FBI's Richmond office, I couldn't miss Kevin's entrance into the parking lot in his cherry-red Tesla roadster, his "fun" car. All electric, the Tesla went from 0-60 in under four seconds. The first time he took me out in that thing, it had taken considerable effort to keep my pants dry.

Kevin carried his computer case, no doubt holding his laptop with today's presentation. I carried a beat-up cardboard box containing all the hard copies. Old school, I had to admit, but I was pretty sure the agent would want hard copies of the paper trail. In any event, I was pumped. We had ourselves a case.

Once inside the building, we were greeted with a serious security checkpoint. I put my box down on the conveyer belt, and proceeded through the metal detector. The instant I stepped in, I had an "oh shit" moment. And sure enough, seconds later, I found myself pressed face-first into the wall, a beefy security guard removing my .38 revolver before I'd had a chance to say a word.

Note to self: Never, ever, try to bring a concealed weapon into an FBI office again.

After an hour delay, including a strip-search, numerous phone calls and a meeting with FBI security, we were finally issued visitor badges and chaperoned to the conference room, where we were joined by Special Agent Griffiths. Still thankful that they had opted against a full body-cavity search, I was suitably apologetic, but the agent was not exactly reassuring, giving me what appeared to be a suspicious onceover.

Kevin went right into his presentation. His slides explained the entire chronology of events, starting with Frankie's death, our work breaking into the laptop, getting into Frankie's email accounts, the timeline correlating the bank account records with email exchanges, the conversation with Trevor, the storage unit, the seemingly erroneous golf club registrations, my investigations into the shady real estate dealings, the sexual harassment lawsuit, and the failed attempt to involve the police in an investigation.

He also mentioned how we believed I'd been set up in the phony drug sting, and, as a pièce de résistance, he included a segment of the surveillance video from the attempted break-in at my house, where we'd identified Detective Reed as the intruder.

Griffiths wouldn't show it, but I could tell that he was impressed. I was ready to give Kevin a hug, but decided that I'd wait until after we left the building.

"From what I've seen," the agent deadpanned, "and obviously we'll have to verify all the information, but assuming for the time-being the information in this presentation is correct, this case is about much more than counterfeiting. Ordinarily, blackmail and murder investigations are usually handled by local authorities. However, if they occur as part of a violation of another federal law, the FBI can claim jurisdiction."

"What's your feel?" Kevin asked.

"It's too early to say," Griffiths answered, predictably, "but we'll take it under advisement."

He looked pretty eager to me. We had just dropped this baby right into his lap, complete with hyperlinks. There was one way to tell if he serious. He'd want copies of everything.

"We're going to need copies of all your documents," he said.

Bingo.

"We'll also need Mr. Brooks' laptop for our forensic

analysts."

"Copies of all the documents are in the box," I said. "The laptop's in there too. The new passwords for the laptop and email accounts are on the top page."

"Also, Mr. Thomas," he said, turning to the other Mr. Thomas, "would we be able to get a copy of your presentation?"

Kevin held up a thumb drive. "It's all here."

"What do we do next?" I asked.

"Nothing. If we need more assistance from you, we'll be in touch."

Outside the building, the security agent brought out my revolver, unloaded, the five rounds now contained in a zip-lock evidence bag. He just shook his head.

At least I had a story to tell my children, someday.

Chapter 19

Sharon's call announced a visitor to my office, at 11:45, not the usual time for a client consultation.

"You have a Ms. Haywood to see you. If you don't need me for anything, I'm headed out for lunch."

"I'll be fine," I said, pondering Sharon's unusual brevity.

The name didn't ring a bell, but then again I wasn't totally familiar with all of the hundreds of employees at the Bluffs.

I didn't usually get too many walk-ins in my role as in-house counsel.

The dark-haired woman who entered was outfitted with scarf, sunglasses, and a long coat, projecting the image of Jackie Kennedy or Audrey Hepburn from those iconic sixties photos.

Ms. Haywood made herself right at home, melting sensually into my guest chair.

"Let me get right to the point," she said, in a deep throaty voice. "This may take a little while. Have you got time?"

"I might. Depends on what you need."

"Excellent." Extracting herself slowly from the chair, she moved to the entrance of my office and casually shut the door. Then, with a sly smile, she turned the lock.

I was about to object, but she put her fingers to her lips, and I was mesmerized into quiet obedience.

She proceeded to saunter around the perimeter of my office, closing the blinds on each window, until it was just the two of us. I wasn't sure where this was going. Well, actually I was pretty sure, but I needed to be certain. No need to jump to any conclusions.

"It's warm in here," she said, "I don't think I'll need this."

She began to unbutton her jacket, starting at the top button and working her way south at a slow, deliberate pace. After three buttons, I realized that she was either wearing a very, very low-cut top or....

After one more button, I had no doubts. As I watched with rapt attention, my legal instincts were waging a ferocious battle with my primal urges. And the urges were winning handily. I sat paralyzed, fascinated.

She was almost to the final button. So far, there had been no sign of anything underneath her jacket, but my burden was to prove it beyond any reasonable doubt. There was definitely something familiar about her.

And then I saw the proof. Of course, she'd known all along that I would.

I smiled, and she knew too.

"What gave me away?"

"You're still wearing the tennis bracelet I gave you for your birthday."

Darby made a pouty face, but quickly recovered.

Actually, her artwork had been the final giveaway. She had a small "Om" symbol tattooed on her right hip.

"Hey mister lawyer," she said in a sultry voice, "I'm ready to invoke my attorney-client privilege. It's the law you know."

"Who am I to argue with hundreds of years of legal precedent?"

"Do you have these consultations with all your new clients?" she whispered in my ear.

"Only the ones that make the grade."

"Well, there are a few perks to this job."

"I thought about calling to apologize for our 'misunderstanding,' and to thank you for the flowers, but then I figured it would be better to do it here, you know, with a personal touch," she said. She did have a way with words.

"It was understandable, considering the circumstances," I said. "And I'm glad you liked the flowers."

"If there's anything I can do to thank you in a more meaningful way," she said while loosening my tie.

"You can keep the wig on."

"You're a rotten, rotten man," she said. "But you're in luck, I love rotten men."

It was in the afternoon when the FBI called. My consultation with Ms. Haywood had been consummated over an hour ago. Happily, she'd decided to retain my services indefinitely.

"Mr. Thomas. This is Special Agent Griffiths. Can you talk now?" he asked.

"Sure," I said, getting up and closing the door to my office.

"Based on the information you provided, I've obtained authorization to proceed."

"Excellent," I said.

"In order to move forward, we're going to need your cooperation."

I'd been around long enough to know that "cooperation" had a much different meaning to the FBI than it did to most people.

"What will that entail?"

"It's probably better if we discuss that in person. When would be a good time today for us to come down and talk to you?"

They're not fooling around.

I checked my schedule. "It looks like I could be free around four this afternoon. How long do you think it will take?"

"Most likely a couple of hours. We have a suite at a hotel just a few minutes from your place. We'd like to meet there."

Agent Griffiths then gave me the relevant contact information. My mind raced.

What will they want me to do?

I'd seen my share of detective shows. I had a mental picture of myself wearing a wire, trying to appear composed while attempting to coax incriminating statements from shady characters.

After my afternoon lessons, I swung by my house to get cleaned up and then headed to the hotel, room 105. Griffiths opened the door before I even knocked.

How do they do that?

He had been joined by another agent, Special Agent Lewis.

Lewis was almost a clone of Griffiths, but a little bit younger. He had a New England accent, which contrasted interestingly with Griffiths' native Virginia drawl. We sat around the table in the small suite.

"The best plan of action is to utilize your current position in an attempt to simulate a blackmail of the counterfeiting organization, similar to that which Mr. Brooks was doing on his own, apparently illegally."

"Yeah, we thought of that. But Frankie ended up—"

"Right," Agent Lewis said. "We'll provide a security detail at all times. But, we're not going to lie to you. There is some risk in what we're asking you to do. If these people murdered Franklin Brooks, then they may have little compunction against doing the same to you."

"That's comforting. So what is it you want me to do?"

"We want you to approach Trevor Dunne, the purchaser at Chesapeake Bluffs, and tell him you are aware he is procuring counterfeit equipment and getting kickbacks from the distributor. Insist on talking to his source and working out a deal for payments in order to keep this quiet, otherwise threaten him with exposure and jail time."

"Do you know for sure that Trevor's getting kickbacks?" I asked.

"We've uncovered regular wire transfers of close to five thousand dollars per month into a bank account registered in his name over the last three years."

"How about the mis-registered golf clubs?"

"The MacKenna Corporation has been very helpful in providing records to the FBI. Obviously, they're interested in cracking down on any illegal counterfeiting activity. It appears that one distributor of the MacKenna equipment, GolfLinx Corporation, is involved in the importation of counterfeit golf equipment. They provide equipment to quite a few country clubs in this region. They're headquartered just down the road from here. That's quite convenient, from our point of view.

"The evidence for GolfLinx's counterfeiting seems to be compelling. Now we'd like to pin the murder charge on the principals involved. And if they've done it once, chances are they may have done it before. Our best bet is to use you to draw them out with the fake blackmail scheme."

"By 'drawing them out,' you mean using me as bait?"

"You already have a connection to the counterfeiters through Dunne, so you're the logical choice. Plus, you've expressed an interest in solving Mr. Brooks' murder. Have you told anyone else beside your brother about your murder theory? Mr. Brooks' widow? Anyone else at Chesapeake Bluffs?"

I thought for a while. I was pretty sure that I had never mentioned the murder theory to Lisa. There was Cody, however.

Kevin was right. I should have left Cody out of this.

"Nobody else knows about the murder theory, I'm sure. I'm currently working for Lisa Brooks, preparing a lawsuit against Frankie's insurance company. They've denied payment on the basis of suicide. Lisa knows about the secret bank account payments, however. She's also aware of the gambling debts, the ones we put in the presentation."

"Plus," I continued, "I am housing a golf intern in my home, Cody Corrigan. He helped me track down the counterfeit serial numbers, so he's aware of my concerns in that area."

The agents looked at one another. "We'll need to talk to him, and make sure he understands the gravity of the situation. We're pretty convincing when we have to be."

"You're not married, I see," said Griffiths, shuffling his paperwork, presumably information about me, "but it says here you have a girlfriend, a Ms. Darby St. Claire. I see she occasionally sleeps at your house."

What the hell? Do they know our favorite positions, too?

"Sometimes I go over to her place," I said, dismayed by the latest revelation of government intrusion into my private life. "But you probably knew that already."

"We'll have to talk to her too, so she knows to expect some changes in the routine while this goes on."

I suppose I'd have to tell Ms. Haywood, too.

After Sharon delivered the latest Monday report, she hung around for a while. It appeared as if she wanted to say something more.

"Take a look at this," she finally said, handing me a business

card.
"This is a joke, right?"
"I'm afraid not," she said.
This was too much. They got points for creativity. The card
read:

Chesapeake Muffs
Premiere Escort Service
"Where everyone gets a hole-in-one"

A figure drawing of a partially-naked woman's torso was
overlaid as a graphic, covering most of the card. They had
appropriated the Chesapeake Bluffs' logo in the corner of the card,
with large letters in blue and gold, changing only the second letter,
but keeping an identical style.
"Doesn't anyone just think about golf anymore? Don't tell
me you got this card from your husband," I said.
"Lloyd doesn't need to go out looking for mu...," she said,
stopping suddenly after realizing what she was getting herself into. "I
mean—"
"I'm kidding," I said. "Where *did* you get this?"
"A caddy. Apparently, they're everywhere. He said they were
even giving them out on street corners."
I was reminded of my last trip to Vegas, where aggressive
card snappers congregated at every corner on the strip, attempting to
hand out their escort service invitations to every male passerby, even
those travelling in couples or families.
The morality of this business didn't particularly bother me,
but the takeoff of our name and logo was an infringement of our
trademark and intellectual property. It tarnished our brand, which
was one of the most valuable and well-respected in the country.
One fact had been drilled into us in law school. "If the
owners of trademarks do not vigorously enforce their marks, they
risk loss of the trademark rights."
And one thing was for certain, I intended to enforce our
rights vigorously against the Muffs.
"I'm on it," I told Sharon.
I was pretty sure I could shut those Muffs down for good. I

called the number on the card.

"Chesapeake Muffs. How can we handle your... *needs* today?" The voice dripped with sensuality.

I explained who I was, and why I was concerned with their appropriation of our intellectual property.

"Why don't you come down here? Maybe we can work something out that would be mutually beneficial. You know, you help us, we help you...."

Clearly, she wasn't one to give up easily. I did need an address in which to send an official cease-and-desist letter, so I played along.

"Ok, can you give me directions to your place?"

That finally got me the address instead of another come-on.

"When can we expect to see you, Desmond?"

"You can expect a letter from Chesapeake Bluffs requesting that you immediately cease use of your company name and our logo. If you don't stop immediately, you will be the recipient of a lawsuit demanding damages and punitive penalties."

"You're no fun at all," she said, "but the punitive part does sound kind of kinky."

"Do you understand what I'm staying?" I said, undeterred by her flagrant overtures.

"I understand perfectly, Mr. Thomas," she said, abruptly dropping the sensual tone. "We need a new name and logo. If you have any suggestions, please let me know. I need all the *input* I can get."

With that last bit of innuendo, I hung up.

Who said trademark law was boring.

At the end of the day, I sat in my living room, notes splayed on the table in front of me, wondering if any of this was worth risking my life. How much did it matter whether someone used authentic clubs or not, especially considering that most of the victims couldn't tell the difference, and would be content to remain ignorant of their exploitation.

I'd learned far too much about my friend in the past few months, things that I never would have wanted to know, disheartening things. Gambling, depression, an affair, blackmail. Each new piece of information had come as a shock.

The root of the problem, the gambling compulsion, was what drove Frankie toward his downfall. I wished he'd talked to me about his problem, but it's not in the nature of the disease. Addicts' brains are wired differently.

Two months ago, Frankie was my oldest and closest friend, the guy who always had my back, the one who had offered me a hand when I was at my lowest point, my college roommate.

It was too late to change his fate, but I could still do this one thing. I could find these people, and make them pay. The people who'd killed Frankie weren't struggling addicts, they were cold-blooded murderers.

I called Trevor. All of my phones were now being monitored, of course, so the FBI would have a record of everything that was said. This particular phone was a pre-paid cell, supplied by the agency. I had the full power of the US government's top investigative experts at my disposal, watching over me, guarding my person.

Why was it then, immediately after tapping the final digit, that I no longer felt safe?

"Hello."

"Hello, Trevor. This is Desmond Thomas. You got a moment?"

"Uh-oh. A phone call from the Club lawyer after hours. That can't be good. Yeah, sure. What's up?"

I glanced down at the first note card on the table.

Stick to the script, don't improvise.

"I know that you guys are selling counterfeit equipment. I've run the serial numbers on sets of clubs that were sold in the pro-shop, and I know that they're fakes with duplicate numbers."

"I don't know what you're talking about." His voice changed to a whisper. "Why are you calling me at home about this?"

"Would you rather I call you at work?" I made my best attempt at a snarl.

"I know you're getting kickbacks, so you're making some pretty good money on this scheme. I want my share, or I'm going to the police."

"You're crazy," he stammered. "You're a lawyer. What do you think you're doing?"

"I want a meeting with your connection."

"I don't know if I can do that," he said, clearly unnerved at such a prospect.

"You will make it happen, and I want the meeting in a public place. Call me tomorrow with the details, on this number, not any other number. Got it?"

"These people," he said haltingly, "you don't know them."

I glanced down at the script. There was only one more line before "hang-up."

"Get me a meeting tomorrow, or I go to the authorities."

I ended the call.

The two agents in my living room relaxed for a moment. Griffiths was still on the line with someone else. Finally he nodded and took off his headset.

"Good job," he noted. "We've got all his home and cell lines tapped, plus we're recording all electronic data coming out of his home and office, so if he calls, texts, or emails, we'll know what he's saying. We should know pretty soon if he's getting in touch with someone, unless he goes out and buys another phone, a burner. My bet is he'll do something within the next ten minutes."

I wondered how long this saga would go on, now that the process had been initiated. I reached down and picked up the script for tomorrow's meeting. In addition to golf pro, attorney, and private-eye, it appeared I would soon be adding actor to my list of occupations.

I grabbed a table by the window, arriving a little early for the 7:00 p.m. rendezvous. I was told that agents would already be positioned both inside and outside the restaurant. I glanced around without any sign of recognition, but I had to assume that was intentional, so that I didn't lock eyes with a familiar agent, arousing suspicion. I wasn't wired. Instead, the FBI was using software that allowed them to eavesdrop on my cell phone, even while it was powered-off. I refused to consider the ramifications of that for my personal life, at least for the time-being.

My new position as bait left me feeling vulnerable. The nice thing about a worm is that it doesn't realize when it's being used as bait. Being bait that's self-aware is much more troubling to the psyche. But at least I didn't have a giant hook rammed up my ass.

I went over the lines in my head. Playing against type, I rehearsed my new persona—demanding, rude, and corrupt. It was a total makeover.

An attractive woman sat down at my table, coming out of nowhere. I'd seen her before. Dark hair, mid-forties, well-heeled. She was the one who'd been locking horns with Frankie in that 8x10 glossy Bull had shown me. No mystery now about the topic of their little conference.

"You've got some balls," she said. "What is it that you want from us?"

"Just my fair share, so you can keep your business going. And stay out of jail."

"Your fair share of what? I don't see you taking any risks. What makes you think you can shake us down?"

"I'm a little uncomfortable talking to someone whose name I don't even know."

"You can call me Ms. Green."

"Ok, *Ms. Green*, to answer your question, knowledge is power. I seem to have all this knowledge rattling around inside my head, and I can't make it go away."

"What do you think you know?"

"I know enough to bring your whole operation crashing to the ground, and I've got lots of connections who'd love to do it."

The waitress interrupted. "Would you like anything to drink, Ma'am?"

"Water," she barked, refusing to even make eye contact.

"Be right back," the waitress responded cheerfully.

She continued, "You're bluffing. What's in it for you if you bring us down? You'll get nothing."

The agents had prepared me for this line of reasoning.

"This can be a win-win, or lose-lose. I take it you don't want to lose everything, neither do I."

"How much do you want?"

"Fifty thousand every month, starting tomorrow, wired to my account."

"50K? You're insane. That's more money than we take in."

"You forget. I'm the attorney. I have access to all the records at the Club. We sold 1.2 million dollars of your shit last year. Now you've got what, a dozen other country clubs? Let's say you gross ten million, and that's conservative. Now you're buying the stuff on the cheap, so to speak, so maybe your costs are three, four million tops. That's six million a year net, or five hundred thousand a month. All I'm asking for is a measly ten percent. Think of it as a tithe. You give cheerfully, good things happen, like you get to stay out of jail."

"You're a greedy son-of-a-bitch. I can't authorize that kind of payment. I'll have to talk to my people."

"At least I'm just a *son*-of-a-bitch. And if I were greedy, Ms. Green, I'd ask for twenty percent. I don't care if you need to talk to the Dalai Lama or the Pope, just as long as you get it to me tomorrow."

I slid her a piece of paper with the numbers to the bank account that the FBI had created for me. She looked at it.

"It'll take a miracle to get you that much money by tomorrow. I hope you know that."

"What I know is that it's entirely possible, if you get your ass in gear. The Swiss banks open in a few hours. You've got my number. Nice doing business with you. "

Indignant, she snatched the paper off the table and shot up from her chair. She hadn't anticipated that the waitress would arrive at that very moment, our drinks on her tray. The tray exploded into the air, glasses and water flying in all directions, the glasses finally smashing on the tiled floor. Every eye in the restaurant turned to the calamitous scene.

Green recovered, looked around, and quickly made a beeline to the door, without so much as a word to the dripping waitress, who stared at the retreating figure with shock and disbelief.

It's been said that you can tell a lot about a person's character by the way they treat the help.

There just might be something to that.

Chapter 20

The wire transfer hit my new Swiss bank account in the morning. $50,000 in less than twelve hours.

Clearly I'm in the wrong line of work.

This extortion business was way too easy. I should have thought of it years ago. A few hours of work and bingo, guaranteed income for the rest of my life. Of course, the rest of my life might only be a few more days, but still, the underlying concept was totally valid.

According to the FBI, I needed to carry on with my work as if nothing odd was happening. The agents were surreptitiously scattered around the premises. How they managed this, I'm not totally sure, since any official cooperation with the Bluffs' management would have been sure to alert Evan, who was, to my knowledge, one of the prime targets of the operation. But the FBI had their "ways," and whenever I inquired about it, they gave me their standard response—"Don't worry, we've got it covered."

We even had a code name: "Operation Knee-Knocker." That was cute, since a knee-knocker was golf slang for a putt in the three to four foot range that caused many golfers to become nervous. It was a putt that you should make, but still long enough that it was by no means a gimme. Somebody at the FBI obviously thought this applied to my role, although I thought I'd been handling things pretty well up to this point.

I was pretty sure that there wouldn't be agents inside the Club offices, where I worked mornings. The FBI assured me they had agents outside to cover me on the driving range. I made sure my cell phone was operational. After they told me about their snooping software, I searched the web and discovered that the feds had been using this technique for quite some time. There was even a commercial version available now. Kevin and Bull would love to know about this. Hell, they probably had it already.

There were civil liberty questions with this kind of surveillance, but in my case, I was sure my right to stay above room temperature trumped anyone else's right not to be overheard via my phone. I kept the battery well charged. I even kept a spare one on me at all times. I wasn't being paranoid, just proactive.

I asked the agents about assassins hiding in the woods. I was visualizing a crack shooter, ex-military type most likely, hidden in the trees with a telescopic sight, taking aim at me while I was occupied with lessons on the driving range. That thought always ended in a shudder. Of course, the agents told me that they "had it covered." They also mentioned that most likely, the perpetrators would be trying to make it look like an accidental or self-inflicted death. An assassin shooting a golf pro on the driving range would tend to draw a lot of publicity and a subsequent investigation, precisely what these people didn't want.

I felt so much better.

However, they also told me, in no uncertain terms, not to play on any of the courses while Operation Knee-Knocker was ongoing. "We can't guarantee your safety while you're traveling up and down the fairways, especially if you're by yourself. There are far too many places for them to hide, and way too many places for us to cover."

Bummer.

I thought about explaining to them how the Bluffs' annual pro-intern golf tournament was coming up next weekend, and how it would be a major disappointment if I couldn't attend. Rather than argue about it now, I'd hold off and see how things panned out. Maybe this would all be over. One could always dream.

The FBI had even given me a safe word, the panic word to indicate trouble. Sticking with the golf theme, my safe word was "ball washer." The word, or words in this case, had to at least be plausible to use in a conversation, but not so common that I would say it by accident.

To avoid such a situation, I was told I had to mention my safe words twice before the agents would come, avoiding, for example, the awkwardness of having the FBI barge in during a golf lesson where I had accidentally mentioned the sacred phrase. It might be somewhat difficult to restore the operation's secrecy after such a mishap.

My use of the safe word had to be purposeful, direct, and nonchalant. I tried to work on some examples in advance, "I'm thinking about ordering some more ball washers. You just can't have too many ball washers." Or perhaps: "What's your opinion of ball washers? I haven't used my ball washer in quite some time."

Clearly, I needed to work on that.

Despite all the precautions, I was left wondering if I was the proverbial sitting duck. I asked the agents if they were tapping the bad guys' phones with the same surveillance tools they had on mine. They just gave me the FBI look, which I came to learn, translated to "you know better than to ask that."

For whatever reasons, the agents were confident that the bad guys would make their move within the next few weeks. This knowledge didn't leave me with a warm fuzzy feeling. Did they have some legitimate intelligence on these people? And if they did, wasn't that enough, in and of itself, to bring them in for attempted murder? How far did they have to string them along before they could charge them?

I don't like long strings.

In an attempt to ease my frayed nerves, the FBI gave me a smattering of information. They had twenty-four hour surveillance on me and my property. They had agents equipped with infrared and night vision goggles stationed in the woods and the golf course at night around the house.

And they did let me in on one other major tactic. Actually, they kind of had to tell me. This one would prove to be an effective antidote for a serious case of knee-knocking.

"We need to talk."

The voice at the door startled me. I'd thought I had the office building to myself.

Despite the FBI's precautions, I still felt jittery, every day, almost continuously. At any instant, I knew I could be a target. Most likely, I wouldn't know it until it was too late, if at all. My safe word wouldn't do me a whole lot of good after getting plugged in the back of the head by a .45.

Much to my surprise, I'd found nothing in the company rules that forbade me from packing my own heat, so I had taken to wearing my gun and holster inside my jacket. I hadn't mentioned this to anyone. No sense in creating a situation, and forgiveness is much easier than permission, especially with the FBI. I tried very hard to remember not to take the jacket off during the day.

Given the restrictions on my social life that this operation entailed, I'd gotten into the habit of returning to the office after lessons to try to catch up on my ever-expanding backlog of legal work, which was where I found myself now, getting ready to settle in for a thrilling evening of contract reviews.

Evan entered the room, closing the door behind him.

Uh-oh.

"Trevor talked with me today," he said, as he took a seat directly across from me.

I hadn't expected it to go down like this. Maybe he wanted to talk some sense into me, to get my demands down to an acceptable level, rather than just trying to get rid of me, like they'd done with Frankie. Maybe he was the designated middle-man between the murderers and the retail conspirators who were just in it to get a few more bucks.

"What's this thing with Trevor all about?" he asked.

I decided to play dumb, having no real idea where he was headed.

"I don't know what you're talking about," I said.

"That's not what Trevor said. He tells me you're hurting our business. We've got a problem, and we need to take care of it, one way or another."

Evan's hand slid into his jacket.

Oh my god, he's packing too.

As I'd practiced some thirty-odd times in front of the mirror at home, I made my move, jamming my hand between jacket and shirt and grabbing the handle of my gun, finger on the trigger. No second chances.

Our hands came out simultaneously, mine holding a handgun, his, a handkerchief.

It was too late for me to hide it. I hadn't actually pointed it at him, but it had gotten very close.

He stared at the revolver, then at me, then back at the gun. I finally had the presence of mind to put the damn thing back in the holster.

Without saying another word, he stood up and calmly walked out of the room, leaving me alone to ponder what had just happened.

I had just pulled a gun on my boss.

I could probably kiss that raise goodbye.

4:00 a.m. Five minutes after pulling the Jeep off the old dirt road that formed the western boundary of the Chesapeake Bluffs' property, the two men had almost made their way through the wooded area that would bring them to the fairway on course No. 5. The new moon helped conceal them from anyone who, by some odd chance of circumstance, may have been looking out in their direction at this early morning hour.

Billy Walker, the older of the two, had led the pair through the woods with the ease of an expert, which of course, he was. The area still smelled of the fire that had laid waste to so many acres a few short weeks ago. The night vision goggles that both men now wore helped them to avoid running headfirst into one of the oaks or other hardwoods that populated the terrain. Trained as Special Forces, Billy had superb outdoor survival and navigation skills, but even more so than that, he was a natural outdoorsman. Growing up in western Tennessee, he had spent the better part of his youth exploring.

Things hadn't gone well for Billy after his dishonorable discharge from the military. It wasn't that he hadn't been able to handle the work in the service. That was the easy part. He just didn't take too well to having people telling him what to do all day long, when he knew well enough that there was a better way to do it. The Army, being the Army, didn't see it that way.

His job as a contractor in Afghanistan had gone well, while it lasted. The money was great, but after a year, his company had lost its contract—something about fraud, waste and corruption—and he wasn't picked up by anyone else. Billy came back home and hung out at the farm, his old stomping grounds. But as always, he got bored, and when his old Army buddy, Charlie Peterson, said he could fix him up doing some contract work in Virginia, Billy jumped at the chance.

"Good money, if you can handle it," Charlie said. "I'd do it myself, but that's not my area of expertise."

Billy was not one to turn away from a challenge, and the good money was just gravy. He hadn't asked Charlie what kind of "contract work" he would be doing, and in truth, he hadn't really wanted to know. He figured that when the time came, he'd find out. Killing a man for hire wasn't much different than killing a man in combat, he'd told himself when he got his first assignment. It would be a private war. Just follow orders and don't get caught. Tonight's job would be his seventh so far. At $10,000 a pop, Billy wasn't complaining.

When the men reached the edge of the trees, they paused and gazed across the fairway, assessing their target. They had to take off the NVG goggles now, as the outdoor lights totally washed out the scene. Ahead of them was their destination, 638 Player Drive, the current dwelling place of one Desmond Thomas. Although Billy would have liked to have claimed credit for the expert navigation, he had to acknowledge that their success was almost totally due to the use of a popular GPS app running on his smart phone.

Billy and his partner, known only as Scrubs, had rehearsed their plan many times over before ever stepping foot in the woods. There was a reason why he'd never been caught. It all came down to planning, rehearsal, and execution. He'd gotten the blueprints of the house. He knew the layout of the rooms, including the master bedroom where Thomas would be sleeping.

They knew there was a dog, a bulldog to be exact. A quick shot in the head would take care of that problem. On to the master bedroom to quickly rouse the sleeping man and shoot him. Silencers would keep the noise down. Take the wallet, grab any valuables, and be off quickly.

It would look like a burglary, pure and simple, one where the homeowner surprised the burglars, who then ended up shooting him during the confrontation. They'd grab his wallet, and not much else, simulating panic after the shooting. They'd be out of there in less than a minute, and long gone before anyone, especially the police, could answer the call.

The men scrutinized the golf course and all the houses within visible range, and saw no signs of activity. Of course, at four on a weekday morning, they hadn't expected to find too many people up. A few insomniacs might still be awake. It was rare to find any populated area where someone wasn't alert these days. The men were careful as always, not taking anything for chance.

They quietly made their way across the dew-covered fairway, their black clothing and painted faces barely discernable in the darkness.

Scrubs used his long metal crowbar to pry the patio door up and away from its track. As soon as the door was clear, Billy rushed inside, light now blazing from a helmet lamp, enabling him to see his way in the dark and also temporarily blinding anyone whom he might encounter.

Billy was surprised when no alarm went off.

Once in a while we get lucky.

He was expecting a dog to be barking and possibly charging at him, but none appeared.

Must not be a guard dog.

Within seconds he made his way to the master bedroom, where he saw the sleeping figure on the bed.

"Get up," Billy yelled at the slumbering form. He had his pistol drawn and ready to fire, if necessary.

Nothing stirred.

Scrubs entered the bedroom seconds later.

"Get your ass up!" he hissed. Scrubs was not, by nature, a patient man. And during a job, where seconds could mean the difference between success and life in jail, his patience dwindled. He wanted to get this job over with and get out of that house, fast, before bad things started happening.

He aimed the gun at the man's head, trigger now cocked.

"No," Billy yelled. "Shit, that's not the way—."

Scrubs squeezed the trigger, directing the 9mm round squarely into the sleeping man's head.

5:45 a.m. A county away from the Bluff's resort, the fourth shot of bourbon put Charlie Peterson in a suitable frame of mind for the task at hand. Well, that along with the two muscle relaxers he'd downed a few hours earlier.

As assistant equipment mechanic, Charlie, along with his boss and three other mechanics, handled repair and maintenance of the entire array of tools, equipment and vehicles used at the Bluffs. They were the people you called when anything mechanical broke.

Charlie was one of those individuals whose lone skill in life lay outside of commonly accepted legal, moral, or ethical boundaries. A professional might have labeled him a mild sociopath. But in general, people liked Charlie. He wasn't the sharpest tool in the shed, but he never went out of his way to deliberately hurt anybody. He just liked to try to take advantage of things.

Taking advantage of things, to Charlie, meant hatching a scheme. Such schemes had allowed him to get through high school by doing a surprisingly small amount of work. Charlie could assess any situation, determine its weak links and devise a plan to utilize them for his own advantage.

While others might have labeled these plans as scams, fraud, or even crimes, Charlie saw no wrongdoing. In his mind, he was using his natural abilities to his best advantage. His efforts were almost always aimed at large organizations, schools, the military, insurance companies, large retailers, and of the most concern lately, his current employer, Chesapeake Bluffs Golf and Country Club.

The Bluffs' maintenance job was generally within his capabilities, and, during the peak summer months, kept him very busy, including overtime, but some of the more routine maintenance tasks, especially during the winter off-season, were mundane and repetitive. Charlie had trouble motivating himself for this type of work.

Last month's big push to prepare and test the new KG golf carts had been hard work, until he'd figured out his own way to beat the system.

His increasing dependence on alcohol and his nagging addiction to pain-killers ate away at what little work resolve he had possessed, and the number of days he called in sick had increased at an alarming pace. In fact, it was only the beginning of July, but Charlie had used up his entire year's allotment of fifteen sick and personal days.

In his own mind, he was justifiably sick. He was sick of having to get up at six to be at work at seven, head pounding from a horrific hangover, mind still dazed from painkillers working their way through his system.

His work performance had slipped drastically. His boss, Dan Waters, who also happened to be his brother-in-law, could no longer count on Charlie to show up. And when he did come in, Dan could rarely give Charlie a task to do that was unsupervised. It would take Charlie two hours to do a job that someone else could do in fifteen minutes, and even then, someone would have to check the work to make sure it was done properly.

Dan liked Charlie, but, even as family, there was a limit to how much longer he could cover for him. He'd forced Charlie to attend a treatment program last year, under threat of termination. It had worked for a while, until Charlie had once again fallen off the wagon.

Even after his wife and kids had left him, Charlie insisted that he was in control and that he could stop the pills and the drinking whenever he wanted. He just needed time to work on this latest ploy that would land him back on his feet.

And "on his feet" was exactly where his latest plan promised to land him. As he stood woozily on the roof of his ramshackle house, he mentally rehearsed.

His goal was to break his own ankle. That, he figured, would be at least enough to get him three months of workers' comp. A nice, long vacation during the hot summer months, with the added benefit of refillable prescriptions for high-quality pain meds.

Of course, the incident had to appear to have occurred at work, so he would just have to endure the pain while he drove there. He knew exactly where he would stage it, the large pothole in the maintenance workers' parking lot. He would park in his usual spot, hobble over to the pothole, sight unseen, then just pretend to trip and fall into it. This, coupled with a scream, would draw people from the shed to serve as witnesses to the event. Since it would still be almost dark at that time, his story would be entirely plausible.

Who knows, he might even be able to come up with a personal injury lawsuit. Lack of good lighting in the parking lot, coupled with an unrepaired pothole that had been known about by management for some time, sounded like a pretty good case to him.

A settlement might set me up for years.

He steeled himself for the jump, vaguely remembering that his goal was to land on his left leg so that he would still be able to drive to work. It looked higher from his current vantage point than it had from the ground, but he needed to make sure that he broke the ankle, not just caused a sprain. It was now or never.

Closing his eyes, Charlie jumped from the sixteen-foot height. On his way down, he pushed his left foot out as far as he could, landing on the concrete driveway to the sound of a sickening crack. He fell to the ground and attempted to roll his body to reduce the secondary impact. An agonizing pain immediately radiated up his leg. He tried to avoid screaming, but the pain was so intense that he could not stifle a yell.

In the dim light, he reached for his lower leg. He felt something odd, and only after a few moments was he able to see the source of his current torment, a huge lump in his lower leg where his bone was now threatening to push its way out of the skin.

6:23 am. I tried to focus on the alarm clock while I fumbled for my phone, the current source of the disturbing noise that awakened me from my blissful and assassin-free sleep. Being roused from a sound sleep usually left me in a disoriented state, but I woke quickly when I realized who was calling.

"Agent Griffiths here. We've apprehended two suspects who broke into your house. They shot your dummy likeness."

I liked the sound of that, my "dummy likeness," although I wasn't sure if they meant that it was like me, a dummy, or just a dummy, like me. Now I was confused.

"Is it over, then?" I asked. "Can I go back home?"

"Not yet. We don't want any lingering potentialities."

"Roger that," I said, appropriating his vernacular. Who was I kidding? I was overjoyed they'd caught the guys. I certainly didn't want to run across any lingering potentialities either, although I'm not sure I'd recognize a potentiality if I saw one.

The FBI's grand deception had gone according to plan. Sensing, as they did, that the plotters would strike in my home at night, the FBI had surreptitiously moved me and Bertha into a safe house a block away. Leaving from work, I swapped vehicles with my FBI double. He drove my car back to my house, while I took the FBI car to my new temporary place. Cody had also been relocated to another residence while the operation was in process.

They even had a dog double for Bertha, a pale imitation a best. No ordinary bulldog could match Bertha's magnificence. My double walked Bertha's double every day at lunchtime, just to keep up appearances. My double wasn't quite as good-looking as I was, but with sunglasses on, and a little makeup, he could pass from a distance.

The FBI had agents stationed both at my house and at the safe house. The dummy likeness slept in my bed, and even wore a pair of my pajamas.

"Are you going to charge them with attempted murder?" I asked the agent.

"We can't divulge details," Griffiths said. "Even if we could, I don't know the whole story yet. To insure your safety, you're going to have to remain in the safe house."

"How about Frankie's murder? Can we pin that on them? It's important for the insurance."

"Like I said, I can't divulge any details."

You're a veritable fount of information.

There was one more thing. Having recently threatened Evan with my pistol, I was more than a little interested to know if my boss was one of the bad guys. I had let the FBI know about my little incident with the gun. Much to my chagrin, that had prompted them to take the gun away, for "my protection," until the operation was over.

"Is Evan McDermott involved?"

"We have no evidence of that. I'm going to talk with him in a few hours. I think you'll be ok. You'd be surprised what a visit from the FBI can do."

"Keep me posted, because I am not going to work with him thinking I pulled a gun on him, which I did, but, you know what I mean."

"By the way," Griffiths added, "you shouldn't be too worried about any more visits from Detective Reed, or Lucas Bennett. We've got them under surveillance, part of a new operation."

The concerns of the past months began to drain away. No more murder plots, drug charges, arsonists, counterfeiters, break-ins, conspiracies or threats. The FBI had it under control. I vaguely recalled what it was like not to live every moment in constant fear. Maybe Darby could help me get back to those days of innocence. On second thought, I rather enjoyed Darby's lack of innocence....

"Lingering potentialities be damned," I said to Bertha, who was awake with stump wagging and tongue flapping.

"Time to take you out, princess." It would be the first time outside in a long while. I could tell she was getting tired of talking her walks on the artificial turf in the garage.

I yanked on the sliding doors that led out to the back yard from the bedroom, only to be reminded that the FBI had fastened them securely to prevent just such a thing from happening. I'd have to go out the front door, past the agent stationed there.

"Good morning Agent Morris," I said cheerfully. "I heard the good news. I think it's about time I take Bertha for a walk."

"No can do, Mr. Thomas. What I'm hearing is that we're keeping the cover going until we're specifically told to halt operations. That means no appearing outside in this yard. Sorry about that, but those are the orders. Sorry, Bertha."

Agent Morris scratched my dog behind her ear, as if this would make the news more palatable. Bertha, clearly not as indignant as I, rolled over in a shameless bid for more affection.

You're way too easy, woman.

I knew better than to argue with the agents. They were pleasant enough if you stuck to their plan. If you tried to deviate, even by the smallest degree, they tended to get serious. And when these guys got serious, they weren't much fun to hang with.

I was anxious to bring my relationship with Darby out of hibernation. But that wasn't going to happen until the FBI officially shut down Operation Knee-Knocker.

Until then, I could only hope and dream. But there was nothing to say that they couldn't be incredibly, fantastically realistic dreams. Even the long arm of the law had its limits.

Chapter 21

Three long, excruciating days after the untimely demise of my dummy likeness, Operation Knee-Knocker was officially declared complete. My first responsibility was to inform Lisa. Rather than sending their agents, the agency showed a little bit of heart by allowing me the privilege.

I wasn't even sure she would answer the phone, after the way our last visit had ended, but the first thing she did after answering was apologize.

"I was just in a bad place that day," she said. "I didn't mean to take it out on you."

"No need to apologize. I understand. But I've got some news."

I wanted to wait until I met with her in person to tell her the whole story, but I did let her know in our phone conversation that she'd be getting the insurance money in a few weeks.

In person, she had a hard time absorbing all the information, but I was able to impress upon her that her husband's killers had been apprehended, and that the FBI had proof that Frankie had been murdered.

Of course, she wanted to know all about the operation, and I revealed what I could, including her husband's involvement with the extortion scheme and his subsequent murder by the same people that attempted to do me in. I decided not to tell her about the affair. She'd had enough bad news about Frankie already.

To say she was stunned would have been an understatement, but instead of the multitude of questions I expected, she had only a single response.

She gave me a hug.

That was reward enough.

As a result of the FBI's operation, Trevor Dunne had been taken into custody as part of the counterfeiting conspiracy, the only employee of Chesapeake Bluffs known to be involved. Apparently, they'd arrested him at his home, discreetly.

Ms. Green, aka Elizabeth Norris, President of GolfLinx, had been apprehended, along with several of her partners, and charged with counterfeiting and murder. From what I'd heard, their arrests hadn't been quite so discreet. In addition to Trevor, the buyers at several other well-known country clubs had been implicated in the counterfeiting ring. The operation had turned into a major coup for Special Agent Griffiths. I think he owed me.

As I'd suspected, buyers at these country clubs sent defective equipment back to GolfLinx for exchange. GolfLinx kept extra counterfeit stock on hand, and replaced the clubs. Never sending any clubs back to the manufacturer, they bypassed registration, thus keeping their scheme intact.

I waited until Griffiths had his heart-to-heart with Evan before going into work. I had no idea what Evan was going to say when he saw me, but as I entered the lobby, there he was.

"Desmond, I had no idea," he said.

"Well, that *was* the idea," I said. "We had to be secretive. I was under orders. And we weren't exactly sure who was involved. It might have been someone in management. Sorry I pulled a gun on you, man. I was a little paranoid."

Evan didn't comment on the insinuation or on my apology. Likely still dazed over the news that his buyer was under arrest, that his pro-shop had been selling counterfeit golf clubs, and worst of all, that a murder had taken place on course No. 3, he let it go.

"Take some time off," he said. "You've earned it."

"I might just take you up on that," I said, feeling that if I'd ever earned an extended break, this was it. I guess putting your life on the line has its advantages.

But the big news was that I could return to my own house, complete with sleepover privileges. And I intended to take full advantage of those privileges. Bertha was thrilled to, once again, be able to pee in the great outdoors. I was also allowed to play golf, and not just any golf. I was playing in the annual Van Avery Cup, *the* golf event of the summer.

The tournament, held always during the first week of July, had been the highlight of my student internship at the Bluffs. It had been recently renamed as the Van Avery Cup to honor the longest-serviced employee at the Bluffs. As one of the course pros, I would get to participate, this time from the pro side. I was more than ready.

Each pro paired with his intern. The tournament used the "alternate shot" format. Playing the same ball, pro and intern would alternate shots. This was a format that was used in many Ryder cup matches.

As a result of my pairing with Cody, our team was the distinct underdog. Apparently, the general perception was that his handicap had rendered him, and therefore our team, as a less-than-serious threat. The truth of the matter was that Cody had been practicing every single day he'd been here. He was still acclimating to the Handygolfer, which meant that his proficiency was increasing at a much faster pace than all the other interns.

I had seen him at the driving range countless times, routinely hitting drive after drive 250 yards down the middle of the fairway. Not a great distance by pro standards, it was extraordinary considering he was using his upper body alone.

With our six course-pros and interns, we had three foursomes. Much to my regret, we found ourselves matched with Rodney and his intern, in the final group. Rodney smirked when informed of the pairing. Of course, he smirked at just about anything, that's the way he was. He was smirking a little less lately now that I was investigating him for sexual harassment. Clearly, he was primed for revenge.

We would be playing on No. 3, the Bluffs' signature course. Viewing had been opened to the public, and the match had been publicized in the local papers, which usually meant it hit the wires and the internet golf sites. People had heard about the "wheelchair player," as Cody had become known. He was a curiosity factor.

The tournament was a popular local event. I estimated at least 500 spectators, probably more. Darby, of course, was watching, and I was pleased that Kevin brought Jessica, his current flame. Evan, Dan Waters, Sharon, Milton and of course Van Avery were there. Trevor Dunne was noticeably absent. Kerry Boggs had made the drive from the university. Valu-U was dedicated and supportive of its student interns, and Cody clearly deserved that support, along with any alumni who happened to be playing.

Sadly, pets were not allowed, so Bertha, by far my most enthusiastic supporter, had to remain at home, watching the match on TV. I limited her to two beers.

No. 3 at the Bluffs demanded pinpoint accuracy. Its constricted fairways punished those who strayed from the straight and narrow by plunging their shots into the Chesapeake Bay or into tall grass or deep bunkers. Big hitters didn't necessarily fare well here, unless they were extremely accurate. Overhitting the fairway often brought worse results than playing a shorter, more accurate shot.

Cody had the honor of starting for our team. The kids in the crowd were mesmerized by his mechanical maneuvering, becoming instant fans. A significant portion of the crowd lingered to watch our foursome play.

As the crowd watched intently, Cody took his swing, and the ball screamed down the fairway, inches above the ground, bouncing and scorching every living thing in its path, a true, honest-to-god worm-burner.

It was the poorest shot I'd seen him make this summer, and was, without a doubt, totally attributable to first-hole jitters.

Cody was mortified.

"It's good to get that one out of the way," I told him. "I've done way worse in my time." It was true. Plus his shot, even as low as it was, still went about 150 yards, so it wouldn't be impossible to recover a par on this hole. It's not the best tournament opener, but people remember the closing shots a lot longer. That I knew all too well.

Kyle, Rodney's intern, hit next, and blasted a nice drive about 260 yards, keeping it on the edge of the fairway.

From Cody's lie, I was 270 yards away from the small green bordered by water on the left and sand almost everywhere else. It would have been an extremely risky shot to shoot for the green, so I played it safe and laid the ball up, leaving a short pitch over the bunkers which would hopefully let us get up and down in two.

Rodney put his team on the green, ten feet from the cup.

Cody recovered and made a beautiful pitch that landed behind the flag and rolled back to within four feet. The crowd roared. It was clear that almost all of them were on our side, and we'd finally given them something to cheer about.

Kyle just missed his ten footer, after which I holed my putt, so each team came away with a par. Redemption. The crowd buzzed.

Cody settled into his game, playing effortlessly through the next holes. His short, consistent game meshed perfectly with my longer one. Heading into 14, we were up by two strokes on our foursome opponents. Rodney wasn't in such a boisterous mood anymore. Kyle was focal point for his current foul spirit, taking the brunt of Rodney's increasingly caustic verbal abuse without returning a word. Kyle was a good guy. He didn't deserve Rodney.

I had to speak up, even if only to redirect Rodney's wrath away from his young partner.

"Why don't you lay off the kid, Rodney? He's been playing great today. Can't say the same for you."

"Why don't you mind your own fucking business," Rodney replied, predictably. "He's my intern, and I get to say whatever I want, whenever I want. If he doesn't like it, and he can stand up for himself, unlike *your* buddy there."

My blood boiled. I moved in close, inches away from his face. "You will never talk to my intern, or anybody else that way when I'm around, understand? You're a short-timer here Collingsworth. I'm going to make sure of that." I felt like slugging the asshole, and I probably would have, given one more insulting word.

He backed off. I heard him mutter something to Kyle. I was pretty sure it wasn't too complimentary.

I was breathing heavily now, juiced up by the aftereffects of the adrenaline from brief confrontation. I tried to force myself to settle down.

Take a deep breath.

The scenic 14th hole should have been the highlight of the No. 3 course, but it would be forever in my mind linked to Frankie's death. He was an afterthought to most people now, and his legacy, whatever it had been, was working its way toward being forgotten by almost everyone.

Cody teed off, and hit his usual shot, splitting the center of the fairway, leaving us in perfect position to hit the island green with our second shot. Kyle nearly duplicated Cody's shot, hitting his ball just a few yards farther.

As we approached our ball, I paused at the rail, peering down at the rocky shoreline. Surveying the scene, I couldn't help but imagine how it might feel to fall, or be thrown, from such a height.

I lined up beside our ball, playing one less club than the distance dictated, since the drop down to the green gave the ball about ten yards of additional travel. I swung and hit the ball cleanly, maybe too cleanly. I must have swung a little harder than usual; I guess I was still a little pumped up.

The ball sailed over the green, striking the rocks that formed the barrier between grass and water. There was a one-in-a-million chance that the ball would ricochet up in the air and drop back onto the green. This wasn't it, however, and the ball rebounded far away, splashing into the bay. In an instant, we'd lost two strokes.

"Nice one, Thomas," Rodney gloated. "Guess you showed us."

Cody put the next shot on the green and we two-putted for a double-bogey. Our opponents made par, and suddenly, we were tied for the lead.

Each team kept pace over the next three holes, keeping us even going into the final hole of the tournament. We were two shots ahead of our nearest competitors, so barring a total collapse, it was down to one of us for the title.

The 18th hole was another of No. 3's beauties. The right side of the narrow fairway was bounded by rocky cliffs. The left fairway was bordered by bunkers.

Complicating matters was the steady breeze off the bay, which made all balls drift to the left, a factor that had to be accounted for in nearly every shot. Even some of the longer putts were affected by the wind, enough to turn a sure thing into a "lipper."

Kyle hit first, aiming slightly to the right, and smacked a high hard drive. As his shot arced upwards, the offshore winds took over, and the ball drifted, picking up right-to-left lateral speed as it hung in the air. By the time it landed, the ball was almost all the way on the left side of the fairway, and after two more bounces, it was comfortably ensconced in the fairway bunker. Rodney cursed loudly.

"Watch the language," I admonished. "We've got a lot of people watching today, not counting the cameras. There are a few spectators who still don't realize what a loser you are."

He gave me a look of pure hatred, and continued to stare straight at me while mouthing a steady stream of silent invectives, most of which I could understand from basic lip-reading 101. I could easily imagine him exploding at any moment, turning into a whirling dervish like some sort of Tasmanian devil on speed.

Now this is what I call a golf match.

Cody seemed to have taken careful note of the effects of the wind on Kyle's ball. He lined up considerably more to the right than Kyle, adjusting his cart to the precise angle with infinitesimal refinements to his controls. His shot promised to head directly into the bay. I cringed, but sure enough, the relentless breeze swept the ball back into play. It landed on the right side of the fairway and rolled, stopping almost dead-center, 240 yards out. It was not his longest shot of the day, but it was, without a doubt, his best.

I'd played this hole many times in the past, both during my internship and during the practice rounds for the Open. The approach shot at 18 was one of the toughest shots on the entire course. I pulled my five-iron out of my bag, a signal to Cody that we would be going for the pin. He nodded. I had 200 yards to the flag, which today was nestled on the right side of the green, surrounded by bunkers in front, on the right and behind.

Aiming to the right, I tried to account for the ever-present winds. I had only about twenty yards front-to-back to work with on the green. Hitting quickly, I let the shot fly. And at precisely that moment, the winds shut down. Instead of drifting back on the green, my shot stayed right. For a brief moment, I thought it might catch the fringe, but it missed by inches, plunging into the extreme edge of the bunker to the right of the green. It looked to be a terrible lie. We could be in big trouble.

"Tough break, Big D," Rodney yelled, face aglow with new hope. All he had to do was keep his ball out of the bunkers and two-putt, and he'd probably have the win. He hit a nice shot, but his ball, coming out of the sand, didn't have enough backspin to stick on the green. It continued rolling and stopped, some 5 yards off the back edge.

As we approached, I realized we had a huge problem. The ball was located at the edge of the bunker on an almost vertical slope. There didn't appear to be any way that Cody could maneuver his cart into position behind the ball without tipping over.

Stick a fork in us.

Our opponents' ball was farthest away, about 20 yards from the pin. Kyle took his time and hit an excellent chip shot, the ball rolling past the pin by about five feet.

Cody could punch the ball out of the sand trap back in the direction of the tee box, and I could chip onto the green from there. But, barring a miracle chip, that would mean our best hope would be a five.

But Cody wasn't going down quietly. He pulled an unusual club out of his bag, literally the shortest club I'd ever seen. It couldn't have been over two feet long. It was as if he'd swiped a club from a four-year-old's toy golf set.

Rodney took one look and burst out laughing. He started a running commentary.

"Hand me a rulebook. Isn't there a rule against using Smurf clubs? This is priceless, I gotta get this on video. YouTube moment, right here." He pulled out his phone, aiming the camera at the scene.

Undaunted, Cody drove his cart up to the edge of the sand, and unbuckled his chest restraint. I began to see what he had in mind. I gave him a hand as he slid himself out of the seat, and scooted into position in the sand trap. He was going to hit the ball out of the trap while kneeling in the sand. This was why he needed the shortest club in the world.

No one knew what to expect from such a shot, as I'm fairly sure no one had ever seen anyone attempt anything quite like it. Being in the sand, he wasn't allowed to ground the club, as that would result in a penalty stroke. He had only a single attempt, from this awkward position, to get the ball onto the green.

Cody took a full swing with the pint-sized wedge. The sand exploded, and out of the cloud I saw the ball emerge, shooting straight up into the air, reaching a height of perhaps fifteen feet before beginning its descent—straight back down. It looked as if it were going to fall back exactly where it started. We would then be totally screwed. But Cody had managed to put the slightest bit of forward momentum on the ball, and that momentum, coupled with the resurgent breeze off the water, enabled the ball to hit on the lip of the turf, just inches from the trap opening. The ball bounced on the sloped terrain and kicked toward the green, rolling until it stopped, three feet from the hole.

The gallery went wild. Kerry Boggs was practically doing cartwheels. It was the most remarkable shot I had ever witnessed. From his vantage point, shielded by the steep bunker wall, Cody couldn't even see the green, much less his ball, but he knew from the reaction that something must have gone right. He emerged, totally covered in sand, grinning from ear-to-ear.

Rodney threw down his phone in disgust. Payback time.

"Big R," I yelled out, "could you send me a copy of that video?"

Rodney's response could be summarized with a single finger. Symbolic speech, if you will. It was his turn, now to hit his five-footer. The putt was downhill, with a sharp break to the left. Not easy by any means.

He took his time, lined up his shot, and barely tapped the ball. It looked like it might only roll two feet, but it picked up speed as it progressed downhill on a perfect line toward the cup, only slowing as it approached the final inches. And then it stopped, unbelievably, hanging on the lip of the cup only millimeters away from dropping in. Rodney stood frozen, willing the ball to go in. He waited, and waited. He finally walked over to the ball, and stared at it some more.

You can only wait so long, Rodney.

Prayers unanswered, at last he capitulated, lining up to tap his ball in. Before he could take his backswing, the ball dropped. An angel had earned its wings.

The crowd roared, but then quieted when our official

scorekeeper stepped forward and talked to the golfers. As I'd suspected, the situation was covered under USGA Rule 16-2, the so-called "ten-second rule." In short, the rule specifies that when your putt overhangs the lip of the hole, you have to approach the hole without delay. Then, if the ball falls within the next ten seconds, the putt is good. After that, it's an extra stroke.

Rodney had delayed his approach, and after he finally did get to the ball he'd waited over ten seconds, so the stroke was added, giving their team a bogey five for the hole. Rodney, of course, knew the rule, but made a big show of being upset.

After the crowd quieted, it was up to me to putt for the win. I had thought that I was all done with "knee-knockers," but here I was, faced with one final, excruciating, example. The queasy feeling welling up inside me was eerily familiar. I had three-putted on this same green, from almost the identical position, on national television, to lose the US Open championship. It was an epic fail. It had turned from being the highlight of my touring career into the beginning of the end.

As I moved over the ball, my arms began to tremble and shake visibly.

The yips.

I couldn't get a good breath. My chest tightened. I was in the midst of a full-blown panic attack.

I stepped away from the ball and looked up, gritting my teeth. As I did, I happened to catch a glimpse of my foe. Rodney was staring intently at me now, a puzzled look on his face. And in a flash, his appearance brightened.

"C'mon Muhammad Ali," he yelled, mocking my shaking limbs, "win one for the yipper."

Vintage Rodney. Darby caught my eye, making wildly exaggerated arm gestures, arching her back while reaching to the heavens.

Nice form, but what is she doing?

It finally dawned on me.

I returned to the ball, focused on my breath. I don't know how long I stood there, hovering, just breathing, in and out. It could have been minutes. Eventually, I heard no other noise, just the sound of my breath. I began to visualize the club striking the ball, the path that the ball would take toward the hole, and finally, the ball dropping in.

I closed my eyes, and in my mind I saw the putter contact the ball, and then the ball rolling smoothly into the center of the cup.

I opened my eyes again. The ball was gone.

Immediately following the tournament, Van Avery presented our team with the winners' cup, an impressive gold specimen etched with the names of the previous winners. After the ceremony, he took us aside for a private chat.

"Why don't you come by my place this week for a little victory celebration? We'll have lunch."

I could live with lunch at the Van Avery estate. And I *had* been interested in getting Darby out there to try the archery range.

"Thursday would work fine for me. Would it be ok if I brought some guests? My friend is a championship archer. And I'm sure Cody would like give your course a try."

Cody nodded. I'm sure he wouldn't mind a day off work.

"I suppose so," he said thoughtfully. "Yes, by all means, bring your friends, and that dog of yours, too. Come by around ten o'clock. We'll all have lunch. I've got a few papers to give to you, too."

"Thanks. That sounds great."

Darby would have to get her archery gear together, and Cody could drive his SUV and load his cart in the back. Bertha was going to have a great time on the mansion grounds. Maybe there were even foxes to chase. Only one thing struck me as a little curious.

I didn't recall ever mentioning to Van Avery that I owned a dog.

"Anything exciting?" I asked Sharon as she dropped off this week's report on my desk. It was Monday's report, but I was just getting it now on Wednesday, having taken the last few days off for a much-needed, and long overdue, romantic getaway with Darby. We both needed a little R&R. I did my best to appreciate her during our retreat.

Many times.

It had been Darby's suggestion that I use her yoga breathing technique on my last putt. Her sun salutation on the edge of the green had tipped me off. I still had a hard time believing I had hit the winning putt with my eyes closed. The results had been so successful that I was thinking of writing a new how-to book for those poor souls suffering from my affliction. I'd call it: "Yoga, Yips and You." Now I just needed a publisher.

"You're going to like item number three," Sharon said. "Your favorite golf pro got himself into some trouble Saturday. I'm surprised you hadn't heard about it on the news. I copied this right off the AP report."

By the tone of her voice, I knew she had to be talking about Rodney. What had he done now?

Chesapeake Bluffs' Golf Pro Moons Reporter, Video Goes Viral

After losing by a single shot at Chesapeake Bluffs' annual Pro-Intern Tournament on Saturday, head golf pro Rodney Collingsworth put his worst face forward in an interview with a local news reporter, apparently unaware, or unconcerned, that the camera was rolling.

As Channel 6 news reporter Anne Cooper questioned him after the tough loss, Collingsworth became increasingly agitated, leading to an obscenity-filled tirade.

"That f----- scorer stole our par. My putt dropped in. There's no way they charge me with an extra stroke there, And that g------ crippled kid used an illegal club. F----- kid, he shouldn't be out here. If you don't walk, you don't play—those are the rules."

Cooper then attempted to end the interview, quickly turning to the camera and saying, "We apologize for the language; apparently the runner-up in today's tournament is still a little upset."

Collingsworth then shouted out "I've got an apology for you," while turning around and mooning the camera. "Thomas, you can kiss my golf-loving a--!" he said as he pointed to his exposed backside, presumably directed toward competitor Desmond Thomas.

Channel 6 aired the interview live. Replays featured a large black rectangle covering the pro's prominent posterior. The video from the interview has since gone viral on the internet, with more than 2,000,000 viewings to date.

Mr. Collingsworth has been a golf pro at Chesapeake Bluffs for the past eight years. Tournament winner and Club legal counsel, Desmond Thomas, was unavailable for comment.

I didn't have to wonder why Rodney had gotten, as the southern expression goes, a severe case of the ass, with his loss in the tournament and the ongoing sexual harassment investigation, but that was no excuse for going off half-cocked on a reporter, in front of a live camera.

"That's unbelievable," I said. I don't know how I missed that."

"It's gone national. Check out CNN," she said.

There was a link on the front page of their website. I groaned. The Bluffs featured prominently in the story. They had a link to the video, which showed the entire scene in all its glory. This had the potential to be another black eye for the Bluffs, as if we needed any more beating up.

There wasn't anything I could do right away about the issue. It was up to Evan to decide how to deal with Rodney, although I believed the Board might have a few suggestions of their own.

Chapter 22

D an Waters was reciting his version of events related to the Charlie Peterson injury. "Friday morning, around 7:00 a.m., we heard a yell and found him lying in the parking lot."

Evan was also seated in the small conference room, along with Cheryl, our HR manager. We were meeting to determine whether to approve or deny the Workers' Compensation claim Charlie had submitted.

"His leg was bent the wrong way down toward his ankle. Curt actually threw up when he saw it. I had to look away for a minute. It was gross."

"Did he say anything?" Evan asked.

"He was screaming and writhing around in pain. He was cursing at the pothole. Funny thing, though, was that from where he was parked, he should never have been near that pothole."

"What are you saying?" I asked.

"I'm not saying anything," Dan said, "other than from where he was parked, the pothole was out of his way."

"Did you ask him about it?" I said.

"All we did was call 911 and get an ambulance to come and get him. He wasn't in the mood to answer any questions."

"Was this the usual time for Charlie to be at work?" I asked. "It seems pretty early."

"I'm always here by six-thirty to get things going. Charlie

usually rolls in after seven. He's been late a lot. In fact, this was probably the earliest he's been at work in a long time."

"Is that it?"

"Well, there is one more thing."

"What?"

"His breath. He'd been drinking."

"At seven in the morning?" Evan said.

"Did Charlie have a drinking problem?" I asked.

"He's an alcoholic," Dan said. "Last year I was told we couldn't fire him until he went to rehab."

"That's not exactly right," Cheryl corrected. "The ADA requires us to give alcoholics a leave to attend an in-patient treatment program for their disability. In addition, FMLA entitles him to take job-protected leave for a serious health condition, such as alcoholism. According to his personnel file, he went on leave six months ago and completed a two-week program at Ridley Shores."

"From the looks of things, it didn't stick," I said. "How's his work performance been lately?"

"It's been getting worse. He calls in sick all the time, and even when he is here, he's not very reliable. Even though he's my brother-in-law, I've been thinking we need to let him go. We can't handle the workload without four good people, and Charlie is just about useless."

"Have you documented this in any way?" asked Cheryl, seizing another HR moment.

"Well, last review I said he was average. Of course, the other three guys I rated as excellent, so you can see that, in comparison, he came out pretty bad."

"We can't really fire Charlie," I said, "if he's on Workers' Comp, because his attorney will sue for wrongful termination, and without any documented evidence to show that he's been a poor performer prior to the injury, we'd probably lose. Is he still protected under the ADA?"

"After the treatment," Cheryl said, "if he continues to be unable to perform work requirements, he can be terminated. But it needs to be documented. That's one reason why we have the annual reviews, to document an ongoing pattern of substandard performance. It's almost required these days prior to dismissal of any employee."

"And now if Charlie finds the right doctor for his leg," I said, "he can get a note that says he's unable to work for three, four, who knows, maybe up to six months."

"Do we have to pay him during that time?" Dan asked.

"No," I said, "he'd get paid from Workers' Comp while he's disabled and unable to return to work. But our rates might go up."

"Well, we're coming up on the busy season, and we're going to need a replacement for Charlie if he's going to be out all summer."

"Let's get this over with," I said. "Is there anyone who thinks the Workers' Comp claim should be approved?"

Silence.

There was one more factor I needed to add into the mix. "If he takes the Workers' Comp, he's legally precluded from suing us for negligence over that pothole."

"What happens if we deny the claim?" Evan asked.

"Most likely, he'll take it to the next level, a hearing before an Administrative Law Judge."

"It seems like a no-brainer," Evan said. "I think we have to approve. We don't want another lawsuit, do we?"

There were no objections. I had my doubts about the cause of the injury, but it was looking like Charlie was getting a free ride for the summer.

Some people get all the breaks.

"Holy cow," Cody said.

I'd forgotten how impressive that first glimpse of the Van Avery mansion was, and as Cody approached the gate, he and Darby were experiencing some of the same amazement that I had a few months back.

"Can we move here?" Darby asked. "I wouldn't mind the commute."

We cleared the gate and made our way up the meandering drive to the front of the mansion, parking as I did last time, in the circle. And, as also was the case before, Hillary greeted us at the front entrance.

"I see you've brought your equipment. Mr. Van Avery's waiting around back."

While Cody and I unloaded the Handygolfer, Bertha chaperoned the machine down the ramp.

Darby donned her gear, quiver on her hip, a full complement of arrows, along with her impressive bow, now fitted with targeting sight and counter-balance. She looked like something out of a Robin Hood movie. It was hot.

As we made our way around the mansion, she checked out the amenities. Of particular interest was the tennis venue.

"Nice," she said. "Imagine waking up and having a court right outside the bedroom."

We could start out every morning at love-love.

Van Avery joined us in the backyard.

He showed Darby the archery range, and gave Cody a brief rundown on the layout of his golf course. Bertha enthusiastically explored each new location.

"Make yourselves at home." He turned to me. "Thomas, let's head to my office and take care of a little business before lunch."

For a second time, I followed him through the spacious interior into his office, taking my seat in the appointed spot. As was my habit, I scanned my surroundings while waiting for him to get his papers in order. I noticed once again the lone picture on his desk. His daughter, if I'd remembered correctly.

Only this time, she looked familiar, and not just because I'd been here before.

I felt the blood drain from my face. This was not good.

Ms. Green.

The picture must have been taken over twenty years ago. But there was no doubt about it; this was the woman I'd met at the restaurant.

"I see you recognize my daughter, Elizabeth. Elizabeth Norris is her married name."

Van Avery now had in his possession a rather large antique revolver, pointed straight at me.

Elizabeth Van Avery Norris.

Evan316, one last link in this tangled affair.

"She mentioned she had the pleasure of making your acquaintance last week. Apparently, you were somewhat rude."

"I didn't know she was your daughter."

"Would that have changed anything? Thanks to you, she's been taken into custody. But, I presume you know that already. It's only a matter of time before they trace the money flow to me. She won't talk, I'm sure. But the rest of those flunkies, they'll cut a deal. That's inevitable. No doubt the FBI will be knocking at my door very soon."

The FBI.

Were they still monitoring my cell? The safe word. What was it again?

Think, Dez, think. Golf ball, ball sack, sack tear, black bear... best ball, one ball, small balls...

I couldn't concentrate with that gun trained on me.

To hell with the safe word.

"You're not going to shoot me now with that gun that you've got pointed at my head?" I said, as clearly and distinctly as possible.

That should've been obvious enough for any junior G-man who might still be listening in on my phone. To make this ridiculous utterance sound even remotely believable to Van Avery, I had to sell it. I needed a follow up.

"The *gun* would make too much noise, attract attention. Guns are messy." I added, envisioning an FBI agent calling for backup as I spoke.

Van Avery snorted derisively. Where was my .38 when I needed it?

Stupid FBI, they still hadn't returned my piece.

"Thomas, you've destroyed everything. Elizabeth and I worked hard to set up that company. That was a twenty-million dollar business you shut down. A cash cow."

"Did you order Frankie killed?"

"We had no choice. After Brooks found out about the equipment, we paid him off. That only worked until he got greedy. He threatened to turn us in if we didn't meet his demands. It wasn't personal; it was business. But with you, Thomas, now this *is* personal."

"You don't really want to do this, Van Avery."

"That's where you're mistaken," he said. "I very much want to do this. Because of you, I have nothing left. You think I have money, Thomas, you all do, but you're wrong. This estate belonged to my wife Margaret. She left it all, ultimately, to Elizabeth. I can stay here for the rest of my life, but only as long as I remain unmarried. And thanks to you, the woman I love is gone, forever."

Huh?

"Who are you talking about?"

"Carolyn Andrews, of course. We've been together for years. We'd planned to marry after Margaret died, but when Margaret found out, she put a limitation in her will. I lose use of the estate and income if I'm with Carolyn. It was my wife's final act of retribution, you see, so she could torment me from beyond the grave."

Andrews and Van Avery? Gross. Maybe he's a tiger in the sack.

I couldn't see it. But they certainly shared one common interest. Both seemed to hate me with a vengeance.

The old man didn't seem to be paying close attention, lost as he was in his rant, but it still seemed too risky to try anything. That was a big gun.

Keep stalling.

"Your wife must have still cared about you, to let you live here."

"Margaret and I had a love/hate relationship. I loved her money; she hated my dalliances with other women. And she despised Carolyn. But Carolyn has her own money. We planned to disappear together as soon as she sold that property to the Bluffs. Now you've ruined that, too. Carolyn's vanished without me."

Clearly, I was the thorn in Van Avery's side.

I understood now why Van Avery had taken such a significant disliking to me, one which might end in my untimely demise. Despite my best hopes, I was rapidly losing confidence that the FBI would come barging through the door in time.

But my best hope was Darby. If I could call her, she might be able to track me through my phone's GPS. Slowly sliding my hand into my pocket, I hit the buttons on my phone in what I hoped was the proper sequence for voice dial.

"Darby," I said loudly, pausing just long enough for the phone to recognize the voice command, "what about Darby and Cody? What are you going to do to them?"

"Unfortunately, your friends will have to pay for your sins,

Thomas. With everything else gone, revenge is all that's left."

"Why didn't you just leave the country?"

"I'm too old to live life as a fugitive. Plus, if I leave, the trust money disappears. No, my life is over. And yours too, in a few more moments, my esteemed colleague. Let's just say you're going to be 'disbarred' for life. Don't feel bad, I'll be right behind you."

"You're insane. Are you going to shoot me right here, right now, in your office?" I enunciated loudly, praying Darby was listening.

"As you so aptly put it, it's too messy in here," he said. "Too much blood and brain matter flying around. It would be a bit much to ask Hillary to clean that up. My hunting shed is a much better venue. There's lots of blood there already. A little more won't matter."

He was done talking. He waved his gun.

"Get up. I'll be right behind you. Don't try anything." He poked the gun into the small of my back to emphasize his point. "We'll be going out the front door."

Prompted by the business end of his rusty revolver, I headed out. Hillary graciously opened the door for us. Apparently, she didn't notice the gun. Or didn't care.

"We're just going to take a little walk, Hillary. I'll be right back."

Van Avery marched me across the wide grassy lawn toward the woods that presumably housed my final destination. I plotted escape tactics. How hard could it be to get away from an old man? If I waited until he was distracted, I'd have a sporting chance.

But, old man or not, out here in the open lawn, I was pretty much a dead duck. I'd wait until we hit the woods, where trees would provide some cover in case he began shooting.

At that moment, I heard a wonderfully familiar sound. Man's best friend. We both turned instinctively toward the barking, and saw three figures approaching. One was driving a cart, and two were running. My phone call had worked.

"Stop right there," Van Avery yelled, removing the gun from his pocket and jabbing it even harder into my back. "I'll shoot him right here if you come any closer."

Cody and Darby stopped in their tracks. Bertha, apparently not paying close attention, barreled in like a Mack truck on a mission.

Van Avery kept the gun pressed firmly at my back. This left him at somewhat of a disadvantage against my canine friend.

"Go get him girl," I yelled in encouragement, as Bertha closed in, snarling and chugging away as fast as she could on her short, stubby legs. I was praying she could make it all the way to Van Avery before collapsing from exhaustion.

Ever the optimist, I shouted, "Go for his neck! Kill, Bertha, kill!"

Bertha closed in and leaped high into the air, clamping down hard on Van Avery's... kneecap. Bulldogs aren't generally known for their jumping abilities.

Van Avery howled in pain while attempting to shake her off.

Now.

I pushed off from Van Avery, attempting to move my body out of the direct path of his gun. Then I'd be able to wrestle the gun away while Bertha had him distracted.

There was a loud crack, coupled with a searing pain in my side. I was not faster than a speeding bullet.

I collapsed on the ground, at once trying to stem the flow of blood from my new wound. By now, Van Avery had managed to free himself from Bertha. Without hesitation, he took aim at her and fired.

She yelped in pain.

I swear I'm going to kill that man.

But all my resolution couldn't change the fact that I was lying bleeding and helpless, posing no threat at all to the man who towered over me. I looked up and saw only the barrel of his revolver, again aimed at my head.

"It'll have to be right here, messy or not. This is for Elizabeth."

All I could do was silently curse myself for having been so slow.

But instead of a gunshot, I heard only an odd "swoosh," followed by a deep "thunk," and then a sickly groan. I was treated to the sight of Van Avery clutching at the thin shaft protruding grotesquely out of his chest. The tip of an arrow was jutting out of his back. I turned and saw Darby at a distance, still holding her bow in shooting position.

Bull's-eye!

Van Avery fell to his knees, face contorted in pain. But instead of going gently into the night, he reached for his dropped gun, apparently still intent on carrying out this one final act of redemption. Damn this guy.

Just die already.

I tried to crawl away, but my whole left side screamed in pain at any attempt at movement. I was immobilized.

I turned back to look at him, his gun once again in hand, just in time to see his head jerk violently, accompanied by a horrific "squish." From the looks of it, it was a three wood to the right temple, with a slight fade. Cody had come to my rescue.

A good man in an emergency.

Van Avery now lay on the ground, blood spurting from his head wound, body twitching. It didn't appear that he was going to be shooting anybody else anytime soon.

"Call 911," I gasped, "and get that gun away from him, just in case."

I was feeling a little woozy. Suddenly I remembered Bertha.

"Bertha," I asked, "is she…"

"It looks like she got hit in the left ass," Cody said. "I think she might be ok."

That made me feel better, and as things began to get dimmer and dimmer, it felt like a good time for a rest.

Chapter 23

Consciousness returned slowly. That frustrating feeling from the bad dream persisted, like a sour taste in my mouth, barely fading even as sleep dissipated. Taking a deep breath, I opened my eyes, staring at the white ceiling. This wasn't my bedroom.

The safe house? No, that's not it.

A hospital bed. I was in a hospital room.

How did I get here?

Van Avery. I groaned, remembering.

I was alone. There were no nurses, no one holding vigil in the guest chairs, no family or friends staring down at me with caring eyes. I must not have been hurt too seriously, I figured, either that or I had to come to grips with the fact that I was totally unloved.

I didn't have a chest tube, so the bullet must have missed my lungs. I thought back. The last thing I recalled was Cody telling me that Bertha'd been shot in the butt. I looked around, expecting to see a little doggy hospital bed next to mine, with Bertha comfortably lying on her back, hooked up to a mini canine-IV. Probably against hospital regulations. I almost threw up recalling the image of Van Avery's head standing in for a Titleist. I wasn't optimistic about his chances for a full recovery.

I punched the button on the end of the cord clamped to my bed. In my limited hospital experience, I was pretty sure that this would accomplish one of two things. Either it would call for a nurse, or it would inject more drugs into my IV. Right now, both options sounded pretty good.

"Mr. Thomas," the nurse said as she strode through the door, "you're up. You've had a nice long rest after your surgery. How are you feeling?" She looked around the room at the empty seats. "I don't know where everyone's gone off to."

I felt somewhat less unloved. "Who all was here?"

"Your parents, your brother, and there was that nice young lady, and of course Special Agent Griffiths." Her voice had changed to a deeper tone as soon as she hit the words "Special Agent."

"Am I ok?" I asked.

"No, actually you're dead," she said, "but the good news is that I'm your angel." She was most likely thinking that she was the height of wit. I was thinking that it was probably not a great idea to screw with patients' minds when they've just awakened from surgery.

"The bullet hit one of your shoulder muscles. It missed the bone and went all the way through. From what I've heard, you're going to be quite alright. They said the only thing you won't be able to do is play golf again."

"What?"

"Just kidding with ya. I'm sure it'll be fine."

Somebody smack this lady.

At that moment, Agent Griffiths strolled through the door, preventing me from making a nasty remark that I would not have regretted. He was carrying a cup of coffee and some faux pastry that he had apparently procured from a vending machine.

How do these guys stay in such good shape?

"Thomas," he said. "Glad to have you back. I've got a few questions." He looked at the nurse. "Could we have a minute?" She nodded, giving him the "I understand this is top-secret stuff" look, and exited.

What would I do without my angel?

"What's that you told me about lingering potentialities?" I said. "Weren't they all supposed to be gone?"

"We weren't aware of the link between Norris and Van Avery. We would've traced the connection shortly. The good news is that you're ok."

"No thanks to you guys," I said. "Were you still listening in on my phone?"

"We didn't have an agent listening, but the recording software was still in place, so we got everything that Van Avery said on tape. Nice use of the safe word, by the way. I can see I trained you well." He started chuckling, the first time I'd seen even a minor tear in the FBI's veil of seriousness.

"I bet you guys got a kick out of that one in the office."

He was laughing now, trying hard to stop, but tears were coming out of his eyes.

"What about Van Avery? Did he make it?"

Griffiths finally managed to pull himself together.

"No, he didn't. Your peeps did a job on him. Any of those wounds were lethal, well, all except the bites on the leg. They saved your life, all three of them. You owe them, big time."

"How's Bertha?"

"She'll be fine. Ms. St. Claire is taking care of her. Both of you got lucky. Taking those slugs like that, it could have been a lot worse."

"Are we certain there are no other 'potentialities' lingering around? And are you still recording my phone?"

"Van Avery's motive was personal, for revenge. Fortunately, we're not seeing anymore like him. We've managed to secure a plea deal with one of the guys that we arrested. He's given us valuable information. The phone recording's been shut down, officially. "

We had to put our conversation on hold, for at that moment, the rest of my entourage came flooding into the room, all smiles and grins at seeing me awake.

Once again, I was loved.

I was up and about within a few days, with only a sling to show for my troubles. When Kevin saw Darby and me again, he couldn't help but make a quip about, "the slings and arrows of outrageous fortune." Bertha was recovering nicely from her wounded left ass, the slight limp not seeming to slow her down at all.

I went back to work, where my first order of business was damage control. The results of the FBI sting, plus the news of my shooting and Van Avery's death had the Bluffs' grapevine buzzing, not to mention most of the major news networks. Murder and intrigue at a world-famous resort made for quite the juicy story. The Bluffs' involvement in the counterfeiting scandal hadn't been officially announced by the FBI… yet. As soon as they went public, I was sure we'd be in the headlines again.

The Bluff's expansion plans were once again in a legal limbo. It wasn't clear if the property could be sold now, given the crimes committed. And the current owner, Ms. Andrews, now resided in a correctional facility, and was about to have the properties foreclosed. Who knew what the banks would, or even could, do with the land?

Our other lingering issue was what to do about the sale of thousands of counterfeit golf sets to our customers. It was only a matter of time before the owners of the illicit equipment put two-and-two together. I was certain that we'd see a class action lawsuit unless we took immediate action.

The Bluffs' public image had already taken a beating, so it was my belief that we needed to be proactive, and act quickly to salvage whatever remnants of goodwill we had left. I sat down with Evan to discuss our options.

"I think we need to offer an unconditional refund to anyone who bought equipment from us during the timeframe that we dealt with GolfLinx, which, according to my records, has been for approximately three years."

Evan swallowed hard, though from his expression, I gathered that he was not totally shocked at this proposal.

"Well, it's possible that not all the equipment was counterfeit," he said, "and not all of it came from GolfLinx. We've had other suppliers during that time."

"Right, but if we handle it on a case-by-case basis, there will be disagreements and bad blood, even if we're right about any one particular set of clubs. The bad publicity's not worth it. Our reputation will be tainted, and people won't want to buy from us. Plus if we do it all up front, the corporation can take a one-time hit on the financials, and move on."

Evan nodded, accepting the inevitable. "I've got the sales figures here. Over the last three years, we've sold over four million dollars in golf equipment. That's quite a one-time hit."

"It's all about our credibility," I said. "Can people trust us to do the right thing? I don't think we have a choice. Anything else is just a self-inflicted wound."

"I'll present it to the Board," he said. "They won't like it, but you're right, we don't really have any good alternatives. They are going to want to know how we can prevent something like this from happening again in the future."

"I've got some ideas on that," I said.

By the look on his face, Evan appeared to have something else to say.

Here it comes.

I'd been here for only four months, and already I'd presided over an unending string of major and minor crises. It had seemed like non-stop chaos was the order of the day during my tenure as in-house counsel, and a part-time counsel, at that. I wasn't sure at this point the Board of Directors would want me to continue, considering the huge public-image hit the Bluffs had taken on my watch.

"Desmond, I just wanted you to know how much I, and the Board, have appreciated your efforts since you've been here. I don't think we could have done this without you. We owe you a debt of gratitude that we really can't properly repay. But we can make a token effort."

He handed me an envelope. Inside, I found a letter explaining the latest action by the Board. A stock grant of ten thousand shares. My jaw dropped. For once I had nothing to say.

"It's not as generous as it seems. We took them back from Van Avery. There was some kind of clause regarding actions detrimental to the company. It's in the fine print, just for the lawyers, you know. You might want to read it if you plan on setting up your own criminal conspiracy ring in the near future."

So there it was. The rumors of my demise had been greatly exaggerated.

"Now if you could somehow set me up in the Van Avery estate," I told him, "I'd be a very happy man."

It had been a while since I'd had a chance to play a complete round of golf, just for fun, with nothing at stake but the joy of whacking the hell out of the ball.

Apart from me, our foursome consisted of Darby, Cody, and

in a rare appearance on the links, my brother Kevin. Kevin wasn't a bad player, but he rarely played, or even practiced, and so was lucky if he managed to hit in the nineties.

But he kept us entertained with non-stop commentary on almost every conceivable topic, and of course, his signature bad puns. It never ended.

On the fourth hole, we encountered the beverage cart. Caitlyn Ross, I saw, was back on the job, looking healthy and happy, and very pregnant.

I was still recovering from the bullet wound, which had torn through muscles in my left shoulder. On the outside, the wound appeared to be almost completely healed. I no longer felt any pain when I swung the club, but I could tell that my distance was short by a few percent, and anything that affected distance could throw my game off considerably, since knowing how far any given shot would travel was of vital importance in golf.

Darby had been facilitating my rehab. She worked with me for about an hour each day, going over the arm and shoulder exercises, range-of-motion drills, stretches and weight training needed to get my shoulder back to peak condition.

When she put on her physical therapy hat, Darby was one tough taskmaster. A few weeks ago, she'd finally given up and moved into my place. It was heaven for me, but it also allowed her to get me up at six each morning, without fail, to oversee the daily regimen.

"How about we skip today," I'd mumble when the alarm would go off.

"If you do your whole therapy without complaining, I'll make it worth your while," she'd say.

"Oh yeah?" I'd reply, my hopes getting aroused, along with other animal instincts.

"I'll make you pancakes."

I'd fallen for it again.

I had yet to find any area in which Darby did not excel. I guess we had a lot in common in that regard, except perhaps that she may have lacked my natural humility. I had no doubt that if she had concentrated her talents in the golf arena rather than tennis, she would have been an exceptional player. As it was, she was merely excellent.

Next week, we were going to start archery lessons. You never knew when proficiency with a bow and arrow might come in handy.

Cody had blossomed during the summer. He was bright, personable, a hard worker, and an excellent golfer, with no qualifiers attached. He planned on playing for Virginia Lutheran in his senior year. He had already filed for an exemption from the NCAA to permit use of his cart. He was hopeful, given the precedent provided when they allowed future PGA golfer Casey Martin to use a cart while a student at Stanford, due to his congenital leg condition.

A lot of people had been asking me lately whether or not Cody had a chance to make it all the way onto the tour. I always told them the same thing, that the chances of anyone making it onto the tour are extremely slim, given the small number of slots, but that if I were betting money on anyone, it would be Cody. It was hard to imagine anyone working harder or being more disciplined.

As for me, I loved my job, or should I say jobs, at the Bluffs. In the back of my mind, however, there was always that nagging question. Could I make it back on the tour? In the past, the memory of my humiliating failure at the Open and its aftereffects had always provided an immediate answer.

But if my latest success in overcoming the yips was for real, there wouldn't be any more barriers to another go at the show. In order to do so, I'd need to start with the Q-school pre-qualifiers in September, which were right around the corner.

Evan had given me the green light to take whatever time off I needed. In fact, if it didn't work out, he even offered me a backup plan, actually several. I could keep my job as is, or take over as fulltime counsel for the Bluffs, or take over as the head golf pro. I certainly couldn't ask for much more than that.

As I sat in the cart, contemplating my future, I realized that I still had to prove to myself that I could succeed at the highest levels of golf. Before I devoted the next four months of my life to prepping for and playing in the qualifiers, I had to be sure that I was up to the task, and that even if I made it there, I wouldn't wilt again under pressure.

It took me all of thirty seconds, sitting there, to formulate the plan. Tomorrow morning, I'd play another round, right here at the Bluffs, on the toughest course, from the championship tees, and I'd have to break par in order to start the process. No if, ands, or bad putts.

The morning sun reflected brightly off the Bay waters, providing the perfect backdrop to the most glorious golf hole in existence.

I looked down over the famous green and felt the cool breeze on my face.

Check the wind.

I knelt down and grabbed a few sprigs of dried grass, tossing them lightly in the air. They landed a few feet to my left.

Nothing to worry about.

I stood over the ball, visualizing the gallery that lined the fairways, watching my every shot. I took a first deep breath, and the throngs slowly faded. With a second breath, I closed my eyes and saw the ball arcing its way to the hole, dropping perfectly on the green. With a third and final breath, the rest of the world disappeared completely, leaving just the ball, and me.

For a moment, this *was* the world. This was golf.

I brought back my club, and swung.

Epilogue

As every lawyer knows, the wheels of justice turn in their own sweet time. But eventually, after all the deals, plea-bargains, hearings and trials are said and done, the wheels grind to a halt. Pending appeal, of course. Here, in no particular order, are the results.

C. Alexander Van Avery

Van Avery was DOA after our final encounter. Pursuant to his will, his faithful housekeeper Hillary spread his ashes over the 9th green at his estate. Per Margaret Van Avery's request, the estate became the property of daughter Elizabeth, who, for various reasons, was unable to establish occupancy. The property did provide a sizable piece of equity that could prove very useful in the Bluffs' ongoing civil action against the family.

Carolyn Andrews

Carolyn Andrews finally admitted everything, after cutting a deal with the prosecutors. Too many years of living the good life with little regard to money management had left her finances in tatters. Her high-leverage real-estate plan had left her on the brink of financial ruin, which fueled her desperate schemes, which, interestingly enough, had not involved counterfeit golf equipment.

Had she waited just a few more days before giving the burn

order, she would have discovered the much-improved prospects for her property sale to the Bluffs.

Her real estate shenanigans, while a breach of her fiduciary duty as a Board member, were not a violation of any state or federal law. She may have been sued for breach of fiduciary responsibility, but she wouldn't have gone to jail.

One couldn't say the same thing about her other offenses. In exchange for reduced sentences, she pled guilty to three charges, conspiring to bring false charges of sexual harassment, conspiracy to commit arson, and conspiracy in the murder of the late Wallace Andrews. She wouldn't be getting out of prison for at least 40 years, which for her, would probably mean a life sentence. At least her money woes would be over.

George Robinson

George Robinson's secret account was uncovered by his wife's attorney during a nasty divorce battle. Once the Bluffs got wind of kickback scheme, George was terminated. The Bluffs are currently pursuing a civil suit to recover damages.

Darrell Parker, Michael Squires

Michael, the wounded arsonist, made a quick deal with the prosecution. He ratted out his pal Darrell, including disclosing all their previous arsons, in exchange for a fifteen year sentence. Darrell Parker got thirty, plus an extra ten for the attempted murder charge. They are no longer the best of friends.

Beverly Sargent

Beverly Sargent had the misfortune of being collateral damage in Carolyn's downhill slide. Her previous careers as exotic dancer, female escort, mistress, and part-time cocaine dealer were things she had wanted to bury and keep buried in a very deep hole. The fact that Beverly had been, some ten years prior, Carolyn's sole supplier of "nose-candy" had given Carolyn all the ammunition that she needed for blackmail. Carolyn threatened to divulge all the dirty details to Beverly's fiancé, rightly assuming that this might derail her developing career as gold digger extraordinaire.

Not surprisingly, after her fiancé got wind of all this, the big rock slid quickly off of Bev's finger. Then, she vanished, perhaps moving on to find another sucker, aka fiancé, somewhere far away.

Her affair with Frankie had been presumably that, just an affair, and there was no evidence that she had been involved in Frankie's death.

Detective Reed

Detective Reed became the target of an FBI sting operation, which led to his arrest for grand theft, breaking and entering, official misconduct, and distribution of illegal narcotics. Reed was caught stealing and "recycling" drugs from the evidence room. The night of the break-in at my house, he had apparently been attempting to plant drugs in my car, at the behest of one Lucas Bennett, with whom he had enjoyed a symbiotic relationship for quite a number of years. Reed was sentenced to 25 years in the federal penitentiary. He is no longer employed by the Chapman County Sheriff's Department.

Lucas Bennett

Bennett, aka Tom Jones, cooperated with the FBI in the sting operation that nailed Reed, and as a result received a lighter penalty for his participation in the efforts to frame me for drug possession, and for running an illegal gambling business. Bennett received a sentence of five years. The odds were good he'd get out sooner.

Rodney Collingsworth

My pal Rodney's "moon shot," along with his sexual harassment malfeasance, finally earned him the heave-ho he had so richly deserved. Rodney didn't go down easily, though, threatening and bad-mouthing Evan and every other person at the Bluffs who had had the misfortune of crossing his path. In the end, he had to be escorted off the property while still uttering threats of lawsuits, personal retaliation, and even divine retribution.

Rodney's ethical and legal issues also violated the PGA's Rules of Professional Conduct, and earned him an automatic expulsion from its membership ranks. He did manage to land another job as director of golf. Unfortunately, it was of the miniature variety. And, as Caitlyn's baby daddy, he will be on the hook for child support obligations for the next 18 years, one year for every hole.

Elizabeth Van Avery Norris

The FBI's operation and subsequent investigation into GolfLinx's operations resulted in the convictions of Elizabeth Norris and four other executives in the company for violation of federal anti-counterfeiting laws and violation of the RICO act. Norris was sentenced to life in prison for ordering the murder of Frankie Brooks, along with the attempted murder of yours truly. Norris claimed that Van Avery was the mastermind behind the entire operation. I suppose that claim was inevitable, since it's hard to defend yourself when your remains are fertilizing the ninth hole.

"Evan316" got a total of life plus 30.

Billy Walker and Lenny "Scrubs" Holmes

Billy Walker turned state's evidence, and received consecutive life sentences for his participation in the murder of Frankie Brooks, as well as six others. Billy's cooperation enabled prosecutors to charge the women who'd retained his services to "terminate" their marriages, including Carolyn Andrews. All members of this exclusive ex-wives' club now resided behind bars for life. His partner, Lenny Holmes, received the death penalty, and is awaiting execution on Virginia's death row.

Trevor Dunne

GolfLinx's gross revenues exceeded $20,000,000 annually, with connections to dozens of country clubs in the mid-Atlantic and Southern regions. All of these clubs had head-buyers who were involved in the counterfeiting scheme, receiving kickbacks of various amounts.

Trevor was sentenced to three years as part of his involvement in the kickback and counterfeiting conspiracy, in addition to owing thousands in back taxes on the monies he received illegally, which, for some reason, he failed to report to the IRS. The

FBI had been more than happy to supply the missing paperwork. Trevor was dismissed by the Bluffs.

Charlie Peterson

Charlie Peterson recovered from his broken leg, came back to work and was fired two months later, the week after his performance appraisal. His next attempt at self-injury on the job was unfortunately his last. Charlie bled to death after a chain saw "accident" gone wrong.

Lisa Brooks

Last, but certainly not least, Lisa Brooks ended up on the positive end of the legal machinations. I had the pleasure of accompanying her to the bank to deposit the insurance settlement. She collected the full insurance payment, but not the double indemnity for accidental death, since murder is not considered by the insurance companies to be accidental. It seemed to me that it all depended on your perspective.

Nonetheless, the half million dollars she received would be more than enough to keep her in good stead for quite some time. She had settled nicely into her new routine, working as a teacher's aide, her kids now in public schools.

My only advice to her was that she not tell anyone about the insurance money. Money only brings out the worst in people.

I should know.

About the Authors

Donna K. Pelham, JD, CPA: Donna is a FL attorney and a NC CPA. She is a graduate of Texas Lutheran University (B.A. in Accounting) and The University of North Carolina School of Law (J.D.). She currently teaches both undergraduate and graduate level courses in accounting and business law at Methodist University in Fayetteville, NC. Her love of teaching and constant search for ways to engage students was the genesis of Twisted Links.

Anthony J. Pelham, BS, MS: Tony is a software engineer by day, comic and writer the rest of the time. He is a graduate of MIT (B.S. in Electrical Engineering). Tony has written a full-length screenplay and several short stories. You can read his semi-regular blog at http://bowelsinanuproar.blogspot.com/. His writing skills, research talents, unique sense of humor, love of sports, and patience with Donna made Twisted Links a reality.

CPSIA information can be obtained at www.ICGtesting.com
Printed in the USA
LVOW040805121011

250159LV00001B/231/P